D0571021

ENERGY-EFFICIENT ARCHITECTURE

BASICS FOR PLANNING AND CONSTRUCTION

ROBERTO GONZALO
KARL J. HABERMANN

BIRKHÄUSER – PUBLISHERS FOR ARCHITECTURE
BASEL · BOSTON · BERLIN

CONTENTS

FOREWORD

Utopias and experiments are important forces that drive the development of our technologies. In the course of time, Jules Verne's visions of space travel became reality, as did Eugène Hénard's on urban design. The idea of energy-autonomous buildings has resurfaced in recent years. Buckminster Fuller, Norman Foster and Richard Rogers are but a few names that come to mind.

Experimentation is followed by applying the positive experiences to construction and everyday building practices. The authors' goal in this work is to build a bridge between the available knowledge and expertise of the specialists in building sciences and technologies on the one hand and the great majority of those working in the sector on the other.

"There is no energy-saving style. Building of that kind does not call for a uniform aesthetic or universally binding rules, unless it be those rules of common sense to preserve (or at least avoid polluting) the environment." (Robert Kaltenbrunner in *Bauwelt,* 1993)

Original material from the architects has been included in the project documentation and the theoretical chapters for good reason. This alone preserves the individual aesthetic imprint as a whole. CAD programs have long since been mastered to such a degree that drawings can once again be rendered with greater individuality. In this book, we have therefore deliberately abstained from visually coordinating the detail information. It also seems important to note here that in the area of innovation there is some risk associated with borrowing details all too readily and perhaps rashly. Only direct contact with a colleague in the field can offer safety through an exchange of valuable experiences and set into motion the technology transfer that is as vital as it is desirable. To this end, the appendix contains a list of all major planning partners and a selection of interesting manufacturers. The book is organized in familiar fashion: starting off with an analytical overview of the history of building up to the current state in architecture, the theme is explored step by step, beginning with urban design through to energy-efficient building planning and innovative detail solutions. The featured projects from Germany,

Austria, Switzerland, Spain and Great Britain were selected with great care and form an important component of this work. A particularly beautiful example of sustainable architecture in the context of development aid is given with the school in Ladakh, where the elements from the pioneering stage of solar architecture were sensibly applied. Consideration of local building traditions, in this example shaped by the extraordinary climate, and of local resources, is a key element in energy-efficient building.

No effort was spared to introduce as broad a palette of different categories as possible. Without claiming to be complete, this volume presents a multitude of possible solutions for a wide variety of different requirements.

The authors are indebted first and foremost to all those colleagues who made their material available and patiently answered all their questions. As experts in technical completion and building physics, the engineers offered additional data that were invaluable for the purpose of achieving the density and depth of information we had set out to present. We would like to extend our special thanks to John Berry, Klaus Eggert, Helmut Krapmeier, Andreas Lackenbauer, Clemens Pollok, Wolfgang Schölkopf, Peter Schossig, Matthias Schuler, Michael Weese and Jan Wienold. Finally, this book could not have been completed without the advice, practical support and patience of our wives, Susana Gonzalo and Ulla Fulde-Habermann.

Munich, January 2006

Roberto Gonzalo
Karl J. Habermann

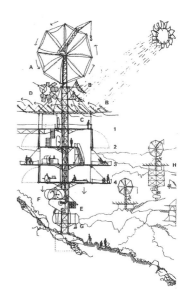

left:
    Facade section of student residence in Wuppertal, first stage of construction; architects: PPP Architekten in partnership with Christian Schlüter and Michael Müller

top:
    "Autonomous House," Aspen, Colorado, Richard Rogers, 1978. An idea of autonomous buildings operated solely by renewable energy sources.

RESOURCE-CONSERVING AND ENERGY-EFFICIENT BUILDING: ORIGINS

Christian Lenz, Hermann
Kaufmann: Office and
residential building in
Schwarzach, Vorarlberg.
Solar panels
are integrated
for warm-water processing
in the balcony balustrade.
See also p. 122

RESOURCE-CONSERVING AND ENERGY-EFFICIENT BUILDING: ORIGINS

"In setting out the walls of a city the choice of a healthy situation is of the first importance: it should be on high ground, neither subject to fogs nor rains; its aspects should be neither violently hot nor intensely cold, but temperate in both respects …"(1) With his famous treatise *Ten Books on Architecture*, Vitruvius created an early cornerstone for a tradition of architecture and urban design. In it, he refers to the architecture and urban design of the Greeks, which had come before his time and plays particular attention to the influence of the sun on the various functions of the city, elaborating on this topic in great detail. For both the Romans and Greeks had long been aware of the link between building orientation and building use.

When we look at the selection of appropriate building materials described by Vitruvius, we can discern early ecological approaches. The differences in the local availability of such materials – be they natural stone, timber, lime or clay – led to an entire spectrum of different types of wall construction until the advent of *Opus cementitium*, an early version of concrete. The Romans were less successful in handing down their discoveries in building technology to future generations: their elaborate floor and wall heating systems were largely forgotten until they were rediscovered by archaeologists in the modern age.

As we search for traces of other useful basic principles of resource-conserving and hence early attempts at energy-efficient construction, the broad field of so-called autochthon, traditional or vernacular building is particularly fruitful. In addition to revealing the prototypes of basic constructional forms, this field also allows us to study the beginnings of house technology. However, it is important to understand the comfort conditions of these early low- or zero-energy habitations in clear relation to the specific climate zone, the achieved living comfort and the average life expectancy of people at that time.

The Blackhouse, an archaic dwelling on the Outer Hebrides, a group of islands off the coast of Scotland, seems to merge with the sparse, treeless landscape because of the rubble masonry and sod-covered roof. Local materials were utilized in a sensible and natural manner. Two parallel narrow rectangles accommodate humans and livestock, and also provide space for a barn. Living room and bedroom lie across from the stable on the other side of a central hallway. Aside from an open fireplace, in which peat was burned, the livestock served as an additional source of heat in winter: according to current knowledge, a 600 kg cow generates a thermal output of roughly 1,200 watt. In those days, people rarely left their homes during the cold season. There was no chimney; the smoke escaped through narrow hatches in the roof and the permeable roof covering. The interior was blackened by smoke. The only technical item in the home consisted of a fire hook, suspended from the ceiling on an iron chain. Every component of the building was reusable or recyclable, as we would say today. Nevertheless, given the harsh climate, life in this primitive "ecological" house could hardly be described as healthy. The average life expectancy was thirty years. A brief description provides some insight into the living conditions and the few romantic moments of life in the archaic Blackhouse of Lewis: "During winter, many neighbours come in each night. We form a circle round the fire and we discuss many subjects. The fire can be built as high as you like because there is no risk of a chimney catching fire."(2) The house was erected circa 1875 and inhabited until 1964. It was refurbished and has been open to the public as a museum since 1988.

The cave dwellings found in the temperate Mediterranean climate represent another form of habitation in harmony with the natural environment, albeit in a completely different manner than the one described above. The cave settlement in Guadix, featured as an example here, has been a tourist destination for some time and therefore includes a perfectly adequate hotel. Nevertheless, this settlement deserves closer study. The whitewashed entrances as well as the chimneys that project above the ground here and there are the only visible manifestations of the development in the landscape. The habitation as such is hidden

(1) Vitruvius: Ten Books on Architecture, http://penelope.uchicago.edu/E/Roman/Texts/Vitruvius, chapter 4, paragraph 1 (original: "In ipsis vero moenibus ea erunt principia. Primum electio loci saluberrimi. Is autem erit excelsus et non nebulosus, non prunio-sus regionesque caeli spectans neque aestuo-sas neque frigidas sed temperatas...")

(2) Alexander Fenton: The Island Blackhouse, Edinburgh 1978, p. 6

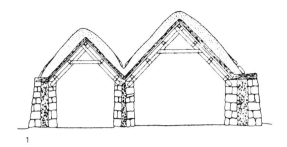

1 Cross section of Blackhouse with barn and living quarters. A narrow strip of grass on a thin layer of earth forms the upper completion of the enclosure wall built of rubble masonry.

2 Blackhouse in Arnol on the Island of Lewis, today a museum

3 Historic photograph of an interior: Family in Ballallan 1934, by S.T. Kjellberg, with kind permission from the Museum of History, Göteborg

4

4 Section and plan of a
cave dwelling cut into
the loess ground in the
Province of Henan,
China

5 Cave dwellings cut into
rock in Guadix, Spain

6 Sun-dried brick housing
settlement in
Humanuaca, Argentina

7 Ventilation chimneys in
the Baris development
in the oasis town of
Al-Kharga, Egypt,
Hassan Fathy, 1967

5

6

7

from view. Constant year-round temperatures of roughly 18 to 20°C ensure natural comfort in the interiors, which have in the meantime been outfitted with the standard home equipment. In winter, the internal climate is perceived as adequately warm, while the same temperatures are experienced as comfortably cool in summer.

The cave dwellings and their courtyards in the loess belt on the Yellow River (Huang He) in China are dug into a layer of clay. The ground above this layer and its natural vegetation remain intact for cultivation. Here we find another, roughly 6,000 year old building method that is impressive for its resource-conserving use of the site. In a climate zone known for extreme temperature fluctuations, indoor temperatures are equalized by up to 10°C in summer and in winter. Due to extreme damp during heavy rainfalls and the resulting condensation caused by poor ventilation, the living quality leaves much to be desired. Housing density is also limited in this case.

In hot and arid zones, clay is often the building material of choice for non-nomadic peoples, if the top layer of the earth consists of clay or the clay-sand-mix known as loam. The excellent mouldability of this clay (weathered feldspar) when water is added and the many variations in its application are chiefly responsible for the popularity of various building methods with clay around the world. The simplest methods employ rammed earth and sun-dried clay bricks. Depending on bulk density, this building material can be utilized for heat storage; the insulating properties are further improved when straw is added to the mix. The moisture-balancing character of this building material can have a positive influence on the interior climate.

Hassan Fathy, the renowned Egyptian architect, revived the traditional clay building technique in his housing projects, most of which were constructed for the socially disadvantaged. He achieved remarkable results in New Gourma (1946) and in the oasis town of Kharga (1967). The minimal use of windows prevents any direct sunlight from entering the building. Fathy employed ventilation chimneys to ensure air circulation throughout the interior by utilizing the ascending convection currents that occur naturally. The buildings are not only oriented toward the sun but also toward the principal wind direction. The constant flow of air offers comfort in the interior despite sweltering temperatures outside. Fathy documented the practical experiences he gained throughout his career in his seminal work *Natural Energy and Vernacular Architecture, Principles and Examples with Reference to Hot Arid Climates.* (3)

In Central Europe, traditional building methods have also been influenced by local climate, on the one hand, and resource availability on the other. The half-timbered house is a natural construction method in timber-rich regions. Depending on the subsoil, such houses are either erected on piles, on level ground or on a solid plinth story. The infilling is executed in a variety of ways with straw, clay, brick or natural stone. In plan, these homes adapt to a variety of needs. The only common element in all structures of this type is the solidly constructed core with fireplace and chimney. It occupies the center of the house and acts as a storage mass. Roof covering, incline and overhang are chosen in response to local precipitation patterns. The window orientation is still very much geared toward minimizing heat loss in winter.

When we look at the use of natural resources, we invariably encounter sophisticated mill technology powered by water or wind energy. We would benefit greatly from not only admiring these models – most of which survive only as exhibits in open-air museums – with a sense of nostalgia, but from carefully analyzing the remarkable sustainability they achieve.

New technologies and devices were developed for house and home during the Industrial Revolution. Traditions handed down through the generations were no longer considered appropriate for the time and replaced, giving rise to new visions for housing.

In 1910, the French urban planner Eugène Hénard (1849–1923) formulated a preliminary conclusion in his essay "Les villes de l´avenir": two sketches illustrate the rapid advances in

8

9

10

8 Windmill in Spiel, Düren district, 1782

9 Half-timbered house in Altenburg, Neuwied district, circa 1700

10 Half-timbered house with hemp infilling near Hennef, Rheinisches Freilichtmuseum Kommern, 1688; Window detail: the opening is reduced to the smallest necessary size in order to minimize heat losses during the cold season.

(3) Hassan Fathy: Natural Energy and Vernacular Architecture, Chicago 1986

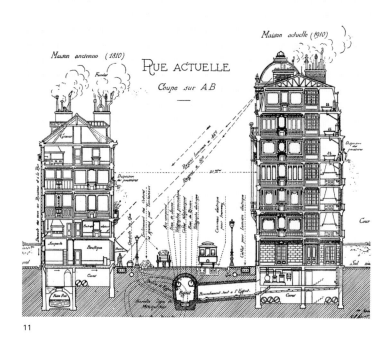

11

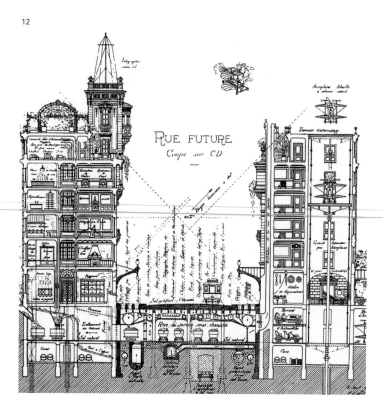

12

technology in the years leading up to his work and Hénard's vision for the future. (4)

The changes in technology and hygiene over the course of the nineteenth century are documented in the sketch of the "*rue actuelle*" or contemporary street. While the left side of the street is still equipped with gas lamps for illumination, the right side has already been provided with electric street lighting. In this sketch, the large sewer is already designed to accommodate supply pipes for compressed air, potable water, pneumatic mail, telephone cables and similar services along the ceiling. Every floor in the homes features bathrooms with hot and cold running water, while the homes on the opposite side still dump their waste in the street. The emissions from the dense forest of chimney heads are clearly depicted on both sides. This problem seems to have been solved with the help of district heating in the image of the "*rue future*" or the street of the future. In addition to a lushly verdant roof patio and a crowning antenna for "telegraphy," the only remaining task seems to be a provision for private air traffic with sufficient space for take-off and landing on the roof. A second street level, the "*rue de service*" or service road, represents a great improvement in urban comfort unlike anything we experience even today. Some reservations aside, Hénard's vision is therefore still current today.

Today, the "*ensanche*" (Catalan: *eixample* means expansion) is Barcelona's central urban quarter. Its attractiveness lies mainly in the many surviving structures in the Catalan version of Art Nouveau. Antonio Gaudí crowned his cleverly ventilated buildings with fancifully designed ventilation stacks. The uniform nineteenth-century block structure is somewhat monotonous. Still, despite the criticism sparked by the project upon its opening in 1867, it remains an important testimony to the beginnings of modern urban planning and design, shortcomings in the execution notwithstanding.

The expansion of Barcelona began in 1854 with the demolition of the city's Gothic fortifications. The road engineer and theoretician Ildefonso

Cerdà, who was committed to social reform, undertook a series of studies on the living conditions in the industrial society. His principal work, the *General Theory on Urbanization and the Application of its Principals and Theses to the Renewal and Expansion of Barcelona* (1867), contains the technical solutions he had developed. Cerdà was not only familiar with the theories of British and French utopians, hygienists and economists, he also had an open mind toward progress in technology. He developed technical solutions for political and social problems, the origin of which he identified as lying in urban concentration, the catastrophic hygienic conditions, land speculation and the lack of urban design in the interest of public needs. The urban grid adopts the axial lines of the old city and reflects Cerda's requirements for space and light. The original plan consisted of two block edge developments on opposite sides. The courtyard was to be kept open as a green space and for the cooling breeze from the sea. The pressure of development nowadays makes hardly any allowance for this type of consideration. The glass verandas that run across the entire height of the buildings on the courtyard side characterize the development to this day and continue to serve as climate buffers. Glazed loggias and glazed oriels are not exclusive to Barcelona. They also dominate the streetscape in southern Spain and in La Valetta on the island of Malta. During the day, the glazed areas are covered by mats and awnings, and the recessed doors are closed. At night, cool air is allowed to flow through the buildings. In winter, the warming sun can penetrate into the interior. These early double-skin facades also act as an effective barrier against street noise.

In the *Well Tempered Architecture* (5), Reyner Banham explored the origins of modern house technology and discovered one source in Catherine Beecher's concept for the "American Woman's Home" (6) from 1869, which offered an interesting evolution of traditional housing models: Beecher organized life in the home around a central service core. In addition to other functions, the entire house was supplied from this core with "healthy" air at comfortable temperatures by means of a cleverly designed forced-air heating system.

13

14

15

11 *"Rue actuelle"* from "Les villes de l'avenir," Eugène Hénard, 1910

12 *"Rue future"* from "Les villes de l'avenir," Eugène Hénard, 1910

13 Palacio Güell, Antonio Gaudí, 1889, ventilation stacks

14 Large glazed veranda in Barcelona

15 Street front with balconies and glazed oriels, La Valetta, Malta

(4) Jean-Louis Cohen: Eugène Hénard. Etudes sur les tranformations de Paris et autres écrits sur l'urbanisme, Paris 1982, pp. 345ff.

17

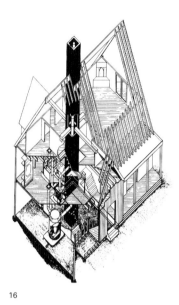

16

Frank Lloyd Wright always paid attention to technical details and the greatest possible comfort for users and inhabitants. The Larkin administration building was located next to a railway corridor and had to be hermetically sealed because of the smoke emanating from passing trains. These conditions brought about the first air-conditioned building in the United States. The four building corners are marked by stairwells with adjacent supply air ducts. Daylight falls into the building through a skylight in the central atrium, which is surrounded by additional offices linked via open galleries: an open-concept office across several floors.

Wright's early residential houses are characterized by projecting hipped roofs as an effective means of sun protection on the south and west sides. The floor plans, which are designed in an open manner in contrast to the vernacular architecture, offer comfort not least of all due to the excellent natural ventilation and a central heating system with warm water that is designed to fit around all facade openings. In an article entitled "Prairie Architecture" and published in *Modern Architecture* in 1931, Wright stated: "All heating-, lighting-, and supply lines must be integrated in such a manner that these systems become essential components of the building itself." (7)

Banham contrasts Wright's dedicated yet pragmatic use of new technologies with Le Corbusier's "machines for living." In this comparison, the author discovers several contradictions between the generous promises and the built results. Le Corbusier supplies his ideal house – the "house with the correct air for breathing" – with warm air at a temperature of 18°C by means of a "factory for exact air"! "Neutralizing walls" were to maintain this temperature. They consist of two layers with a cavity for air conduction. "In Moscow, hot air is conducted through this membrane cavity, in Dakar cold air. Result: in this way, the internal wall (the internal membrane) remains at a constant temperature of 18°. There you have it! The Russian house, the house in Paris, Suez or Buenos Aires, the luxury steamer crossing the equator: all will be hermetically sealed. In win-

18

19   20

16 "American Woman's Home," Catherine Beecher, 1869

17 Willis H. Carrier standing next to the first turbine cooling and refrigerating machine, 1922

18 The Larkin building, Frank Lloyd Wright, 1904, exterior

19 The Larkin building: interior

20 Willits House, Frank Lloyd Wright,1902

(5) Reyner Banham: "Well Tempered Architecture," Arch+ 93/1988

(6) Catherine E. Beecher and Harriet Beecher Stowe: American Woman's Home, complete text available online courtesy of The Project Gutenberg: www.pjbsware.demon. co.uk/gutenberg/gtn-letB.htm

(7) Frank Lloyd Wright: Modern Architecture, Being the Kahn Lectures for 1930, New York 1931

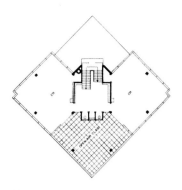

21

ter, it will be warm, in summer, cool – in other words: in the interior, there will be a constant supply of pure and good air at a temperature of 18°. The house is hermetically sealed! In future, no dust will penetrate into the interior. No flies or mosquitoes will enter. And no noise!" (8) "Air conditioning" had already been invented at this time, although it had only proven itself in industrial applications. The idea of the hermetically sealed space is gaining renewed currency in today's passive house technology.

"Sun, air and a home for all" was the motto of a 1932 exhibition at the foot of the radio tower in Berlin. The result of the competition, "the growing house," was presented in model buildings on a scale of 1:1. Elements such as inclined glass facades and winter gardens signal early initiatives of passive solar energy use. (9) In 1930, Johannes Duiker created an early example of innovative thinking in school construction with his Openluchtschool in a densely developed area of Amsterdam. The building is a rigorous expression of new ideas on childhood education. Light, air and sun are recognized as key elements that promote health and learning and are translated into architecture. The moderate Dutch climate allows for a generous use of glass. Some time would pass before the British architect Emslie Morgan successfully translated the use of glass facades in a school building as a deliberate energy-saving approach with his project in Wallasay. (10)

"From the interior, there is uninterrupted contact with the outside world. Sun and moon will illuminate the landscape, and the sky will be fully visible, but the unpleasant effects of climate, heat, dust, vermin, blinding light etc., will be regulated by the skin in such a manner that the interior is transformed into a Garden of Eden." (11)

From the early 1950s onward, Buckminster Fuller explored the idea of covering entire cities with a dome. It began in 1950 with the project for a dome over Manhattan, followed in the 1960s by concepts for settling the Arctic and Antarctic. Complete separation from all climatic influences has been a dream of humankind. In

22

23

24

21　Openluchtschool in Amsterdam, Johannes Duiker, 1930, floor plan

22　"Sun, Air and a Home for All," exhibition, Berlin, 1932

23　Same as 21, elevation

24　School in Wallasay, Emslie Morgan, 1961; Facade detail: The heating concept is designed to heat the building exclusively with solar heat and the waste heat from artificial lighting. (UK Patent Specification 1022411)

(8) Le Corbusier: Remarks, 1929, p. 72

(9) Thomas Katzke: "Netzwerken in Berlin," Bauwelt 17/2004, p. 12

(10) Brian Carter, Peter Warburton: "Die Entwicklung einer Solararchitektur," in: Detail 6/1993, p. 671

25

26   27

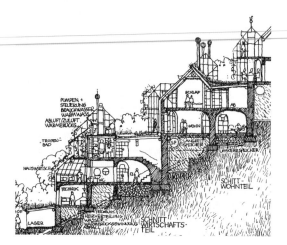

1967, Fuller was able to achieve this dream on a small scale at the EXPO in Montreal.

The technological euphoria seems undiminished. All that remains since a fire in 1976, which destroyed the synthetic skin, is the structural grid. The effect is imposing; yet the idea of being completely cut off from the natural climate has something oppressive about it.

As early as 1968, the Club of Rome emerged as a "circle of dedicated world citizens, unified in their care for the future of humankind and understanding their task as effecting change as an impartial, global catalyst." International interest was aroused in 1972 by Denis L. Meadow's report to the governing body, in which one subtitle read "The limitations of growth."(12) The resulting call for "developing a global social-economic market economy" has occupied the efforts of numerous institutions and committees ever since. With the oil crisis of 1973, the gravity of the situation deepened more quickly than had been anticipated. Responsible management of available resources became the subject of further investigation in the years that followed. The planning and construction sector has long been recognized as an important key area. Some time would pass, however, before the book *Ecological Building,* printed modestly on recycled paper and published by the German Federal Ministry for the Environment, became available as a first compendium with an abundance of basic information on new approaches to building.(13) The authors Althaus, Gabriel, Krusche and Weig-Krusche had the courage to investigate the entire sphere of building with a view to possible alternatives. Fundamental and detail-oriented topics are explored without reservations. Climate-, natural- and material lifecycles are analyzed. Options for passive as well as active energy generation are explored. The efforts of others with similar goals are also researched and included in the work. The Swedish architect Bengt Warne used his own home to test possibilities of minimizing energy requirements and the impact of building on the natural environment. It seems only natural that author Per Krusche and his comrades-in-arms followed suit and started their own experiment. They personally converted a barn step by step into a combined home and office building, and trans-

28

formed it into an experimental laboratory. The buildings created by the hippies and drop-outs in the United States in the 1970s also served as inspiration. Steve Baer succeeded in creating an especially clever, energy-autonomous shell in New Mexico: old oil barrels filled with water were used as solar storage components.

The aforementioned book ended with the presentation of an opencast mine, which had been abandoned in 1977 and was converted into a housing project (see illustration). "The renewal of biologically impoverished or abandoned sites can occur everywhere, even in large cities (New York, etc.), for houses, squares and streets are biotopes, too, and can be revived," thus the statement on the motivation behind the project.

When Peter Sulzer and Peter Hübner set out to build a student residence together with their students at the Technical University in Stuttgart, they were similarly motivated. The buildings were conceived as light-weight timber structures with a view to future reuse. Solar aspects were still neglected in this first initiative, but were taken into consideration for subsequent projects. This was complemented by the idea of practical training and the participation of the future users in all stages of the realization.

The Landstuhl project in 1982 was the first of its kind where a series of residential buildings was equipped with alternative solar systems that were subsequently tested and evaluated. The garden courtyard house by Eissler, Hoffmann and Gumpp is conceived in such a manner that it can also function as part of a group. Solar energy is to be utilized in a carefully considered manner through the south facade, which is largely glazed and equipped with adjustable solar panels and internal moveable insulation – both elements are operated manually. The solar energy is stored in the heavy building mass and released, when needed, via free convection or radiation. An analysis carried out by R. Gonzalo revealed that the system chosen for complementary heating was too sluggish and the dependency upon correct user behavior was relatively high. (14)

It is true that the single-family house is generally speaking not an energy-efficient form of housing. Nevertheless, numerous solar technological components were developed, launched,

29

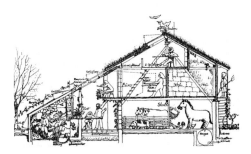

30

31

32   33

28 Bengt Warne, Naturhuset, 1976

29 House in New Mexico, Steve Baer, 1972. Heat stored during the daytime is utilized to provide warmth on cold nights.

30 same as 29: detail with opened solar wall

31 Office building incorporating an old barn, Arche Nova group (Per Krusche, Martin Schaub, Claus Steffan, Maria Weig-Krusche), 1983, cross section

32 same as 31: exterior

33 "Bauhäusle" student residence in Stuttgart Vaihingen, Peter Sulzer, Peter Hübner, 1983

(13) P. und M. Krusche, D. Althaus, I. Gabriel: Ökologisches Bauen, Wiesbaden/Berlin 1982

34

SÜDANSICHT

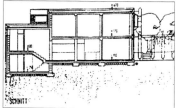
SCHNITT

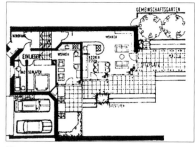

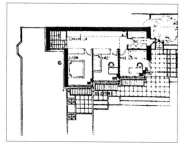
GEMEINSCHAFTSGARTEN

35

36

37

tested and refined in single-family house applications. The project presented here should be seen as representative of a great number of similar pilot projects. In an essay on "Minimal-energy houses," Horst Küsgen remarked in 1983: "Most development plans prevent energy-efficient building design, often without the awareness of the authors." Consequently, Küsgen rules out the single-family house and makes the case for high-density multi-story housing. In an overview, he provides a summary of the experiences with alternative energy systems to date, from forced ventilation with heat recovery to air collectors and mass storage. The effect of glass structures in front of the facade – a characteristic of solar building at the time – is critically questioned in terms of energy efficiency. (15)

The earth-mound houses on the grounds of the University in Stuttgart-Hohenheim, a student residence with 158 units, were not realized as a self-directed project. In this case, experts provided the design. The principles of activating passive solar energy were applied to low-energy building. A high daylight ratio was considered, as was intensive roof planting. Rainwater is collected and allowed to seep away. The facades are planted as well in order to prevent overheating in summer. The imbedding into the site corresponds to the ecological concept of partially compensating for the intervention into nature through building.

In addition to quality and cost-efficiency in building, Denmark is equally focussed on energy-related topics. The housing scheme in Greve, realized by Bente Aude and Boje Lundgaard, emerged from an architecture competition. Clear divisions in the plans, combined with effective dividing elements that are easy to handle, allow for effective energy savings. In winter, only the northern zone with high thermal insulation values is inhabited, while the middle zone is reserved for habitation in good weather. Solar heat is collected in the glass structures fronting the building and conducted to the center of the house. During the transitional seasons, inhabitants can use both the northern and the central zone, and in summer they can enjoy the entire cross section of the building. Considerable savings in energy consumption are entirely dependent on the correct use of French windows, blinds and insulating shutters. Other housing projects function according to similar principles.

In Austria, solar architecture is very much at the forefront especially in the province of Vorarlberg despite – or perhaps because of – the challenging climate. A strong desire for ecological and economical homes has led to multi-family house designs, often developed on a co-operative basis. Great value is placed on the creation of additional interior spaces for shared use. These are realized, on the one hand, as large projecting glasshouses or as internal atria with glass roofs, resulting in valuable buffer zones that offer multiple uses in winter and during the transitional seasons. The continuation of the tradition of building with timber, which is still very much alive in the region, supports the efforts in search for more energy-efficient solutions. An important factor in this case is the active communication of the experiences gained in conferences and numerous publications.

The international building exhibition (IBA) in Berlin brought energy-efficient solar architecture to the inner city. A comprehensive report on the row of five energy-efficient buildings on the Landwehrkanal, published in the journal *Bauwelt,* demonstrates the confidence of the state in this initiative: "The goal of the energy-efficient houses in Berlin is not to erect experimental buildings for energy-saving technologies, but to demonstrate the current state of technology and to explore it under the aspect of utility and usefulness for the tenant." The critical analysis openly discusses the problematic conditions in the context of urban planning. A closed block edge would have greatly increased the energy efficiency from the outset. Further cutbacks had to be made to the alternative technical equipment during the realization stages. In 1993, Robert Kaltenbrunner carried out some follow-up research that confirms the initial concern. Moreover, he finds himself compelled to remark: "The residents have obviously failed to understand the intentions of the builders or decided to reject them." (17)

38

39 40

34 Residential building created as part of the Landstuhl project, Eissler, Hoffmann, Gumpp, 1982, south elevation

35 same as 34: south elevation, section and plan

36 Student residence in Stuttgart, Kaiser, Schmidtges, Minke, 1984

37 Housing complex in Greve, Denmark, Bente Aude, Boje Lundgaard, 1985

38 Residential district in Copenhagen, Faellestegnestuen, 1987

39 Multi-family house in Fussach, Mittersteiner, Larsen, 1988, view into the communal winter garden

40 same as 39: exterior of winter garden

(14) *Roberto Gonzalo: Passive Nutzung der Sonnenenergie – Grundlagen für den Gebäudeentwurf, Munich 1990, p. 89*

(15) *Horst Küsgen: "Minimalenergiehäuser," arcus 3/1983, pp. 137ff.*

41

42

41 Five energy-saving
   buildings in Berlin,
   by Gerkan, Marg and
   Partner; Pysall, Jensen,
   Stahrenberg; Faskel,
   Nicolic; Schiedhelm,
   Axelrad; Klipper +
   Partner, 1985

42 Solar house in Berlin,
   Schreck, Hillmann,
   Nagel in collaboration
   with Kempchen,
   Güldenberg, 1988

43 Exemplary ecological
   renovation in Munich,
   Per Krusche, Arche
   Nova, 1989

44 Apartment building in
   Stuttgart, Christian
   Gullichsen 1993

45 Apartment building in
   Stuttgart, Michael
   Alder, 1993

(16) Axel Jahn, Klaus
    Sommer: "Fünf
    Energiesparhäuser am
    Landwehrkanal in
    Berlin," Bauwelt 4/1985,
    pp. 126ff.

(17) Robert Kaltenbrunner:
    "Die Energiesparhäuser
    der IBA in Berlin,"
    Bauwelt 38/1993, pp.
    2056ff.

43

44

45

Another IBA-project, the so-called solar house on the Lützowstrasse, was more successful. Here, the block edge is closed and the south wall is faced with glass-enclosed winter gardens, air collectors and internal insulated sliding panels. In the passive system of the winter gardens, the floor acts as a storage mass. Warm air is pressed through ventilators into the adjacent cavity ceilings with the help of air collectors located between the winter gardens. Regulating systems control the operation in winter and during the transitional seasons, all the while providing sufficient sunlight in the interior.

In Munich, the exemplary ecological restoration of a heritage house, built in 1898, has unfortunately remained a unique effort. The rundown structure was retrofitted with great optimism and dedication with a series of technical components: partially glazed balconies as climate buffers, solar collectors for water heating, a heat exchanger for exhaust air from kitchens and climate buffers, a gray water processing plant and a composting system for biowaste. The author's repeated requests for information from the client with regard to the operation of the building have remained unanswered, even though subsequent monitoring of projects of this kind is as important as the initial determination to implement new approaches to building. We can only surmise that investors and users were ultimately overwhelmed by the task.

The housing projects realized for the IBA in Stuttgart in 1993 is another case where subsequent monitoring of the initial vision was never carried out. The architectural quality of the buildings designed by Gullichsen and Alder has stood up to the requirements of contemporary habitation despite reductions to the innovative technologies employed.

The guesthouse at the youth education center in Windberg remains one of the few exceptions. The clear integration into the urban plan, the rigorously differentiated facades and carefully calibrated building systems justify the numerous domestic and international publications dedicated to this project.

The oeuvre of the Danish architecture firm Tegnestuen Vandkunsten includes many housing projects distinguished by quality of living combined with aesthetic design. Aspects of energy efficiency are only integrated into projects that benefit from special promotions or subsidies, for example, the Skejby development. Solar collectors integrated into the facades play as important a role as the orientation of the houses, the floor plan organization and the facade design based on orientation.

The residential building by Fink and Jocher in Coburg is similar in appearance. While the north side with its small openings is rather closed in appearance, the large glass surfaces on the south side open the building to the sun. Cleverly integrated TIM elements are part of a collector: excess heat is diverted to a storage facility in the basement through prefabricated concrete components with integrated heat exchangers behind the facade. The urban parameters were set by HR2 architects (refer to the project featured on page 56) and were the subject of a competition.

This brief overview of highlights in the history of energy-efficient building can only address a few important aspects and is by no means intended to make any claims to being complete. What is important, however, is the insight into current trends in architecture we can gain.

The interconnectedness between local resources and vernacular building tradition has been lost in the wake of the rapid expansion of transportation routes around the world. Thus, natural stone from China and South America can be offered at more favorable cost in Europe than locally available stone. Renzo Piano built his museum in Riehen near Basel with red porphyry from Patagonia, a material that creates a reference to the locally available sandstone while being far more durable. Clearly there are no simple and immediate answers to the question of sustainability.

The comfort provided by house technology has evolved mostly during the last three centuries. Increased life expectancy is directly linked to this evolution. However, the constantly rising energy demand that goes hand in hand with technological development and the plundering of available resources were ignored for a very long time. It was only gradually and under pressure – reflected in political milestones such as the Charter of Athens, the oil crisis, the accident at the reactor in Chernobyl, the Rio Conference and finally the ratification of the Kyoto Protocol

46

47

48   49

46 Guest house of the youth education center in Windberg, Thomas Herzog in collaboration with Peter Bonfig, 1991

47 same as 46: entrance facade

48 Housing complex in Skejby, Tegnestuen Vandkunsten, 1998

49 Housing complex in Coburg, Fink + Jocher, 1999. The energy balance is 40 percent below the value stipulated in the current heat protection act. The non-glazed area in the image shows the surface of the prefabricated concrete component tinted a dark blue: the heat exchangers are integrated in this section.

– that public awareness of ecological issues began to develop.

Many of the technologies available today were developed and tested by experimenters in their own homes. But the single-family house in the guise of a passive or zero-energy house cannot be the ultimate goal. There should be greater political will and resistance to the destruction of our landscape through urban sprawl. Building skins with high thermal insulation in combination with the necessary, intelligent ventilation systems only make sense in high-density development. The examples that follow have been chosen to demonstrate that the phase of developing new technologies can be followed by integrating these methods into architecture as a matter of course. Aesthetics are part of sustainability too, as a look at the history of architecture illustrates.

50

51

ENERGY-EFFICIENT URBAN DESIGN:
PRINCIPLES AND STRATEGIES

ENERGY-EFFICIENT URBAN DESIGN: PRINCIPLES AND STRATEGIES

Point of Departure/Status Quo

There are general basic rules and principles for energy-efficient building. However, if one were to seek a correspondence in the field of urban design and planning, the situation that emerges is less clear. On the one hand, urban design and planning are affected by a vast number of factors that must be taken into consideration and on the other hand, valuation and implementation in this field never fail to provide ample material for debate. The palette ranges from the political determination of the conditions, including zoning or aspects related to access and traffic, to technical considerations such as the type of energy supply or the use of renewable energies.

The following is true in principle: the greater the scale of a system, the more complex are the mechanisms that govern the system as a whole. On the plane of urban design, the number of influencing factors increases proportionally to the number of decision-takers, which in turn diminishes the power of enforcement of the control and regulatory mechanisms. It is not uncommon that these circumstances result in situations where the planning task as such is carried out in a context that is contrary to the principles of energy efficiency. Efforts aimed at energy-efficient, sustainable planning are barely sufficient, in such a situation, to compensate for the negative effects that result from the demands for mobility, access, supply, etc., which have already been established at the outset.

In most cases, the architect's options of bringing any influence to bear on the total system of urban design by means of planning turn out to be limited and largely ineffective. However, this experience should in no way act as an excuse for a mono-causal approach that does not do sufficient justice to the responsibility of the architect. Regardless of whether they are changeable or not, contexts and issues must be revealed to the full extent. In the interest of further development it is important, therefore, to not only utilize the urgently needed feedback but to correct erroneous decisions of the past as much as possible. Sustainable urban design and planning set signals that inspire a new way of thinking. By establishing the framework for

potential sustainable developments, the built realization can help to identify the limitations and possibilities inherent both in the buildings themselves and in the public spaces they generate.

Political and social parameters are important aspects – albeit outside the sphere of planning – that fundamentally define the framework for all urban development in advance. In the following, these aspects are mentioned only briefly; for a more detailed exploration of this topic, readers are encouraged to consult the comprehensive literature. Far-reaching decisions are extremely difficult to achieve on a practical level. Even if a consensus on the overall goal is reached in society and although the importance of a commitment to the promotion of sustainable processes may be recognized, the willingness to provide the necessary support quickly evaporates when personal interests are at stake.

Over the past decades, the longing for nature and the subsequent flight from the city have resulted in an amorphous, unregulated urban expansion. The uncoupling of functions – a belated consequence of modernism – inspired a trend that was later carried forward by a misguided ecological movement. Cities were abandoned because they were supposedly unsuitable for living in harmony with nature. On the other hand, the dream of living in the countryside was to be realized without relinquishing services related to supply and infrastructure. Proximity to the city as a service center, moreover, was seen as a guarantee that all additional needs and employment resources would remain secure. Having arisen from a consumer society, in which ecology is but another marketing ploy, this attitude can in long term be little more than a privilege for eco-yuppies, who can afford to indulge their fancy. For the house as a one-of-a-kind object cannot represent a universally valid solution, no matter how energy-efficient it may be.

The consequence is urban sprawl with the result that the desire to live in nature can, ultimately, no longer be fulfilled. What we are left with, instead, are reduced strips of green resulting from the prescribed distances between single-family houses that are hardly energy-efficient.

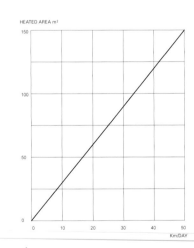

1

1 Energy consumption of a car (5 l/100 km) depending on average distance travelled per day compared to the energy required to heat the corresponding living area in a residential unit built to low-energy standards.

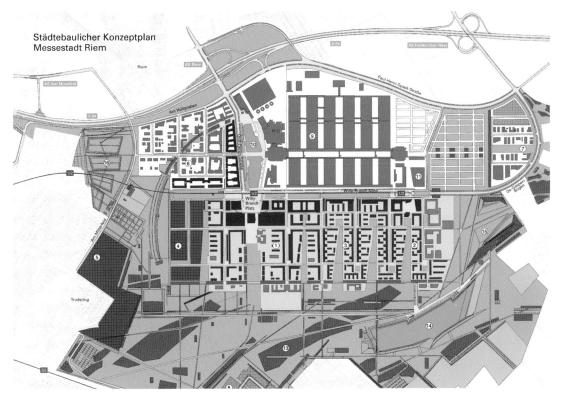

Städtebaulicher Konzeptplan
Messestadt Riem

2

3

The negative side of this trend, which is moreover promoted by tax initiatives (e.g. lack of differentiation in funding for housing development, tax relief for the drive to work, etc.), is exacerbated by the energy consumption and the toxin and noise emissions of daily commuter traffic.

In recent years, efforts have been stepped up to seek solutions that could reverse the trend. In several large cities such as London or Paris, comprehensive studies and projects are being carried out to find ecologically sensible, sustainable and socially just solutions for habitation within the configuration of the city. It is generally agreed that the most important aspect is to increase the appeal of living in the city. Political leadership can send a clear message in this regard.
To keep guidelines simple, aspects of urban design and planning are rarely considered as criteria in the decision whether energy-efficient developments should be promoted or not. Rather, they tend to be limited to individual building objects. Building typologies such as

the single-family house are supported as soon as the calculated energy balance for the individual building meets the requirements. What is overlooked in this context is the fact that the negative, type-related consequences cannot be compensated with energy-saving measures, no matter how efficient. For the growing urban sprawl that is obliterating our landscape, the expensive infrastructure required as a result of wide-spaced development and the dependency on private vehicular transportation are all linked to additional energy consumption that is never reflected in the energy balance of the building. Building strategies chosen for promotion and subsidy should be evaluated in a differentiated manner according to their urban (and sustainable) effect. Shifting funding from new construction to renovation and renewal, urban densification and the improvement of open urban areas, would strengthen the revival of old buildings and urban districts. Reducing traffic volume, expanding pedestrian and cycling paths, utilizing the existing infrastructure (roads, access, supply and waste management, linkage to the public transportation system) as well as

2 Urban planning concept, Messestadt Riem, Munich: the parameter plan offers excellent options for the creation of different building forms: passive house, low-energy house, assisted living, etc. Good public access, social services, shopping and leisure facilities promote energy-conscious living.

3 Apartment building with childcare built to passive house standard, Messestadt Riem, Munich, NEST GmbH, 2002

4

5

6

7

4 Woningbouw Kiefoek in
Rotterdam, JJP Oud,
1925–30. The complex
has been renovated to
meet the new standards
for housing.

5 Residential building
built to passive house
standard, urban devel-
opment project Am
Ackermannbogen,
Munich, A2-Architekten,
NEST GmbH, 2004.
Conversion of former
barracks complex.

6 Housing development in
Passau-Neustift,
H. Schröder and
S. Widmann, 1989. The
development, created
within the framework of
the Bavarian initiative
for housing models,
demonstrates the princi-
ples of energy conserva-
tion and the passive use
of solar energy.

7 Office and apartment
building in Wiesbaden,
A-Z Architekten, 2002.
Closing a building gap
with a new structure
built to passive house
standard (see p. 68).

avoiding urban sprawl across the landscape, strengthening neighborhoods and providing easy access to services and cultural institutions are all additional advantages of this develop-ment, which enhance the living environment while reducing energy consumption.

In most medium-size and large cities the avail-ability of open spaces for new buildings is decreasing. Future development is therefore only possible by expanding the city boundaries or renewing the existing fabric. Growth in the periphery is less desirable for the reasons we have already discussed. Renewing existing fab-rics through demolition and new construction can achieve higher density and/or better use of areas that are already developed. Even without demolition, increasing the density of existing structures is a highly relevant approach from the perspective of energy efficiency. Measures to increase the density tend to go hand in hand with upgrades in the energy balance of existing fabrics.

The conversion of buildings and areas to new uses, for example former industrial areas or barracks, is a significant factor. Ecologically, these areas, which are often centrally located, offer ideal conditions due to the existing infra-structure and possibilities for integration. They represent a growing potential for creating new housing developments in which sustainability is uppermost in the approach to realization.

Evolution

The recent history of architecture abounds with forerunners of ecological housing, for example the garden cities or the housing initiatives dur-ing the Industrial Revolution. Energy consump-tion in the context of building was not the pri-mary concern in these historic examples, how-ever. The focus was on creating a social envi-ronment rather than reacting to the profound impact of industrialization. At that time, atti-tudes toward energy consumption were char-acterized by an optimism that was still free of thoughts of relinquishing services or accepting restrictions.

Energy-conscious attitudes and the concept of utilizing solar radiation to reduce the heating requirements in housing came to the fore in so-called solar architecture. It would take until the

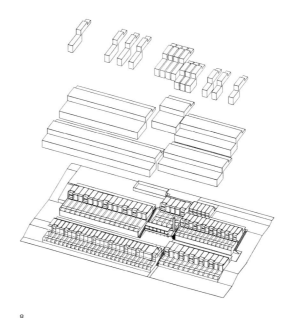

1970s, however, before the breakthrough from purely experimental and isolated projects to a broader consideration of the linkages between architecture and energy took place.

In the beginning, measures aimed at the passive utilization of solar energy in residential buildings were almost exclusively employed in detached houses. This is explained in part by the experimental nature of these measures, which would have translated into too high a risk had they been employed on a larger scale. Monitoring and subsequent optimization of the solar systems by eliminating other factors with a negative influence (shading, unfavorable orientation, etc.) were also more easily achieved when working with detached houses.

The experiences and intense research in the years that followed provided the basis of accumulated knowledge that induced architects to apply the proven principles on a broader scale. The technical equipment (solar collectors, ventilation systems, etc.) became more sophisticated and achieved higher levels of efficiency when applied on a larger scale. Energy-efficient building was finally able to establish itself in architecture and to leave its "alternative" character behind. The prejudices that were a legacy of the era of development and experimentation, namely that any sensible application of these principles would always be restricted to isolated objects and small developments, were overcome.

The years that followed saw an increase in the development of row housing with greater density. The row house has a much better ratio of external surface to volume (S/V ratio) than the detached house. Early examples are the housing schemes in Halen and Thalmatt realized by Atelier 5 in the 1960s. They are masterful models of making the advantages of a freestanding house available to a wider circle of users by means of higher density in building; these schemes combine compact planning with optimized orientation to achieve excellent energy standards.

What these first housing projects have in common with the experimental projects that preceded them is that limited solar incidence as a result of location was able to be overcome to a

8

9

large degree: rural or suburban areas, where orientation and shading from trees did not present a problem, were usually preferred.

Innovative trends in ecological building became a standard feature in the program of international exhibitions such as the International Building Exhibition (IBA) in Berlin (1989), the International Garden Show (IGA) in Stuttgart (1993) and, most recently, the EXPO 2000 in Hanover (2000). In the area of high-density urban housing, the goal was to demonstrate options for responsible energy management. Although the buildings created for this sector were often formal in character, they helped to focus attention on the problems of urban housing and sustainable urban design.

Solar urban design is a fairly expensive experimental field for demonstration and pilot projects. The few examples of this kind illustrate on the one hand how much effort is required and, on the other hand, how rarely the results match the expectations. Too much

8 Halen housing develop-
   ment near Bern,
   Atelier 5, 1955

9 same as 8: aerial
   photograph

10

11

12

13

weight is placed on building design, neglecting the overarching urban design principles. The definition of the parameters, from communal energy management to local and regional energy supply concepts to the zoning map, which blaze the trail for solar architecture, is the basic prerequisite for the successful development of energy-efficient architecture in an urban setting.

Climate Conditions

Sustainable urban design can only succeed on the basis of climate-appropriate planning, which – as the name indicates – must be adapted to local microclimate conditions. The etymological meaning of the word "climate" is "slope" or "incline," in reference to the angle of altitude of solar radiation. This "incline" varies both over the course of a day and throughout the year and influences the entire spectrum of climate parameters. However, only those weather factors that directly influence people or the utility of a building are relevant to the architect. These factors are, broadly speaking, temperature, wind and solar radiation.

The heat losses of a building are largely determined by external temperature. In this context, transmittance heat losses are dependent on three equally important factors: the heat-transmitting surface, its insulating properties and the difference between internal and external temperature. While the first two factors translate into measures related to design (compactness) and construction (insulating properties), the third factor is a characteristic of the local climate that cannot be influenced. The more extreme the external temperatures are, the more important is the optimization of the first two aspects.

Glasshouses, the so-called "house-in-a-house" principle, or enclosed atria and courtyards, create a buffer zone between interior and exterior. Newly discovered for large, usually multi-story foyers and access areas in the development of office and commercial buildings, the concept is based on predecessors such as the atria or public, glass-enclosed arcades of the nineteenth century.

10 Passive house development Lummerlund in Hanover-Kronsberg, Rasch & Partner, 1998

11 Ecological housing created for EXPO Hanover, 2000

12 Apartment buildings in Stuttgart, Tegnestuen Vandkunsten, 1993. Part of the exhibition "Werk-Stadt-Wohnen" during the IGA (international garden exhibition), Stuttgart, 1993

13 same as 12: south elevation

Warmed by solar radiation, these spaces achieve higher temperatures on average than the temperature of the external air. Consequently, they contribute to energy conservation and provide comfortable interior spaces for a variety of activities. Although the concept opens the door onto attractive architectural expressions, the constructional effort of most realized examples is disproportionate to the energy savings achieved. Overheating in summer is often unavoidable without expending additional energy.

Daily fluctuations in external temperatures can also be significant in summer. Carefully designed ventilation overnight can cool the building mass, enabling it to absorb temperature peaks or the internal heat load during the day.

Wind affects the energy balance of a building in two ways: first, by increasing the transmittance heat losses through the convective cooling of the building skin, and secondly, by increasing the ventilation heat losses through leaks in the building skin. Energy-efficient building is therefore based on creating impervious building skins.

The influence of wind is a significant factor in the design of open spaces. Local conditions, above all topography and vegetation, orientation and shape of the built volume or the positioning of buildings in relation to one another, determine the wind conditions in the interstitial spaces and hence their quality as useable outdoor areas. Dense groups of buildings and open spaces or streetscapes with directional breaks prevent a wind tunnel effect. Ancillary buildings (warehouses, sheds, garages, etc.) as well as earth walls or planted wind barriers (trees, hedges, etc.) can fulfill a protective function for the built environment.

For energy-efficient architecture, solar radiation is the most important climate factor. This design concept is therefore known in simplified fashion as "solar architecture." We must understand the solar geometry, both in cold climates where its utilization can contribute greatly to heating, and in warm zones, where the focus is on avoiding solar incidence in summer. Methods for the study of solar incidence in the context of urban design are discussed from page 49 onward.

14

15   16

14 Galérie Vivienne in Paris

15 Nachtgärtle housing complex in Fussach, Vorarlberg, W. Juen, 1993, entrance and access atrium

16 DVG administration building in Hanover, Hascher + Jehle in collaboration with Heinle, Wischer and Partner, 1999. The glass hall offers protection for the office buildings and the access and open areas.

17

17 EXPO 1992 in Seville. Paths shaded with vegetation and evaporative cooling with water.

18 same as 17: shaded square

19 Streetscape in Seville shaded with *toldos* (canvas awnings)

18

19

Dependent on cloud cover, global radiation is composed of a direct and a diffuse component. The diffuse component of solar radiation is non-directional. Hence, even north facades will receive a certain amount of solar radiation, although it is much lower than in all other cardinal directions. Measures for the passive utilization of solar energy are chiefly based on direct solar radiation. It influences the orientation and distance between buildings as well as the conditions for solar incidence in streetscapes and open areas.

In warm climates, protection from the sun is a more important urban design task. The close arrangement of houses that is typical of Mediterranean regions prevents the heating of the building mass by providing mutual shading. Narrow lanes and courtyards are also protected from direct sun by this means.

In addition to the climate factors we have already explored, location, orientation, topography and vegetation are important in the context of defining the local conditions.

The characteristics of the site are vital for the choice of ecological measures. In an urban setting, buildings sites tend to be smaller and more influenced by the surroundings than in rural settings. The topography influences the orientation of the buildings to the sun (slope orientation) or the influence of wind (exposed or sheltered location). A summit location, for example, offers ideal conditions for the utilization of solar energy, while at the same time causing higher heat losses as a result of the greater exposure to wind. A location on a south-facing slope, by contrast, makes it possible to decrease the distance between buildings arranged one behind another, thus enabling a higher building density.

Planting vegetation around the building can improve the climate conditions (solar incidence, wind conditions) for the building skin and adjacent open spaces. Deciduous trees provide shade in summer and allow solar incidence in winter. Rows of trees can also form wind barriers or act as wind channels for natural ventilation where needed. As a result of evaporation, which extracts heat from the environment, vegetation can also be used to cool the outside air in summer and hence promote the effect of natural ventilation.

Building Type and Building Proportions

While there are defined structural and design parameters for energy conservation and energy generation for passive houses, such definitions are only partially established in the area of urban planning and design. There is a lack of concrete requirements for the optimization of the energy balance of urban structures. At the same time, the specifications for urban design (distance, orientation, access, building form, etc.) establish the basis for planning and designing buildings with a view to optimized energy use and hence for the building requirements for energy-efficient architecture.

The heat transmission losses of a building are proportional to the insulating quality and to the heat transmitting external surface. Two aspects are relevant in the context of urban design:
– building type and
– building proportions.

Building type defines the degree of compactness that can be achieved. Given the same shape, the external surface is relatively larger in a small volume than in a large volume. Freestanding single-family houses, even if they are compact in design, are therefore less efficient in terms of energy use than row houses or multi-family houses. While the most compact shape for freestanding houses is a cube, the optimal proportions for row development in terms of compactness are found in a deep prism-shape. In this case the ratio of depth to width of the individual housing units must be considered with regard to compactness, natural lighting and solar heat gain.

The context in which a building is located determines the degree of potential solar incidence and hence of potential energy gains. Two urban design factors play a role:
– building orientation and
– distance between buildings (density).
Furthermore, these two aspects are linked to additional factors in urban planning for energy-efficient architecture. These are:
– access (external and internal),
– parking and
– open spaces.

20

21   22

20 Sun protection with straw mats. The mats are moistened to achieve adiabatic cooling.

21 Hanweiler housing development in Stuttgart, Knut Lohrer, 1982, glazed rooms articulate the row houses built on a slope.

22 Conversion of the old Atocha railway terminal in Madrid, Rafael Moneo, 1992. Micro sprinkler systems between the potted plants humidify and cool the air.

26

Building Orientation

In low-density settlements, corresponding to the situation present in developments in rural environments or on the urban periphery, requirements such as good orientation or sufficient distance between buildings are easier to fulfill. In the urban context, on the other hand, considerations related to energy conservation take on a different dimension. Complex contexts, for example access and traffic volume, noise, urban integration, density, neighboring developments, heat supply, etc., must be taken into consideration. These differing factors should be treated within the scope of the overarching situation and never be optimized in a mono-causal, that is, isolated fashion.

This does not mean, however, that the utilization of solar energy cannot be achieved given the complex conditions presented by urban situations. On the one hand, optimal orientation of the buildings toward the sun is simply not possible in all cases and limited solar incidence in winter has to be accepted in most cases. On the other hand, urban situations are characterized by greater density and more compact building forms, both of which reduce energy losses in the first place. Measures for passive solar use must then be developed in response to the conditions of the specific site and scaled accordingly. In addition to structural passive measures, active systems are a sensible complement (water heating, supplementary heating). These are most effective if they are not employed for individual buildings but for ensembles as a whole. They are usually installed on the roof, since roofs tend to be exposed to the sun even in dense developments. Optimal orientation of the solar systems, independent of building orientation, is also facilitated in this situation. Choosing the appropriate type and dimension of the system is dependent, however, on the overall supply concept. Regional energy concepts and supply structures should also be taken into consideration.

Density

The achievable density is largely dependent on the necessary distance between buildings. In row development with south orientation, all units can benefit from the same conditions for solar incidence provided the necessary distance is maintained between the rows for winter conditions. For a 48° latitude (Munich, Freiburg), this distance equals three times the building height. Based on this prerequisite, the maximum sectional density that can be achieved in multi-storey developments is roughly 1.0.

If the goal is to achieve greater density, these distances cannot be maintained. Roof shape also has a considerable influence on the determination of distances. Even if the goal is to create a fully insolated facade, maisonette units in developments with shorter distances between buildings make it possible that at least part of each unit has the full benefit of the sun even in winter. These and similar planning measures can increase the average sectional density in a south-oriented row development to roughly 1.3 – maintaining the distance of 1 H, which is typical for housing. Greater density can only be achieved through a combination of buildings with differing orientations (courtyard-, block structure). Shadows cast by one building onto another and the various qualities of the location must be studied on a case-by-case basis.

For uses other than habitation, solar gain tends to play a subordinate role. Allocating the lower parts of a building, which receive little or no sun, to commercial uses makes it possible to reduce the necessary distances.

Developments on the periphery should also aim for high density in areas with excellent public access. Savings in traffic and infrastructure are usually much greater than any energy savings achieved by the buildings themselves.

Access

In addition to density, the access system and the differentiated use of open spaces – both public and private – are important aspects for the study of distances between buildings. As urban planning and design evolved, the differing views have divided the planners of Modernism into two camps: those who favor E-W orientation and those who advocate N-S orientation.

As early as 1918, Muthesius wrote on this topic: "The type of road layout also determines, to some degree, the quality of habitability in the

24

25

23

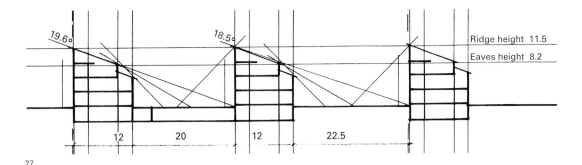

27

surrounding houses, especially as regards solar incidence and wind protection of the apartments. A road running from east to west results in house fronts that are always shaded on one side, and house fronts that are always fully exposed to the sun on the other. Development along such a road could be designed in such a way that all interior spaces that do not require sunshine, for example, corridors, stairwells, laundry rooms, sculleries, lavatories, etc., are planned for the side that is devoid of sun, and, conversely, all living areas would face the side that receives sunshine, regardless of whether this would place them at the front or to the rear of the houses. Yet the modest house does not offer the flexibility required for this measure, which can usually be achieved without too much difficulty in larger houses. Living spaces are located both along the front and the rear. In houses with live-in kitchens, these must receive as much or even more sun than all other rooms. As to the bedroom floor, it is impossible to make a difference between front and rear side. The conclusion is that roads running from east to west are poorly suited for housing developments with small buildings. Conditions are far more favorable on roads running from north to south, for they allow one row of houses exposure to the eastern sun and the other exposure to the western sun, so that each half receives the same amount of sunshine." (1)

Statements of this nature formed the basis for the familiar east-west row house developments of the 1950s and 1960s. In south-oriented rows, the open solar facade will lie opposite to the closed north facades of the row on the other side. A symmetrical composition of the rows would interfere with the required south orientation of living and lounging areas.

The southern exposure can be better utilized if access is provided from the north. One disadvantage is that building rows with access from one side only require an uneconomical increase in the number of individual access routes. This approach also results in nondescript interstitial spaces and the differentiation between access and open space is rendered more difficult. From the social perspective, the possibilities for contact and thus social interaction are also diminished.

Access from one direction only requires a great deal of sensibility in the treatment of the inter-

28

29   30

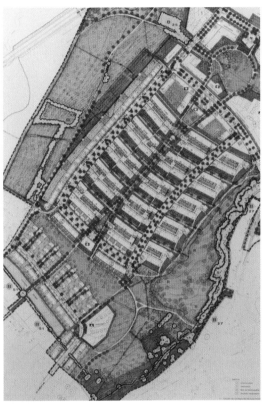

23 Apartment building in Munich, Raupach and Schurk, 1996. The glazed balconies serve for passive use of solar energy and as noise protection.

24 Apartment building in Madrid, Mario Muelas, 2003. Active use of solar energy in the urban core: solar collectors on the roof for water heating.

25 same as 24: air collectors on the facade as solar chimney for cooling in summer.

26 Housing development in Kriens, Switzerland, Lischer, 2001. The hillside location and the staggered arrangement of the buildings make it possible to reduce the distance between houses (see p. 44).

27 Berteldorfer Höhe housing development in Coburg, H2R, Hüther, Hebensperger-Hüther, Röttig, 1992, south-facing rows with optimized distances for solar incidence on buildings and open areas.

28 same as 27: site plan

29 Ried housing development in Niederwangen near Bern, Atelier 5, 1983/1990. Dense building in the form of a block.

30 same as 29: differentiated orientation of residential units depending on location.

31

33

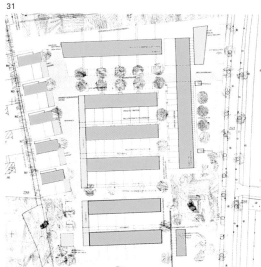

32

34

31 Solar housing in Münster-Coerde, Pollok + Gonzalo, 2000. One-sided access per housing row.

32 same as 31: access to the short rows is provided from a common courtyard.

33 Röthenbach a. d. Pegnitz housing development, Metron Architektur, 1990. Access to each row from a residential village green with play area and community hall.

34 same as 33: access and private yards are separated by a row of garden sheds.

(1) *Notes on planning housing developments by Hermann Muthesius, in: Kleinhaus und Kleinsiedlung, Munich 1918*

stitial spaces and is only sensible for shorter rows, which are linked to a common, superordinate access space (residential paths).

Providing one common access per double row is more economical, especially if it is designed for vehicular traffic as well. In south-oriented row development, however, the preference for south-facing living and lounging areas translates into a variety of access conditions for each row, which must be taken into consideration in the plan. The treatment of the open spaces in rows with southern access also deserves particular attention, as we shall demonstrate. This form of access is a typical feature in east-west oriented rows, whereby a qualitative differentiation between the eastern and western locations would be necessary, although it is frequently neglected.

The internal access or circulation within the building is subject to a variety of conditions, depending on the orientation of the access side.

In a building with access from the north, the following options are available:

– Direct access (row house, direct access via external stairs),

– Covered walkway, and

– Common access per block or building slab.

In a building with access from the south, there are some restrictions, which must be taken into consideration:

– Direct access: here on the sunny side, where a private outdoor space would be desirable. This conflict must be avoided through appropriate measures.

– Covered walkway: on the south side, the walkway interferes with the sunshine penetrating into the rooms behind or below the walkway. Privacy must be ensured between the walkway and the adjacent interiors. If the walkway is located on the north side, it does not interfere with solar incidence but causes a change in the access side. This arrangement means that residents walk through the building to the rear side, which nullifies the clear separation between public access and private spaces. Once again, visual contact into private areas is an irritant.

– Common access per block or building slab: this type of access causes few problems with regard to solar incidence. To ensure that a south-facing outdoor space can be allocated to units on the ground floor, the distance between stairwells should be sufficiently generous. On the other hand, when stairwells are spaced farther apart, one can only build fairly large apartments. A combination of block or slab access and short individual walkways offers an advantageous alternative.

35

Parking

While high density is desirable in the context of ecological town planning and urban development, unnecessary sealing of ground surfaces should be avoided. Access roads and parking lots can result in the sealing of larger areas than the built development as such. To avoid unnecessary paths (e.g., access from several sides), access as a whole should be conceived in a minimal and simple fashion. The type of access is closely linked to the topic of parking. If expensive underground parking or large parking lots are to be avoided, then this issue becomes the most important restriction in terms of urban development.

In the case of lower building height, the necessary distances between building rows are relatively small. The resulting scale is just sufficient for residential access (local traffic only) and an appropriately large yard. Access to shorter rows should therefore be combined with parking at the principal access road, from which the individual homes are then accessed via car-free paths.

If parking is to be provided in the area between structures, the required space is of necessity increased. The necessary distances then correspond to the shading lengths of 3- to 4-story buildings. In these situations, a careful arrangement of parking can contribute to the zoning of the interstitial space, for example, as a protective barrier between public areas and the private yard.

Hillside locations make it possible to integrate the parking area in the hill by modulating the site. If we wish to render life in the city more attractive, we must re-conquer public spaces for people. Alternative parking concepts can make a positive contribution to public spaces. These areas should be designed for multiple uses: a sheltered play area for children, storage, hobby area or workshop, are but some of the functions that can be accommodated in this fashion. This enhances the flexibility of the development and makes it possible to reduce the scale of the individual buildings by providing additional space in these alternative extensions for a variety of uses.

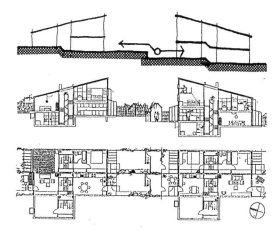

36

37

38

35 Housing development in Passau-Neustift, H. Schröder and S. Widmann, 1989. Access from two sides.

36 same as 35: the areas in front of the rows accessed from south and north differ in situation and layout.

37 Solar housing development in Osuna, Spain, SAMA arq., 1990. North and south facade are clearly differentiated in the narrow courtyards.

38 Siveliuspark housing development in Rødovre, Denmark, Fællestegnestuen Aps. Access to two rows from a common residential path.

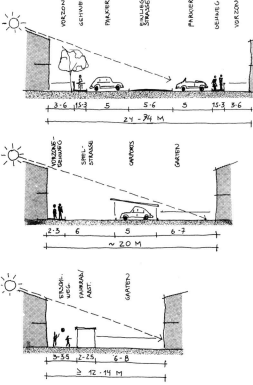

Surroundings and Open Areas

Determining the necessary distances between buildings must always be seen in the context of how these interstitial spaces are designed and used. As sites for a variety of activities – from hobbies to gardening to communal celebrations – the layout and design of the open areas is as important as the access solution. Differentiating between public and private spaces is essential if one wishes to ensure the unimpeded use of the private zones.

Single-sided access to building rows results in interstitial spaces with adjacent access and open areas. When distances between rows are small, it is especially important to clearly separate these areas from the public zone.

When access is combined for two rows, the result is the formation of groupings and an alternating provision of access and open areas in the interstitial spaces. Differing building heights require different distances for solar incidence, thus contributing even further to the differentiation of the interstitial spaces. The monotonous repetitiveness in row housing, a typical characteristic of developments from the 1950s and 1960s, can be alleviated by this means. Mixing building types (row houses, multi-story buildings) is also possible through this approach. Since living areas should preferably face south, the access conditions change for the individual rows and this factor must be taken into consideration in the development plan.

The usefulness of private open spaces as well as the protection of privacy in the living areas of building rows with access from the south is especially affected by this. If this protection is not provided, the glazed area is closed off from visual contact (curtains, etc.) and the desired heat gain from sunshine is eliminated.

"Even though the peek-a-boo hole has long since evolved into a wide window, he (man) has a desire to keep the outside world in sight from his internal retreat. He looks out of the window onto the world, spread out before him in brightness, but the world does not see him hidden in the darkness of the room.

People have tried to enhance the privacy of the window through curtains and blinds, while modern living is at the same characterized by

39

40

increasingly opening the house to the outside world through large glazed areas." (2)

Decisions made in urban development thus influence even the user's behavior with regard to passive use of solar energy. This situation deserves particular attention in environments with increasing density. The closer the buildings are, the more important privacy becomes in terms of visual contact into private open spaces. The effect of the sun should not be studied exclusively from the perspective of the energy it can provide. Architecture is the result of the definition of space within space, that is, the dialogue between interior and exterior. In this relationship between the interior and the exterior space, there are intermediate spaces, transitional elements, which we call threshold.

39 Access, parking and distances between two rows.

40 Housing development in Affoltern am Albis, Metron Architektur, 1998. The hillside location allows for parking below the open outdoor area of the adjoining row. This diminishes distances between rows and separates private from public spaces (see p. 50).

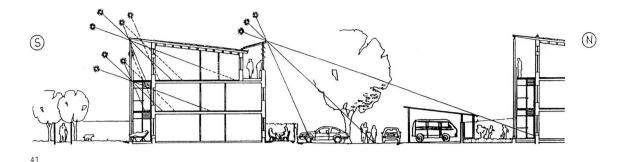

41

42

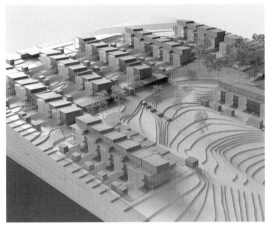

43

whether we are dealing with a new urban quarter, an isolated settlement, development on the periphery or an inner-city situation.

The sun can play a determining role in low-density developments. In inner-city locations, other factors such as conditions at the site, property costs and the related economic density, population structures, etc., will largely determine building structure and placement. Although improving solar incidence can be a goal, the results will rarely be ideal. Nevertheless, densification is the more sensible path in the city with regard to energy savings since it achieves better results, on a global perspective, than developments designed for optimized solar use on the urban periphery.

A sunlit environment offers the ideal framework for individual and communal activities to flourish. This is where the life in the city takes place and as an extension of the living space in the open air, its quality is directly linked to the quality of the apartment. The urge to flee from the urban environment into "nature" is diminished, which translates into yet more energy savings. Living in the city should recapture the charm of times gone by, the public space should be characterized by a rich and varied social dimension, and urban space should be understood as space for public life.

"The outside and the inside are two types of inwardness; they are always ready to revert, to exchange their animosity. If there is a border area between such an inside and such an outside, then this border area is painful on both sides." (3)

The sun allows the outside and the inside to enter into an exciting dialogue, thereby initiating different possibilities of perception, which this relationship communicates to us. The use of the open space and the sunshine it receives should therefore be given the same degree of attention as that accorded to enclosed living spaces.

Ultimately, the scope of the problems we have just enumerated is an issue of scale in urban development. Priorities differ according to the context of a specific project, depending on

41 Optimized distances between rows and differentiated treatment of public versus private space, student work at the Technical University, Munich, 1991.

42 Passive house development Am Leimbacher Berg in Leverkusen–Schlehbusch, tr.architekten, Rössing and Tilicke, 2003. Row housing on a slope, north access. Parking is provided at the ends of the rows along the access road.

43 Housing development in Altötting, Demmel + Mühlbauer, 1994. Parking beneath sheds designed as multi-purpose spaces.

(2) Otto F. Bollnow: Mensch und Raum, Stuttgart 1989

(3) Gaston Bachelard: Poetik des Raumes, Frankfurt am Main 1987

45

Planning Tools

Orientation and the arrangement of buildings with respect to each other are the most important basis for the passive use of solar energy. These aspects must be planned in accordance with solar altitude and the intensity of annual and diurnal solar radiation. Alternative urban development plans can vary greatly with regard to the potential solar incidence on individual buildings. The effect of these differences is not always obvious at first glance and is frequently only understood by an expert.

With regard to shading, both the shade created by the building itself and shading from the surrounding built environment or plants must be taken into consideration. The shade cast from one building onto another is generally easier to gauge than the shade cast by irregular shapes (trees, elevations in the topography). Shading from building components (projections, edges, additions) should not be overlooked.

Rules of thumb for the passive use of solar energy are not very useful for increased density and planning in the urban core. The study of more complex situations requires good knowledge of the solar geometry, and working with models or three-dimensional computer simulation is essential in this context.

The shading diagram (horizontal sundial calculated for the relevant degree of latitude) makes it possible to study solar incidence for different times of day and different seasons in a very simplified manner with the help of a working model. Simple checks carried out on the model are suitable for an investigation of different basic alternatives. Working with a model also corresponds to the architect's standard approach in concept development for urban planning.

Computer studies are essential in the planning stages that follow in order to optimize the results. Most CAD programs also offer the option of calculating a shade profile for a specific time. This provides the basis for a preliminary comparison of different alternatives, although the results are only meaningful to a limited degree. They simply illustrate a specific situation and cannot reveal the changes over the course of a day and throughout the various seasons. To cover the entire spectrum, one would have to

46

spend time- and labor-intensive hours on the computer. Once again, however, the results would yield neither an absolute nor a relative evaluation of the alternatives.

Since more specific stipulations for the building plan are not available, the creation of an energy balance sheet on the basis of an urban development plan is usually a hopeless or at the very least imprecise undertaking. Evaluation criteria can therefore only be applied by comparing different alternatives for an identical situation, for example, in the context of a competition. Several programs have been developed for the purpose of determining the percentages of shading on facades.

Absolute values can only be generated in the course of advanced planning with concrete building definitions. The readiness or the possibility of fundamentally changing the urban development plan at that stage is limited, however.

The different methods are by no means mutually exclusive; instead, they are suitable for different planning stages. A variety of controlling methods accompany the design process, correcting the plan as it proceeds and optimizing the basis for the subsequent planning stage.

44

47

48

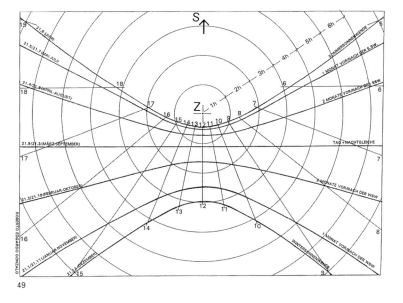

49

Energy Supply

Urban housing is increasingly equipped with alternative solutions for energy supply, for example, combined heat and power plants, solar-supported central heating installations, long-term storage of solar heat, etc. However, the same principle applies to urban planning as to building planning: anything that is overlooked in the planning can only be compensated at tremendous technological cost later on.

When primary energy is transformed into useable energy, there are losses on a differing scale, dependent on the energy carrier. Renewable energies (sun, biogas, environmental heat) can cover a considerable amount of the demand even if limitations in potential are taken into consideration. In the selection of the energy supply system, the ideal goal is to couple minimal energy with optimized use of the energy potential.

Commercial buildings consume large volumes of electrical energy for lighting, power and cooling, and this energy carrier is characterized by a particularly poor ratio of primary energy to supply energy at the user end. Moreover, energy consumption is concentrated on specific times of day, which results in an uneven demand on the public supply network. Central heating systems, large heat pumps and combined heat and power plants can supply energy

to entire commercial districts and at the same time minimize generation and transfer losses. Combined heat and power plants generate power and utilize the waste heat to supply heat, in some cases even for neighboring developments. Decentralized supply plants also allow for a more economic coupling of systems with alternative energy sources (wind, sun), as well as the use of heat sources within the development area (groundwater, air, waste heat from commercial operations).

Solar-supplemented district heat with seasonal storage is one of the options for delivering local supply through the use of renewable energy. Large solar plants have the advantage over smaller installations by yielding greater and more specific levels at lower costs. This type of heat supply is chiefly used for new housing developments. For existing developments or densification projects, the heat in the earth can be harnessed. Depending on the geological characteristics, geothermal installations can supply ultra-modern district heat for entire urban quarters. Although the borehole depths, which range on average from 3,000 to 4,000 meters, represent a high initial investment, they will subsequently deliver energy with tremendous efficiency and reliability, and do so without fluctuations caused by changing seasons or weather conditions.

47 Model study of solar incidence with sun path diagram

48 same as 47: shading study

49 Sun path diagram (horizontal sun dial for 48° latitude) to simulate shading length

51

52

50 Borehole drilling for geothermal heat gain in
Pullach near Munich

51 Windmills in southern
Spain

52 Salzburg housing development Gneis Moos,
G. Reinberg, 2000. Solar
district heat storage with
410 m² collectors and
100 m³ storage tank.

50

Another alternative for energy supply in the
urban area is the formation of virtual heat-
power-stations. Photovoltaic installations feed
the power into the network and are remunerated
for the power they supply. Similarly, privately
operated combined heat and power plants or
fuel cells can be linked in the grid. Regulated via
a grid management, they would behave like
supplementary grid districts based on energy
forecasts. In times when demand on the grid is
at a peak, local generators can be switched to
operate at full load, making the excess power
they generate available to the public grid. They
would thus assume readiness during peak
times, which would allow the supply power
plants to operate in a more economic fashion.
This "part-time job" as a micro power generator
could also serve as an incentive for private
investment in future technologies.

ENERGY-EFFICIENT URBAN DESIGN:
EXAMPLES

Passiv House Construction	**Semi-detached House in Kriens**	Lischer Partner Architekten, Lucerne	
High-density Housing	**Row Houses in Affoltern**	Metron Architektur, Brugg	
Block Edge Completion	**Multi-Family House in Munich**	H2R Architekten, Hüther, Hebensperger-Hüther, Röttig	
Urban Repair	**Office and Residential Building in Munich**	Martin Pool, Munich	
Building Gap Development	**Residential and Office Building in Wiesbaden**	A-Z Architekten, Wiesbaden	
Energy-efficient Social Housing	**Residential Building in Madrid**	Guillermo Yañez, Madrid	
Urban Renewal of an Industrial Wasteland	**University Campus in Nottingham**	Hopkins Architects, London	

Passive House Construction:
Semi-detached Houses in Kriens

Architects:
Lischer Partner Architekten, Lucerne

1

Selected data:

Completion: 2001
NSA: 340 m²
GSA: 423 m²
GRV: 1,780 m³ per two
semi-detached houses

Heating energy consump-
tion 23.6 kWh/m²a

U-value roof:
0.10 W/m²K
U-value exterior wall:
0.105 W/m²K
U-value floor ground floor/
basement:
0.10 W/m²K
U-value window:
0.94 W/m²K

1 Aerial view of develop-
  ment structure

2 View of two semi-
  detached houses show-
  ing the differentiated
  heights

3 Public open space with
  Spanish chestnut trees

4 Floor plans basement,
  ground floor, upper
  floor, penthouse not to
  scale

Kriens is a neighboring community of the city of Lucerne, characterized by a heterogeneous town structure with a rural character. On the edge of the town and yet close to the center, nine semi-detached homes form an autonomous and yet spatially integrated development. They are placed crosswise to the hillside and face south. The elevated location and terraced plan provide an unobstructed view of Kriens and the panorama of the Swiss Alps in the distance. A branch road provides access to the quarter in which the open spaces have been landscaped with great care. There are lanes alternating with small squares and green spaces shaded by Spanish chestnut trees. The investor was committed to creating a sustainable and energy-efficient architecture from the outset, with a plan based on the so-called passive house technology.

The buildings in the ensemble are defined by their simple cubic forms. These ensure an effective reduction of possible heat losses. Another aspect of the design is the sensible distribution of living functions in the floor plan. All living areas face south. The bathrooms, the stairwell and the building systems are gathered in a compact cluster on the north side. This floor plan also provides each homeowner with a great degree of flexibility in terms of internal divi-

sions. The terraced plan creates differentiated external spaces. Each house has its own enclosed, private open space.

The following components play an essential role in the energy-efficient concept of a passive house: in addition to a compact volume and a favorable floor plan, the external skin is impermeable and characterized by high thermal insulation; moreover, the internal ventilation is centrally regulated and linked to a heat-recovery system. In this case, the outside air is prewarmed in an earth pipe, warmed in the heat-recovery system, reheated electrically if needed and then distributed into the rooms.
The decision to realize the concept as a sophisticated timber construction is logical and correct. Timber is the ideal building material in this case. And the choice of Spanish chestnut for the wood boarding of the facades invests the ensemble with a unique charm because the same wood is found in the living trees.

The constructional differentiation between a massive plinth of reinforced concrete and a prefabricated timber superstructure is a sensible response to the slope at this location. Concrete retaining walls are used to overcome the height differences. The timber structure makes full use of the precision that prefabrica-

2

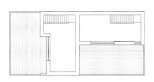

3

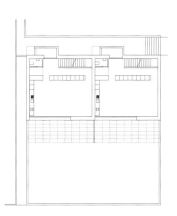

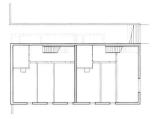

4

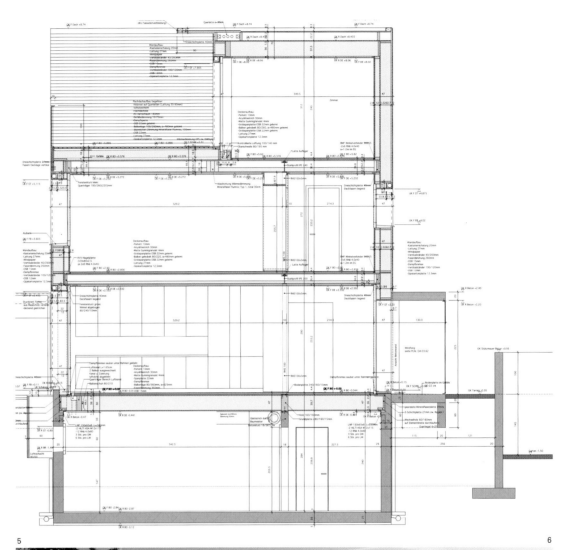

5 Section, not to scale,
  from working and detail
  plan:
  the building cubes in
  timber system construc-
  tion are erected on solidly constructed base-
  ment stories of rein-
  forced concrete and
  masonry.

6 View across develop-
  ment and of the impres-
  sive mountain panora-
  ma to the south

tion can offer. The external walls consist of a 380-mm-thick frame construction composed of glued laminated timber members. The thermal insulation, which has the same thickness, is rock wool with a basis weight of 32 kg/m^3. A carefully applied impermeable vaporproof membrane must withstand the subsequent blower-door-test. The internal shell, composed of a double layer of gypsum fiberboard, is covered in a thin coat of gypsum plaster. The external skin of 21-mm-thick chestnut boarding is installed at the prefabrication plant: this alone can ensure the desired precision in the finishing. The boarding continues along the front of the patio in the form of a screen and enhances the visual uniformity. From the inside, the narrow gaps between the boards allow the surroundings to shimmer through down to the ground, thus avoiding the appearance of a solid balustrade.

The structure of the flat roofs from the outside in starts off with a densely planted protective layer. The membrane lies on a particleboard above a ventilated cavity. The internal roof panel of wood fiberboard provides thermal insulation and rests on the binders and joists below it. Vapor barrier and airtight membrane are installed on the internal OSB panel. A grating provides the installation space required for lighting. The inside is covered in a gypsum stopping coat.

The staircases were also prefabricated and were quickly assembled and installed on site.

The detail section on the facing page (scale 1:20) illustrates the minute treatment of numerous important joints and transitions, while the facade details (overleaf) leave no question unanswered. Clearly, the attempt to accommodate ecology, cost-efficiency and comfort under one roof seems to have succeeded.

7

8

9   10

7 Timber components during prefabrication

8 Photograph documenting the assembly: installing the prefabricated flights of stairs

9 Once the panel construction elements have been assembled, the Spanish chestnut boarding is installed on site

10 View of basement story, solid form of construction

Wall construction
1   20 mm chestnut boarding
2   30 mm Douglas fir battening
3   Ceiling lining
4   40/260 mm vertical members
5   260 mm fiber insulation
6   15 mm OSB3
7   Vapor barrier
8   15 mm gypsum fiberboard
9   100/120 mm vertical members

13

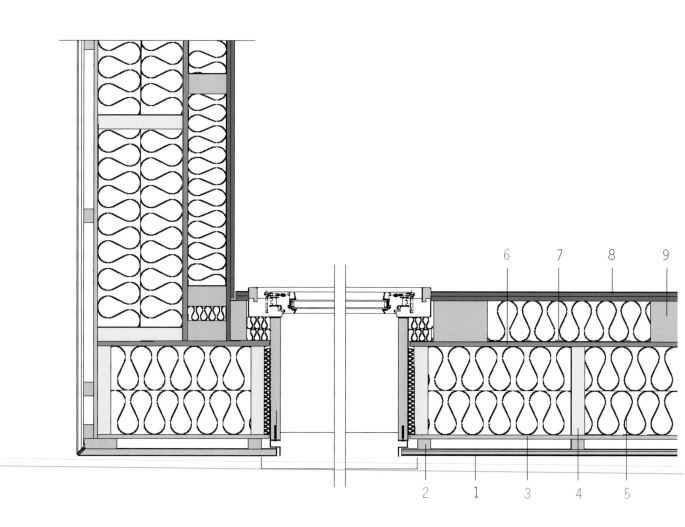

11

Floor construction
10 Floor covering
11 30 mm anhydrite screed
12 Separating and sliding layer
13 22 mm plywood panel OSB3
14 18/220 mm joist frame
15 160/220 mm cross beam
16 Cavity insulation
17 22 mm plywood panel OSB3
18 27 mm battening
19 Gypsum fiberboard

14

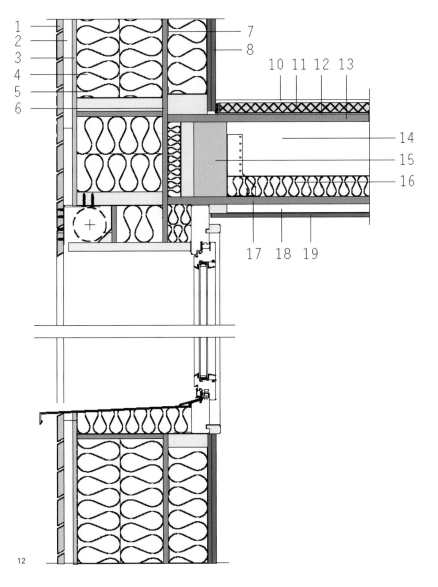

1
2
3
4
5
6

7
8

10 11 12 13

14
15
16

17 18 19

12

15

11 Horizontal section of
    window and building
    corner, not to scale

12 Floor construction

13 Detail: window detail

14 Detail: balcony breast-
    work

15 Detail: building corner

High-density Housing:
Row Houses in Affoltern

Architects:
Metron Architektur, Brugg

1

Selected data:

Completion: 1998
Energy reference area ERA:
6,137 m²
Volume according to Swiss
association of engineers
and architects (SIA116):
29,019 m³

Heating energy
consumption:
51 KWh/m²a
U-value roof:
0.22 W/m²K
U-value facade:
0.28 W/m²K
U-value floor:
0.38 W/m²K
U-value window:
1.40 W/m²K
(incl. frame)

To be successful, environmental building must today meet not only ecological standards, but economic and architectural standards as well. What is in demand is good architecture with a high quality of living and flexibility in a structure that is optimized with regard to ecology and energy consumption – and all of this at favorable financial conditions. The Looren development, one of the largest timber housing developments in Switzerland, is one example of this approach. It was realized on commission for a consortium of private clients and comprises forty units.

The row house development lies on the southern edge of the village of Affoltern, on a sunny, quiet, west-facing slope. The proximity to the railway station and other important infrastructural services as well as the site itself make this a high-quality location. Excellent use has been made of this situation by implementing a high-density plan that meets economic and ecological goals.

The property is accessed via two branch roads running north-south. Parking to the east of these residential and play streets is provided in the form of carports carved out of the hillside. The roof of the parking areas forms the private yard of the adjacent homes, thus minimizing excavation and ground sealing. This approach also saved costs and created additional options for future uses. The open design of the parking area can also accommodate other functions. For example, this area could be envisioned for uses such as a workshop, a hobby room, or a covered play area for children.

The access roads divide the site into three sections on which three different housing types were erected (4.5 to 6 rooms). The houses are distributed across ten small groups of row houses with four units each. The lots along the top of the site are developed with a cluster of three housing groups situated parallel to the branch roads and to

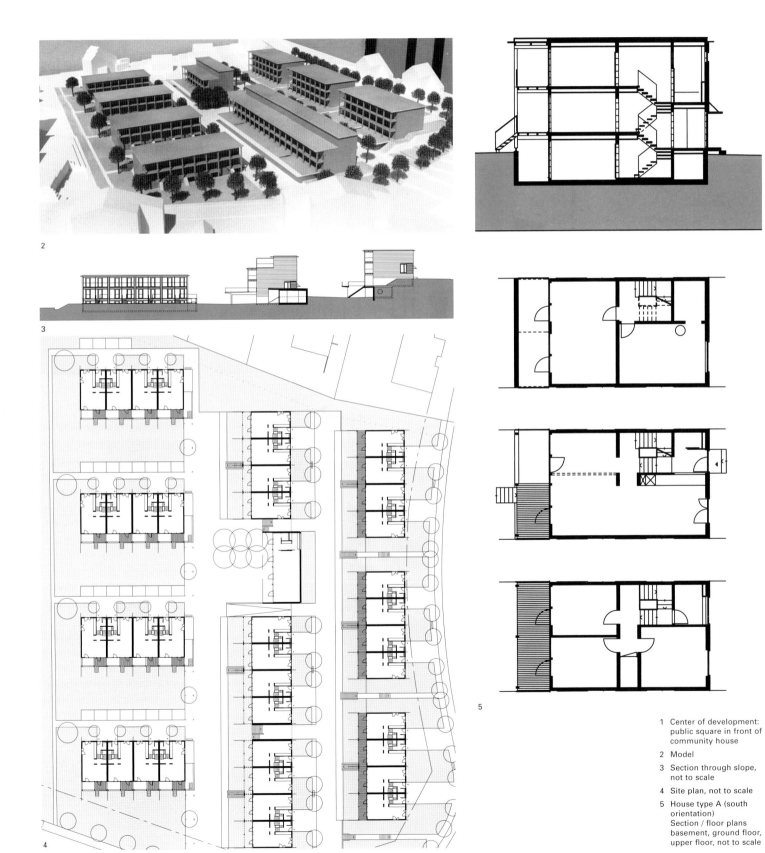

1 Center of development:
  public square in front of
  community house
2 Model
3 Section through slope,
  not to scale
4 Site plan, not to scale
5 House type A (south
  orientation)
  Section / floor plans
  basement, ground floor,
  upper floor, not to scale

6

7

the slope. The living area and garden side of these homes face west. The lots in the lower and more level section of the site accommodate the remaining four housing groups with south orientation. Access in this area is provided via short paths leading off from the branch road; these paths run along the north side of the rows.

The staggered plan of groups on the slope creates a variety of sightlines across the entire development. A network of paths with passages and stairs links the lots.

The living and garden areas are distinguished by a high degree of privacy. In the west-facing homes, the slope creates a difference in elevation between public and private spheres. In the lower section of the site, storage facilities in the form of garden sheds and pergolas act as screens between the access area and the adjacent gardens.

The forty row houses are complemented by a centrally located community house that is conceived to serve as a basis for promoting a social infrastructure within the built development.

8

With a depth of 9 m and a width of 6 m, all three house types are designed according to the same plan. The differing house sizes result from their height: depending on location, each home is 2, 2.5 or 3 stories high. The simple floor plan structure accommodates a variety of internal divisions and uses – meeting the wishes and needs of the users.

The structural design, the facades and the building systems are uniform throughout the development. All homes feature continuous balconies across all floors on the principal living side. These extend the living space and shield the window fronts on these sides from the summer sun. By adapting to the slope, the staggering of garden and entrance area is further enhanced by an additional half story. The internal floor plan results in a split-level solution for the access and sanitary areas. It also creates differing room heights, sightlines and natural lighting schemes.

The development is heated with brine/water heat pumps. Although this increases the investment costs in comparison to conventional heating, the solution causes no CO_2 emissions and

eliminates the need for fuel transport. Each cluster of four units is serviced by a bore hole heat pump, which sucks brine (temp. 20° C) from 180-m-deep bore holes. Heat distribution is conventional through radiators equipped with thermostats. Consumption is billed to each individual household.

Warm water is supplied in decentralized fashion and linked to an auxiliary thermal solar installation for each house. Some units were already equipped with solar collectors upon construction. For others, provisions have been made for retrofitting at a future date.

Healthy, sustainable materials promote an excellent indoor climate and increase the living quality and value of these timber houses. The prefabricated timber structure with large panel components decreases assembly times on site and allows for a dry construction method. Within one week, four row houses could be raised on a reinforced concrete plinth that accommodates the basement and parking. The decision to design the homes as prefabricated timber structures was linked to other important choices relating to the sustainable use of building ma-

6   View of living room

7   Planted roofs

8   Residential and play streets with open carports

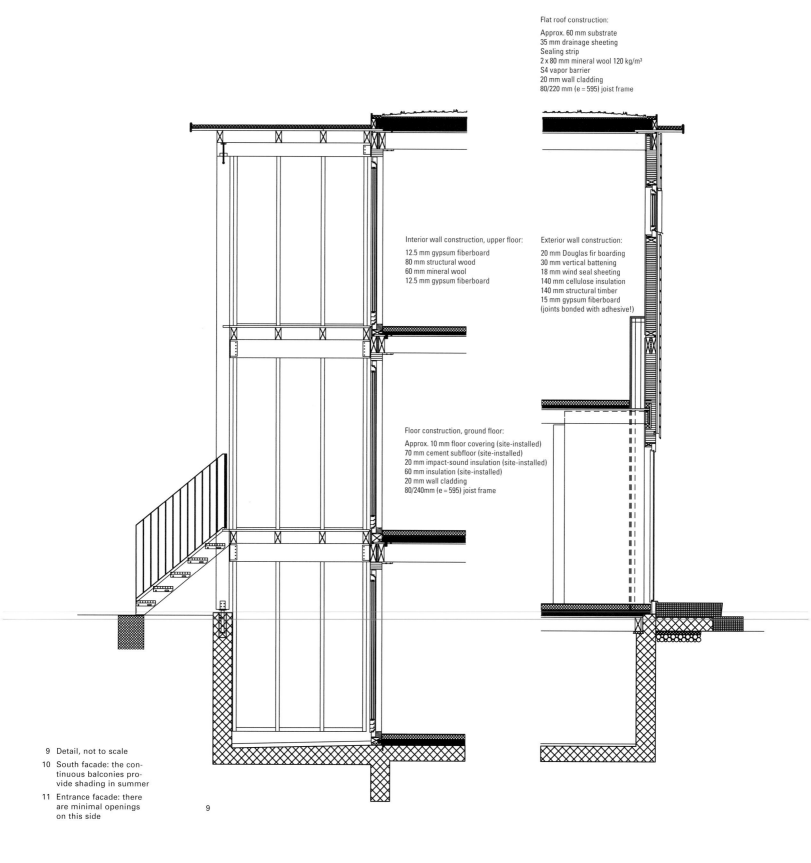

Flat roof construction:

Approx. 60 mm substrate
35 mm drainage sheeting
Sealing strip
2 x 80 mm mineral wool 120 kg/m³
S4 vapor barrier
20 mm wall cladding
80/220 mm (e = 595) joist frame

Interior wall construction, upper floor:

12.5 mm gypsum fiberboard
80 mm structural wood
60 mm mineral wool
12.5 mm gypsum fiberboard

Exterior wall construction:

20 mm Douglas fir boarding
30 mm vertical battening
18 mm wind seal sheeting
140 mm cellulose insulation
140 mm structural timber
15 mm gypsum fiberboard
(joints bonded with adhesive!)

Floor construction, ground floor:

Approx. 10 mm floor covering (site-installed)
70 mm cement subfloor (site-installed)
20 mm impact-sound insulation (site-installed)
60 mm insulation (site-installed)
20 mm wall cladding
80/240mm (e = 595) joist frame

9 Detail, not to scale

10 South facade: the con-
    tinuous balconies pro-
    vide shading in summer

11 Entrance facade: there
    are minimal openings
    on this side

9

terials: untreated wood as the load-bearing structure; visible joists and ceiling boarding; balcony construction and facade boarding.

The clear architecture with compact, simple building volumes, without any projections or recesses in the facade, results in an ideal surface-to-volume ratio. This compact building form combined with high thermal insulation on the roof and facade results in correspondingly low heating energy requirements. The use of timber and derived timber products also established the prerequisites for excellent thermal insulating properties despite the moderate structural thickness. Beneath the green cover on the roof, the thermal insulating layer consists of 160 mm rock wool; the thermal insulating layer on the walls is composed of 140 mm cellulose fiber insulation and 20 mm softboard. The building skin composed of timber and cellulose fiber insulation is permeable to vapor diffusion and creates a healthy indoor climate.

The planted flat roofs act as a dust and moisture screens. They delay water runoff during precipitation and increase the thermal insulation of the living areas in summer. All collected rainwater flows through a system of open gutters to humus-enriched basins from where it seeps gradually into the naturally landscaped grounds of the development.

10

11

Block Edge Completion:
Multi-Family House in Munich

Architects:
H2R Architekten, Hüther, Hebensperger-Hüther,
Röttig, Munich

1

Selected data:

Competition: end of 1996
Completion: 2001
Main Usable Floor Area
MUFA: 2,780 m²
GSA: 3,356 m²
GRV: 13,860 m³

Calculating heating energy
requirement Tower and
south wing:
46.5 KWh/m²a
West wing:
49.9 KWh/m²a
U-value roof:
0.19 W/m²K
U-value exterior wall:
Light: 0.24 W/m²K
Solid: 0.25 W/m²K
U-value floor/basement:
0.20 W/m²K
U-value window:
1.10 W/m²K

Energy conservation and the passive use of solar energy are not the only means of reducing the energy consumption in a residential building. One valuable – albeit quantitatively undeterminable – contribution to the rational use of energy is the product of how the building is used and treated. Specific examples of this approach are mixed apartment sizes in one building to ensure high occupancy rates and flexible, divisible floor plans that allow for adaptation to other uses. These aspects ensure continued use of the existing fabric over the long term and also avoid expensive and energy-consuming refurbishment.

The block edge development in Schwabing, a central district of Munich, was initiated as a cooperative project in which the future users participated in the planning process. Involving residents in all manner of choices including selecting the architects, planning and partial self-administration of the completed building was a key element in achieving the savings potentials. The construction of a new barrier-free multi-family dwelling was conceived as a positive contribution toward social integration in inner-city housing. The concept focused not only on combining living and working; the goal was also to achieve a social mix of different income levels and household constellations within the complex.

The comprehensive user participation resulted in a multitude of different apartments with regard to floor area, accessibility and personal preferences. Twenty-eight one- to four-room apartments (30–120 m²) were created, of which six units on different floors were designed for wheelchair access. The building also includes two offices with wheelchair access, one homecare unit and one guest apartment. Parking is provided in an underground garage, 75 percent of which is in use at this time. The remaining 25 percent can be retrofitted at any time. Communal rooms in the attic and a common, roughly 200-m² roof patio, as well as the landscaped courtyard with barrier-free areas, offer an excellent quality of extended living and complement

2

5

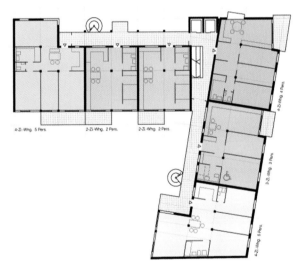

3

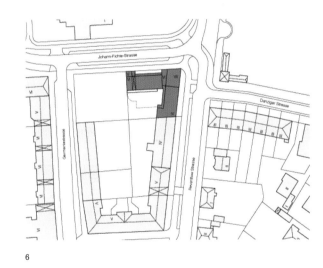

6

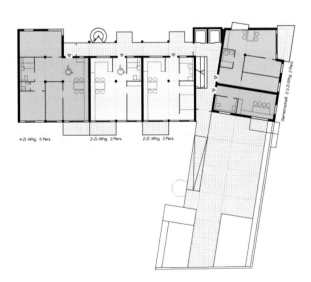

4

1 Northwest elevation

2 Ground floor plan, not to scale, with foyer, therapy rooms as well as guest- and homecare apartments

3 Fourth floor plan, not to scale with individually designed apartments

4 Fifth floor plan, not to scale with communal room and roof patio

5 North elevation, not to scale

6 Site plan, not to scale

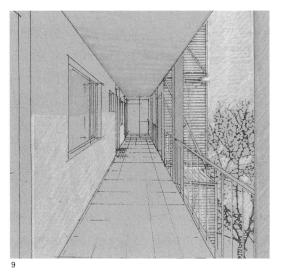

9

7

8

the program for social activities promoted by the cooperative.

The complex is distinguished by a 7-story, tower-like corner structure from which wings extend on both sides. The ground floor of the tower accommodates a spacious foyer, which is also useable for social functions, and provides access to the stairwell and two elevators equipped for wheelchair use. From this tower, every apartment is also accessible along barrier-free covered walkways that serve as a circulation link between units. The walkways of the 4-story, east-west oriented wing run along the west side and overlook the courtyard. Given their size and a widening at the end of each walkway, these elements also serve as patios for the adjacent units. A spiraling escape staircase provides direct access to the courtyard.

The south-facing, 6-story block is accessed from the north side. Here, box-like balconies are suspended from the walkways; these elements define the appearance of the street facade. They are simply constructed as steel balconies and serve as additional spaces for the adjacent apartments: they can be used as open or closed storage areas, as an outdoor seating space or as a play area.

District heat supplied from the municipal network is channeled to the building through tubular heat exchangers in the district heat transfer station.

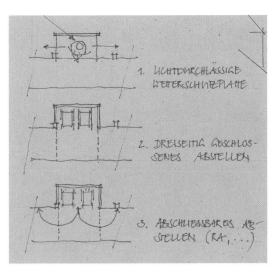

1. LICHTDURCHLÄSSIGE
   WETTERSCHUTZPLATTE

2. DREISEITIG GESCHLOS-
   SENES ABSTELLEN

3. ABSCHLIESSBARES AB-
   STELLEN (RA, ...)

10

Internally, heat distribution is effected by means of a warm-water heating network with 70/50° feed- and return flow temperatures, respectively. The rooms are equipped with door-height tube radiators: they increase heat radiation and create a greater sense of perceived comfort.

In accordance with the client specifications, the link to the district heating system – a cost-efficient energy-conscious solution – is complemented by a solar system for warm water heating. The field of thermal solar collectors, which covers an area of 52 m^2, fronts the south facade where it was mounted over the top of the steel structure of the balconies. The collectors thus fulfill the dual function of providing shade and weather protection for the balconies on the top floors. The energy savings realized during the first year of operation suggest that the total period of amortization will not exceed five years.

The project was geared toward implementing a high ecological standard from the outset, beyond heating requirements that meet the standards of a low-energy house and the active use of solar energy by means of a thermal solar system. This includes an installation for rainwater collection, which is used for lavatories and irrigation. The flat roofs are conceived as membrane roofs with extensive greenery. Ventilation for the underground garage was solved by developing a cost-efficient ventilation concept with integrated floor ventilation ducts.

11   12

7   Communal courtyard

8   Elevation walkway

9   Sketch of walkway with balcony boxes

10 Use diagram for balcony boxes

11–12 South facade with collector area above balconies

6 OG
5 OG
4 OG
3 OG
2 OG
1 OG
EG

13

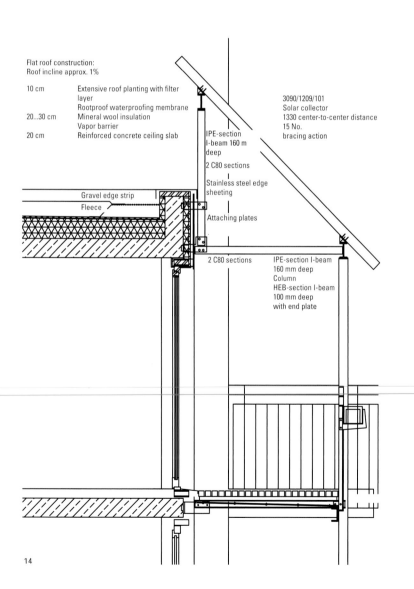

Flat roof construction:
Roof incline approx. 1%

10 cm	Extensive roof planting with filter layer
	Rootproof waterproofing membrane
20...30 cm	Mineral wool insulation
	Vapor barrier
20 cm	Reinforced concrete ceiling slab

3090/1209/101
Solar collector
1330 center-to-center distance
15 No.
bracing action

IPE-section
I-beam 160 m
deep

2 C80 sections

Stainless steel edge
sheeting

Attaching plates

Gravel edge strip

Fleece

2 C80 sections

IPE-section I-beam
160 mm deep
Column
HEB-section I-beam
100 mm deep
with end plate

14

Although the client and the future users expressed the desire to realize a brick building, the plan gradually shifted in favor of a reinforced concrete skeleton structure as the more sensible solution.

Building costs were to be kept as low as possible. Despite this mandate, the brief was to aim for the thermal insulation standards of a low-energy house from the very beginning. The highly compact volume and the homogeneous insulation of the building skin, installed on the outside, are favorable factors in this regard. The combination of these factors made it possible to achieve a reduction of 30 percent by comparison to the minimum heat protection standard at the time of planning.

The external walls overlooking the courtyard are timber frame panel structures clad in fiberboard cement panels. The tower walls and the facades overlooking the street are brickwork and concrete respectively with 16 cm thermal insulation plaster coating. This, too, is part of a comprehensive energy-conserving concept, as is the utilization of the dividing walls between apartments and the reinforced concrete ceilings as storage masses.

13 Cross-section of south-
facing wing with solar
collectors above balco-
nies and suspended
boxes at walkway

14 Detail, not to scale

15 Partial elevation north
facade with suspended
boxes at walkway

15

61

Urban Repair:
Office and Residential Building in Munich

Architect:
Martin Pool, Munich

1

Selected data:

Completion: 2004
NSA: 2,410 m²
GSA: 2,940 m²
GRV: 8,860 m³

Heating energy consumption 20 kWh/m²a
U-value roof:
0.13 W/m²K
U-value exterior wall:
0.13 W/m²K
U-value flooring ground floor/basement:
0.19 W/m²K
U-value glazing:
0.7 W/m²K

The development of a vacant lot that has been covered in rubble for decades acts as an expansion of the lively core of the Lehel district to the north, especially since the new complex offers mixed use and an urbane style. It also provides an opportunity for the State of Bavaria, which owns the property to the north, to exercise a bit of "urban repair" by creating an addition to close the historic block. To the south, the new building also restores the pre-war condition to a large degree. It maintains an appropriate distance to the historic structure on that site and adopts the height established by the existing development. The architectural design and the realization of the upper floors as terraced stories are in keeping with other new buildings in the surroundings. The eaves height of the neighboring building to the south is adopted; the continuity of the street front has been preserved and strengthened.

The distance on the south side means that the corner units of the new building enjoy vistas and excellent exposure to sunshine despite the nearby development on that side. Even on the ground floor and in winter, these corners receive sunshine during a few hours per day. This potential was recognized and chosen as the departure point for the concept. As an early sketch illustrates, the corners are emphasized

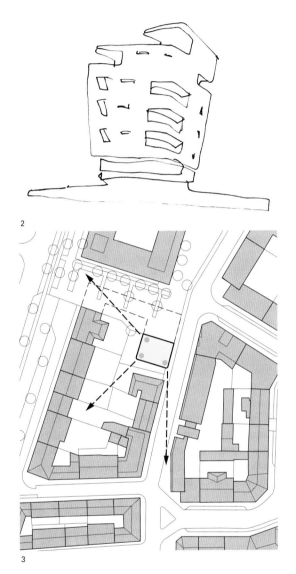

2

3

4

with large openings; the plan is also based on diagonal access and internal circulation. A visual sightline runs from the entrance door located at the core of the building through the foyer, living room and corner window all the way to the street or courtyard space. This is where the living areas and the kitchen are located. The facades overlooking the courtyard are fairly closed. Bedroom and bathroom lie to the rear, facing east and west.

Anticipating the future addition to the neighboring building, the entire north facade was designed as a fully closed firewall. The principal rooms are nevertheless well-lit, since the building core is occupied by an internal stairwell and the usual ancillary rooms. The south-facing living area is bright because light can flow into the large open space from two sides.

The office floors are conceived as open spaces with few columns, allowing for flexible internal divisions. The open-plan space is structured by the different characteristics of the individual areas and service zones within it. These accommodate the server, a tea kitchen, an archive, building services and the load-bearing structure and separate the entrance areas from the work areas. Immediately adjacent to the south side of the stairwell, the storage rooms can be opened up to form a corridor linking the east and west units. At this point, the stories can be

1 South elevation: the corner windows capture the sun and light.

2 Early design sketch

3 Site plan, not to scale

4 Location in the context of the street space

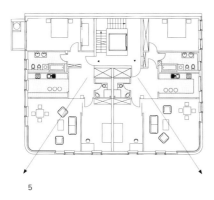

5

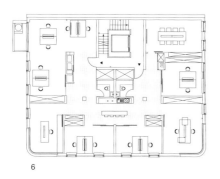

6

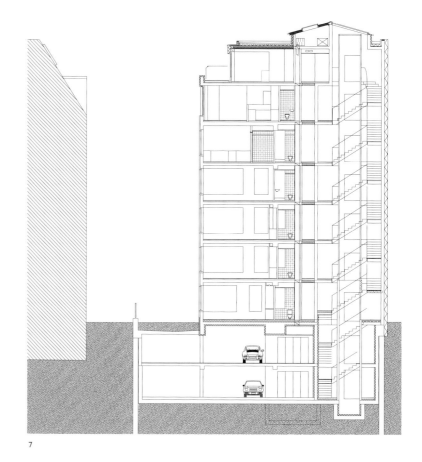

7

linked vertically by a single staircase should the need arise; a ceiling recess has been created for this purpose. This connecting option is provided across all levels.

The upper stories are set back and on these floors the apartments are preceded by spacious patios.

Despite shading from neighboring buildings, the new complex will achieve an energy consumption quotient as low as roughly 20 kWh per m² of useable area per year. It is thus clearly superior to the standard set for a low-energy house (30 to 70 kWh/m²a) and far superior to that achieved by average mixed-use buildings in Munich (200 kWh/m²a). Having lowered the heating requirements for heating and warm water to one tenth of the norm, the operating costs of the building will be diminished over the long term.

The cubic volume of the building is very compact. Since the transmission heat losses of a building are in direct relation to the dimension of its surface area, the compactness alone translates into a considerable reduction in heat losses. Balconies and oriels, projections and recess-

es in the facade – all of which act as cooling elements – were largely avoided. Since the building is fully detached and has an open floor plan, many rooms benefit from light flowing into the space from two sides. A natural oriel that does not compromise the compact nature of the building is formed at the corner. This project appears to be the first of its scale to employ vacuum insulating panels (VIP) as insulation on the exterior walls. The insulation value of these panels is roughly eight to ten times higher than that of comparable conventional insulating materials. The elements employed here are formed in a patented process in such a manner that heat losses at the panel edges are largely avoided. By installing these panels with an insulating thickness of only 2 cm and an 8-cm-thick lathwork panel to protect the insulation, passive-house values can be achieved without the loss of valuable useable area through thick thermal insulation on exterior walls and deep reveals that diminish the amount of sunlight penetrating into the interior. The panels are attached to the facade in a specialized process that was developed by a renowned insulating system manufacturer in collabora-

8

9

10

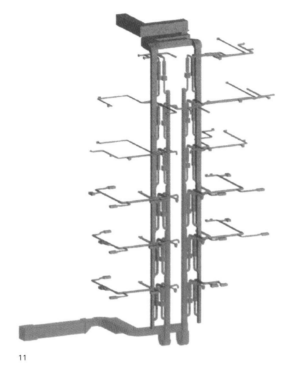

11

tion with the architect and an energy consultant. The approval for the constructional implementation of this innovation was granted.

The large glass areas on the rounded building corners, where shading is minimal, allow for maximum penetration of sunlight. In summer and during the transitional seasons, these windows can be opened across the full height and width, which transforms them into loggias; in winter, the same loggias can be utilized as living areas. All windows are triple-glazed with thermal panes, equipped with blinds in the interstitial space between the panes and fitted with a thermal insulating frame. A unique feature in the frame strip allows for continued thermal insulation across the frame, avoiding the weakness at the joint that characterizes other window frames. In order to prevent heat losses through unregulated window ventilation and improve the indoor air quality, the building has been equipped with a ventilation system with heat-recovery. Fresh air is sucked into the building via the planted roof and distributed to the individual offices and apartments.

Stale, warm air is extracted and used to prewarm the incoming cold air in a heat exchanger.

8 Detail of CHPP engineering room
9 Typical shaft use on standard floor
10 Installing the composite thermal insulation system
11 Spatial diagram of ventilation ducts

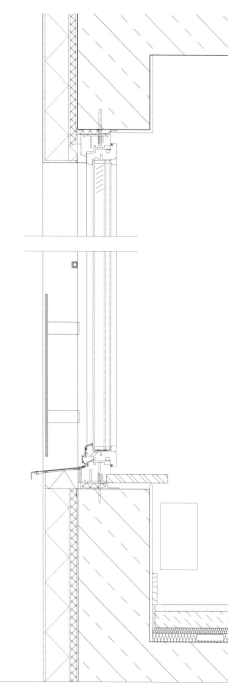

12

14

15

13

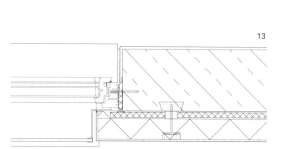

12 Vertical section of facade, structure inside to outside:
rendering, 24 cm reinforced concrete with integrated recycled PU wedges 100/35 mm, 20 mm vacuum insulating panel between 30/50 mm strips of recycled PU-material, strips adhesive and dowel fixed to wedges, 80 mm PU-thermal insulation, adhesive and dowel fixed to strips, 7 mm reinforced mineral rendering, passive-house wood frame window with triple glazing, integrated shading and additional section for installation, laminated safety glass in stainless steel fixings as safety barrier, external window sill of aluminum with sound-deadening coating

13 Horizontal section window connection joint, structure as above, detail sections, not to scale

The residual heating demand is too low to warrant the use of district heat and is therefore met with the help of a small, natural gas-operated combined heating and power plant (CHPP) and an auxiliary condensing value boiler.

Use of the valuable primary energy is optimized by means of co-generating power and heat for the building's own use. At the same time, the small CHPP also serves as a constituent element for a future power plant in Munich with a virtual grid.

Future plans include the installation of a photovoltaic system on the flat roof to generate power from sunlight.

With the help of groundwater that is drawn at a temperature of roughly 8° C, natural cooling is provided for offices and apartments in summer at a very low rate of energy consumption, thus avoiding the installation of inefficient air-conditioning systems. Cooling sails or an induction system can be linked, if needed, to installed fixed pipes and ducts and combined with the ventilation. And finally, the dense urban development itself also contributes to the energy efficiency of the building. Short paths and excellent links to public transport, minimal expendi-

ture in providing access and the provision of workplaces that are in immediate proximity to housing all translate into additional savings in energy consumption, which is comparable to the savings that have already been achieved with the heating system.

In the long term, this project may well serve as a model for energy-efficient, mixed-use multi-story buildings, despite the parameters given by the density in an urban space and the somewhat limited potential for passive solar energy.

14 Detail of facade with
    rounded corner window

15 Office space with a
    view through corner
    window onto street
    space

Building-Gap Development:
Residential and Office Building in Wiesbaden

Architects:
A-Z Architekten, Wiesbaden

1

Selected data:

Completion: 2002
MUFA: 400 m²
GRV: 2,334 m³

Heating energy
consumption office:
17.8 KWh/m²a calculated
according to PHPP

U-value exterior wall:
0.21 W/m²K
U-value basement walls:
0.12 W/m²K
U-value floor: 0.39 W/m²K
U-value windows and post
and rail facade: 0.8 W/m²K

The small 9-m-wide and 20-m-deep lot is located in a renewal district in the center of Wiesbaden. To the south and the north, the narrow building gap is enclosed by high fire-proof walls, and windows are therefore only possible on the east and west sides. These parameters and the shading that results from the density of the surrounding development do not present ideal conditions for the passive use of solar energy. However, the narrow and compact volume that was designed in response to the limited building space is one advantage. This volume allows for a concept with a high percentage of windows (roughly 42 percent) and hence maximum use of daylight combined with minimized energy losses.

The building was to accommodate living and working under one roof. The office of the architects, who were also the clients in this case, occupies the basement, the ground floor and the second floor. The office loft on the third floor is leased to a media agency. Two subsidized four-room apartments occupy the fourth and fifth floor. A narrow bachelor penthouse with large roof patios forms the upper completion. To meet parking requirements, the building is also equipped with a triple garage with car elevators.

All living and working areas are placed near the facade, while the sanitary rooms and the kitchen are gathered in the core of the apartments. The offices as well as the central living and dining rooms extend across the entire depth of the building. In the apartments, light-weight dividing walls allow for flexible floor plans. Rooms are accessed through sliding doors set along the facade; when opened, they create a generous spatial impression.

The office features an atrium on the west side, which allows daylight to penetrate into the offices below. A round skylight above the basement serves the same purpose and doubles as a conference table on the patio in summer. The plan was designed to fulfill a specific list of criteria; these included
– a house with abundant daylight and a view across the city from the upper apartments;

– a quiet office space that offers both protection from traffic noise and good ventilation
– floor-to-ceiling windows unobstructed by radiators
– a sustainable building volume obviating the need for energy-consuming renovations
– minimal operating costs, even in the long term.
And finally, cost-efficiency was the overarching requirement for all of these criteria.

Fresh air for the offices is pre-warmed or pre-cooled by 2–3° C in a geothermal collector. A 20-m-long synthetic pipe was laid in the working space of the excavation. The length of the pipe was limited by the amount of soil remaining on the site. The air inlets and outlets are located in the garden courtyard.

To ensure autonomous operation, the apartments and offices are equipped with decentralized ventilation fixtures. Users are responsible for the maintenance of the fixtures in their units. Each apartment has a separate heat exchanger in the size of a broom closet, which is supplied with fresh air via the roof. Synthetic ducts integrated into the reinforced concrete ceilings distribute incoming air to the ceiling vents in the living areas and bedroom. Spent air from the kitchen, bathroom and lavatory is extracted and vented through the roof, during which process 90 percent of the heat is transferred to the fresh incoming air in the heat exchanger of the ventilation system. One disadvantage of this decentralized arrangement is that individual heat gains, for example, solar heat gains in the attic or internal heat gains in the offices, cannot be utilized throughout the building.

The ventilation ducts are hidden behind the built-in shelving in the office: behind the lighting that is integrated into the shelving, the inlet opening is located on one side of the room and the extraction vent on the opposite side.

In a neighborhood with traditional eaves from the end of the 1800s and the start of the last century, one would expect that the roof on any new development would have to conform to the established plan. In the end, the conservation authorities granted permission – in view of the innovative building concept – for a penthouse with a flat roof set back from the eaves height. A 21 m² solar installation, which pro-

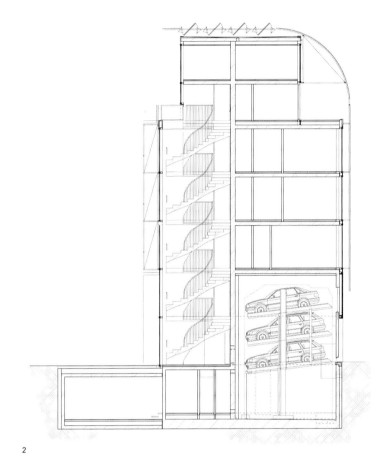

2

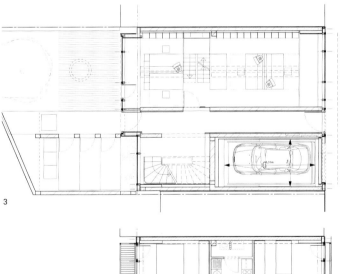

3

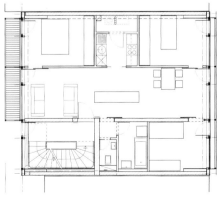

4

1 West facade on street side: it is composed of floor-height, prefabricated components across the entire building width.
2 Section through stairwell and triple garage
3 Ground floor plan with office use
4 Fourth floor plan with residential use, section and plans, not to scale

5

vides heat for three water boilers with a capacity of 800 l, was mounted on the roof. The boilers are located in the services room above the stairwell. They supply the building with warm water and also serve as a backup for emergency heating.

The warm water system was fitted with electric heating rods to ensure safety. The apartments feature radiators in the bathrooms and living areas, the office is equipped with two radiators in the basement. Five years after completion, this has been revealed as a superfluous measure, since the penthouse is the only unit that requires auxiliary heating in extremely cold weather. Waste heat from a transmitting station installed in the garage represents an additional heat source for the architects' office.

The first year of operation demonstrated that the residual energy required for heating was virtually negligible: calculations according to PHPP (Passive House Planning Package) resulted in a balance of 17.8 kWh/(m²a). This balance was further improved after the first year of operation.

The floor plan makes it feasible to cool the undersides of the shallow filigree ceilings by means of overnight cross-ventilation. Conversely, the office facade was optimized with regard to cold weather periods and noise levels; therefore, it does not feature an opening flap on the street side. The ventilation system alone, however, does not suffice to replace the overnight cross-ventilation in summer.

The architects were able to demonstrate that a passive house can also be realized with an east/west orientation on a lot that receives very little sunlight.

The carcass composed of concrete and masonry functions as load-bearing structure, spatial division and storage mass; it is also exposed in the interior and defines the character of the space. Prior to installing the high-quality materials, such as the facade or the building skin, the

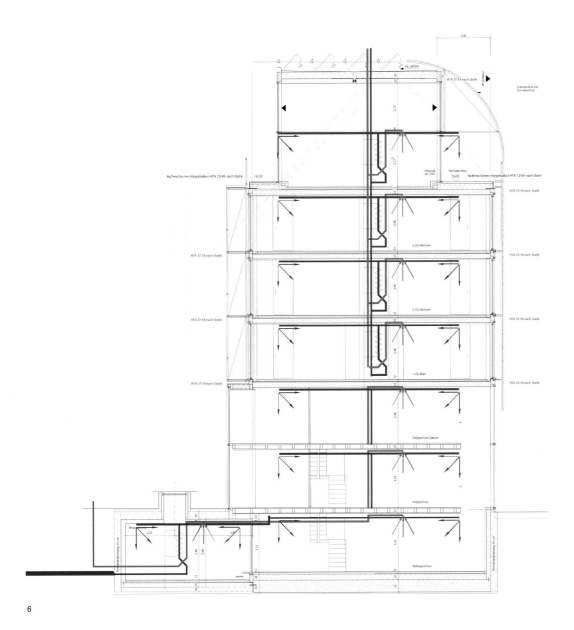

6

carcass is finished with all necessary rendering- and plasterwork.

The most expensive building component in any passive house continues to be the triple-glazed window. However, since maximum use of daylight was one of the priorities, the plan called for large glazed areas. Prefabrication of the large facade components – with dimensions that match the floor height of 2.8 m and the entire building width of 9 m – was chosen in order to keep costs low, while achieving a superior quality and impermeability in the external skin. The post and rail structure of the facade was constructed of wood as a natural material choice.

The facade was prefabricated by a single company which assumed the responsibility of ensuring the high quality of this component, without thermal bridges or leakages. Prefabrication also has the advantage that the facade can be quickly installed, weather permitting.

The entire east and west facades were delivered to the site on a semi-trailer truck. They are bolted to angle brackets at the ceilings and gable walls. The entire facade was installed in two days; in another two days it was fully sealed, a tremendous reduction in labor and time on the construction site.

Protection against excessive heat in summer is especially important when large glazed areas are used. To this end, the facade on the apartment floors is equipped in external shading- and privacy blinds. The offices on the ground floor and the second floor receive sufficient shade from trees and the planted slope on the opposite side. The steel balconies on the east side and those overlooking the garden courtyard, as well as the maintenance bridges on the west side, are suspended from the roof. The few trusses that were required are a negligible factor as thermal bridges. The railings function as framework trusses. They are covered in awning material as a safety feature and to provide a visual screen.

5 Interior view of living and dining area. The open-plan space receives natural day- and sunlight from two sides.

6 Sectional diagram of regulated ventilation with heat-recovery. Apartments and office are equipped with independent systems. The air supplied to the office is pre-warmed in a geothermal heat exchanger.

7

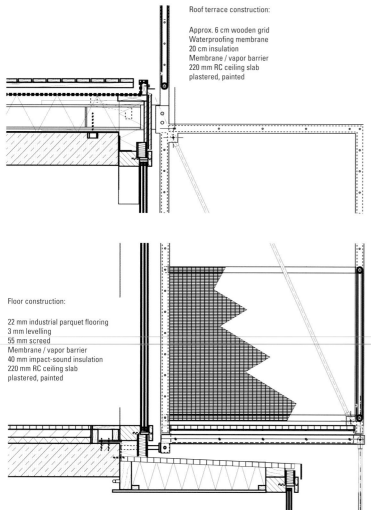

Roof terrace construction:

Approx. 6 cm wooden grid
Waterproofing membrane
20 cm insulation
Membrane / vapor barrier
220 mm RC ceiling slab
plastered, painted

Floor construction:

22 mm industrial parquet flooring
3 mm levelling
55 mm screed
Membrane / vapor barrier
40 mm impact-sound insulation
220 mm RC ceiling slab
plastered, painted

8

With the exception of the penthouse, the fire-proof walls facing the neighboring structures are constructed of concrete and insulated on the inside where necessary. Heat losses were thus eliminated on both sides. A 30-cm-thick external insulation was installed in the basement, on the penthouse and on the roof. The flat roof consists of the concrete ceiling with 32-cm rigid foam insulation. The solar system mounted on the roof represents a superimposed load. Given the total load, the 55-cm-thick floor slab beneath the main building has been insulated on the inside (24 cm), while the 20-cm-thick concrete floor slab of the basement plinth story beneath the patio was poured concreted on top of 20 cm of insulation.

Many of the building materials used for the interior work were left untreated, such as the concrete walls and ceilings and the prefabricated staircase components, or finished in a very simple manner, such as the industrial varnished parquet flooring and the laminated wood shelving in the offices.

7 Office interior

8 Detail, not to scale

9 East facade overlooking
   courtyard: the steel balconies are suspended
   from the roof. Light
   shaft cover doubles as
   outdoor conference
   table in summer

9

73

Energy-efficient Social Housing:
Residential Building in Madrid

Architect:
Guillermo Yañez, Madrid

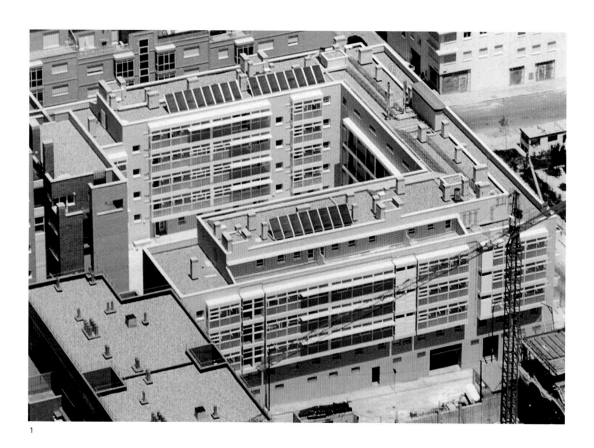

1

Selected data:

Completion: 2004
MUFA:
3,939 m² residential
251 m² retail
GSA: 6,420 m²

GRV: 15,740 m²

Heating energy
requirement:
62.52 KWh/m²a
U-value flat roof:
0.32 W/m²K
U-value wall:
0.43/0.58/0.77 W/m²K
depending on orientation,
buffer effect of projecting
components is not
included
U-value window:
2.18 W/m²K
U-value floor:
0.45 W/m²K

The social housing project in San Fermin, an emerging district on the periphery of Madrid, won the 1999 competition for one of three buildings with a focus on "social housing with a high degree of energy efficiency." The competition was initiated by the Empresa Municipal de la Vivienda (EMV Community Housing Development Agency). The brief called for concepts pertaining to bioclimatic planning in multi-story buildings with integrated active and passive use of solar energy. Despite subsidies provided by the EU for any additional costs resulting from ecological and energy-efficient measures, cost-efficiency and proof of operating efficiency for the solar systems were to enhance the model character of the project.

The building adopts the existing U-shape in the extremely dense development with two parallel north-south blocks linked by one east-west block.
To the west, the block is complemented by a higher, neighboring slab, which protects the complex and especially the courtyard against the noise from a six-lane traffic artery.
Parking for the entire complex is provided in an underground garage, which is lowered into the ground by only half a story and receives natural light through a skylight in the courtyard. Due to the natural slope of the site, the east side of the story provides space for retail units at street level. Raised on top of this plinth, the 4-story structure with a recessed attic story accommodates a total of fifty-four apartments.
In addition to the use of solar energy in winter, shading and natural ventilation during Madrid's hot summer months were essential criteria for the planning and construction concept of this building. Both criteria are fulfilled with constructional means and in the arrangement of the apartments within the plan.
The units are oriented toward two sides to ensure cross-ventilation. Within the three sides of the U-shaped development, the apartments are arranged in a differentiated manner according to orientation: living spaces are located on the south or west side, while bedrooms face north or east.

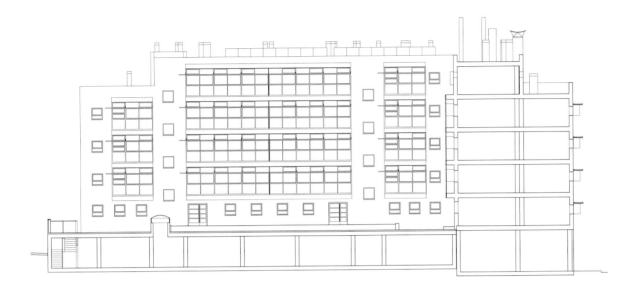

2

3

4

1 Bird's eye view: the
  high density of the area
  gives it an urban char-
  acter.

2 Section – south eleva-
  tion (courtyard)

3 Floor plan upper story,
  not to scale

4 Site plan with sur-
  roundings, not to scale

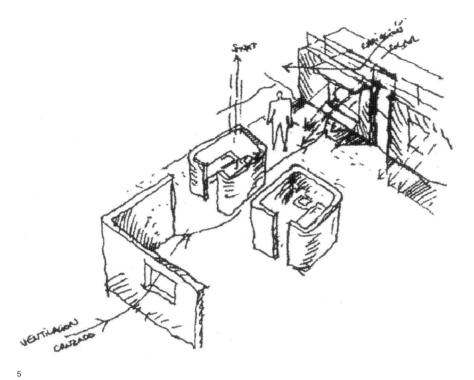

5

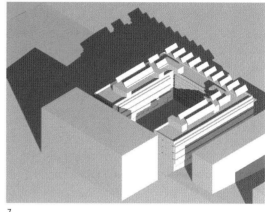

7

6

The building service installations form cores at the center of the apartments, a layout that makes it possible to achieve an optimum building depth. This centralized placement of the installations also allows for the shortest possible distribution for supply and disposal.

Different opening dimensions and the systems provided for solar gain and shading give the facades a varied appearance – always according to orientation and location, and according to sunshine or shading conditions. These variations enliven the rather severe block development and serve as an attractive visual expression of the bioclimatic initiatives.

The courtyard is landscaped with local plant species chosen to improve the microclimate, especially in summer. Irrigation of the plants in the afternoon cools the outside air by means of evaporation. This factor plays a key role for natural ventilation in summer. It enhances the effect of both the cross-ventilation in all apartments and the convection ventilation provided via solar shafts.

Ventilation shafts in the central core provide cooling for the apartments with east-west orientation. As a result of the Venturi effect, air is extracted from the living spaces through the roof, while fresh air from the courtyard flows through the windows into the apartments.

The sum of all these measures resulted in energy savings of over 40 percent and half the CO_2-emissions by comparison to conventional buildings that meet the established standards.

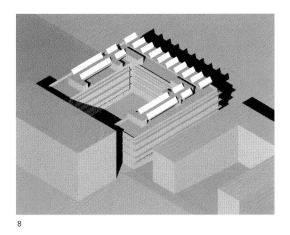

8

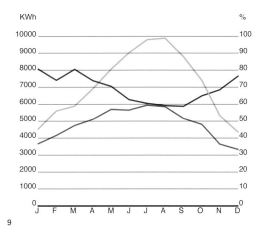

9

10

Heating is provided from a central gas boiler operated in modular fashion. Distribution is conventional, by radiators with individual thermostats in each unit. The heating system is computer-monitored and operated.

Transfer stations with meters are housed in cabinets designed for this purpose next to the entrance doors. The meters can be read from the outside to calculate individual consumption.

A second, also gas-operated boiler is used for warm-water processing, supplemented by a solar system comprising twenty-four collectors, each covering an area of 2.5 m². The collectors are installed on the flat roof at a 40° angle and face south. The system covers roughly 70 percent of the total warm water requirements and has a calculated amortization rate of 12.4 to 9.5 years, depending on the projected costs for the conventional energy sources. The energy contribution of the system translates into a reduction in CO_2-emissions of nearly thirteen tons.

Like the openings, the exterior walls are also designed in response to orientation. On the east and west sides, they are designed as single-skin walls composed of thermal insulating, lightweight and porous brick. On the south and the fairly solid north side, the walls are fitted with an external thermal insulation layer. The buffer effect of the glazed balconies was not taken into consideration in the calculation of the overall energy balance.

In the interior, the solid construction form supports the storage capacity required to compensate for temperature peaks in summer. All

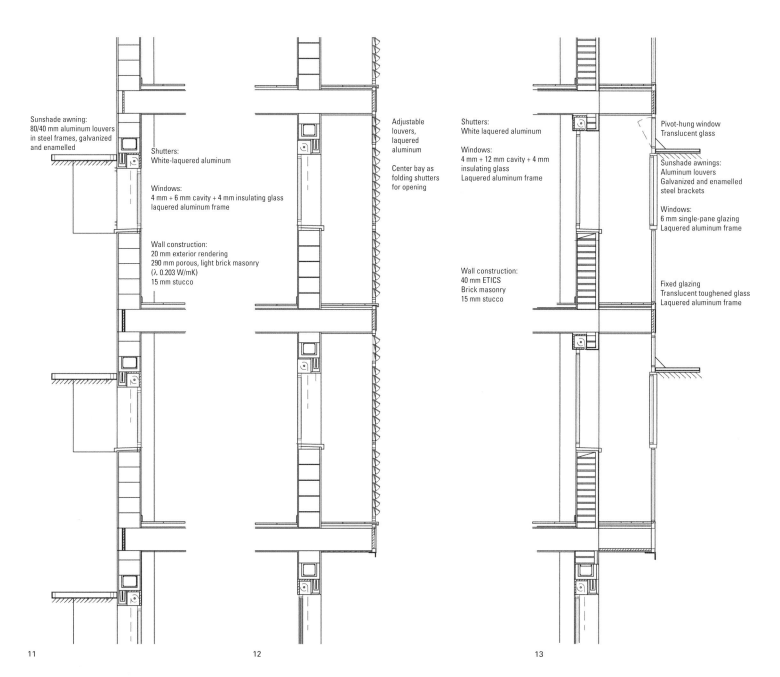

Sunshade awning:
80/40 mm aluminum louvers
in steel frames, galvanized
and enamelled

Shutters:
White-laquered aluminum

Windows:
4 mm + 6 mm cavity + 4 mm insulating glass
laquered aluminum frame

Wall construction:
20 mm exterior rendering
290 mm porous, light brick masonry
(λ 0.203 W/mK)
15 mm stucco

Adjustable
louvers,
laquered
aluminum

Center bay as
folding shutters
for opening

Shutters:
White laquered aluminum

Windows:
4 mm + 12 mm cavity + 4 mm
insulating glass
Laquered aluminum frame

Wall construction:
40 mm ETICS
Brick masonry
15 mm stucco

Pivot-hung window
Translucent glass

Sunshade awnings:
Aluminum louvers
Galvanized and enamelled
steel brackets

Windows:
6 mm single-pane glazing
Laquered aluminum frame

Fixed glazing
Translucent toughened glass
Laquered aluminum frame

11

12

13

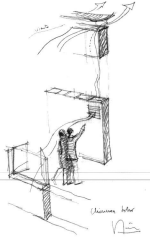

14

11 Detail section east facade
12 Detail section west
facade
13 Detail section south
facade
14 Functional diagram of
ventilation with solar
stack

openings are equipped with shading elements, specifically designed according to orientation. These elements allow sunshine to penetrate into the interior when needed or, conversely, to block it, an essential feature given the extreme conditions in summer. It is important to note that the shading elements do not diminish the efficiency of the natural ventilation. The south-facing balconies, with translucent glass panels in the parapet area, are designed to act as sun-traps. Horizontal louvers provide shading in summer on this side.

Folding shutters with horizontal, adjustable louvers protect the west-facing balconies against the low evening sun during the hot season. Bedrooms facing north and east feature smaller windows, whereby the east-facing windows are equipped with shading in the form of fixed horizontal and vertical elements.

The systems require very little maintenance and are easy for the residents to operate. Since their functions are clearly designated and recognizable, there is no risk of incorrect use.

15

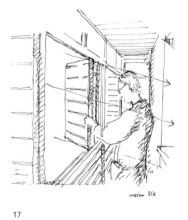

16   17

15 West elevation (court-
    yard): facade with shad-
    ing by means of folding
    shutters and adjustable
    louvers

16 East elevation (street):
    smaller opening with
    combined horizontal and
    vertical shading

17 Functional diagram of
    shading systems in front
    of balconies on the west
    side (courtyard)

Urban Renewal of an Industrial Wasteland:
University Campus in Nottingham

Architects:
Hopkins Architects, London

1

Selected data:

Completion: 1999
NSA: 37,050 m²

Energy consumption:
85 kWh/m²a
U-value roof:
0. 22 W/m²K
U-value exterior wall:
0.287 W/m²K
U-value flooring ground
floor/soil:
0.393 W/m²K
U-value window:
2.4 W/m²K

1 View of central campus
with study- and media
center and lecture halls

2 Site plan, not to scale

3 Isometric drawing of
study- and media center
and lecture halls

In 1996 the University of Nottingham launched an architecture competition for a new campus on the site of a former bicycle factory. The spatial program, scaled to accommodate 2,500 students, called for a study- and media center, a lecture building, three faculties and a student cafeteria as well as the required student housing. The project was to become a model of sustainable urban development in the region and exemplify the renewal of disused industrial land. Another goal was to ensure integration with a suburban residential district.

The dominant idea of the successful design created by Hopkins Architects, the engineers at Arup (building systems and load-bearing system planning) and the landscape architects at Battle McCarthy is the creation of an elongated lake covering an area of 13,000 m²: it serves both as a separating element and a connective element between the new university facility and the adjacent residential district. The new greenbelt sets clear priorities for pedestrian access and orientation on the site. Recreation and

improving the outdoor climate are therefore key aspects of the new complex.

The study- and media center is the visual focal point of the ensemble. The distinctive polygonal, cone-shaped volume invests the new campus with the necessary identity in a natural and unselfconscious manner. The spatial program of the building includes a library and a central computer lab that is available to students around the clock. The levels are arranged in the form of an upward, spiraling ramp. Elevator and stairwell constitute the core of the structure. The dividing wall between library and computer lab is designed to be adaptable to a variety of needs. The three faculty buildings are ventilated in accordance with low-energy standards. The combination of cellular offices and lecture halls with generous atria supports the chosen ventilation principle, which consists of two components: natural ventilation and an auxiliary, low-pressure mechanical ventilation system with heat-recovery. Final adjustments to the system were made during the first year

2

3

4

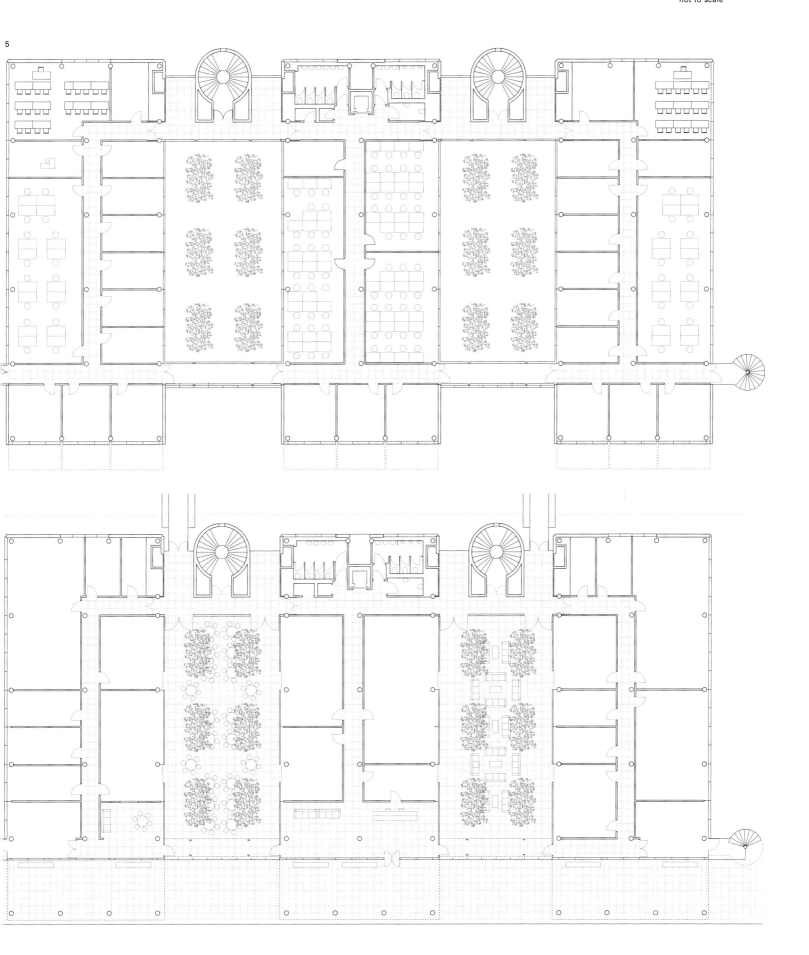

4 View into atrium of
Faculty of Education
building
5 Ground floor and upper
floor of Faculty of
Education building,
not to scale

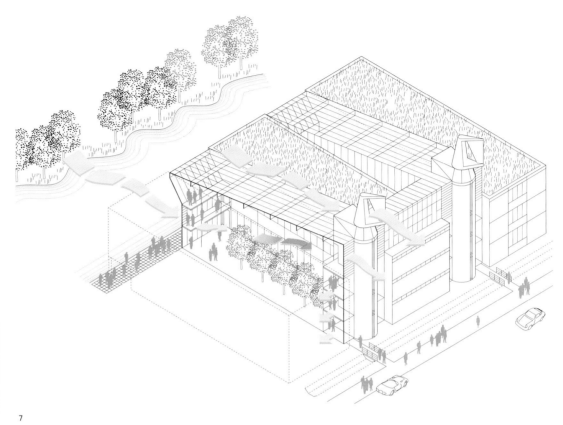

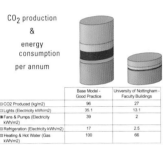

CO₂ production
&
energy
consumption
per annum

	Base Model - Good Practice	University of Nottingham - Faculty Buildings
⊞ CO2 Produced (kg/m2)	96	27
⊟ Lights (Electricity kWh/m2)	35.1	13.1
▣ Fans & Pumps (Electricity kWh/m2)	39	2
⊟ Refrigeration (Electricity kWh/m2)	17	2.5
⊟ Heating & Hot Water (Gas kWh/m2)	100	66

6

7

6 Comparison of consumption data with conventional institutional buildings in the U.K.

7 Ventilation diagram, faculty building: fresh air is sucked in from the park, stale air is evacuated via ventilation towers with rotating caps

8 (Overleaf) Facade section of faculty building with ventilation tower: Canadian cedar boarding panels, galvanized steel and exposed concrete emphasize the deliberately understated canon of materials, while at the same time investing the building with an unpretentious and friendly flair

9 (Page 86) Campus center and lecture hall building at night

of operation. To reduce the energy required for air distribution, corridors and stairwells are utilized as cross-sections: the greater the available cross-sections, the lower the energy required for the operation of the fans. Power for the fans is gained solely from photovoltaic cells installed on the atrium roof. The installation, which covers an area of 450 m², generates 51 240 kWh per year. The solar cells are integrated into the roof glazing with the desirable side effect that they provide shading in summer.

Natural light covers almost all the lighting requirements in the atria and the adjacent teaching facilities – even on overcast days. When necessary, minimal artificial lighting is added via an intelligent system controlled by infrared detectors. The presence of people and the actual daylight strength determine whether the system is activated.

As in some other passive houses, achieving the target for energy consumption is largely dependent on the users. Faculty and students are instructed in how to operate the ventilation system. Environmental aspects also define other aspects of the plan for the campus. These

include: the 22,000 m³ of excavated material used for landscaping; landscape design based on local soil properties; planted flat roof areas; and surface water collection in the lake. The fact that careful planning succeeded in reducing CO₂-emissions by 2,556 t/a speaks for itself.

**ENERGY-EFFICIENT
BUILDING DESIGN:
BASIC PRINCIPLES AND
STRATEGIES**

ENERGY-EFFICIENT BUILDING DESIGN: BASIC PRINCIPLES AND STRATEGIES

Point of Departure and Goals

It goes without saying that the concept of creating climate-conscious architecture was born with architecture itself. One of the reasons for the evolution of human habitation was to moderate extreme climate conditions in order to make life outside of tropical regions possible in the first place.

Climate-appropriate and energy-conscious principles were applied in conjunction with the structural and aesthetic aspects of architecture as a matter of course almost until the mid-nineteenth century. The accelerated development of climate technology "liberated" the architect from these constraints and allowed him to focus his attention entirely on structural or formal themes. Architecture thus gradually became divorced from nature. This attitude led to an irresponsible use of energy resources that cannot continue without resulting in grave ecological consequences.

The buildings that are being realized today should continue to be in use thirty to forty years hence, when energy supply will undoubtedly be an even more critical issue than it is today. In order to clarify the close relationships between man, climate and architecture, a wide range of so-called "solar buildings" was created. The energy performance of the buildings and the impact of the various strategies employed to utilize solar energy constituted the principal factors that were studied in these demonstration projects. Simplified calculation methods, developed for PC application, allow for a quantitative evaluation. The principal goal of these efforts should not lie, however, in optimizing the energy performance of these systems, but in establishing architectural applications for energy-conserving strategies and energy generation in the form of specific design components. Special attention should be given to the influence of these solutions on the design of facade and space and the use of the building, but also on the interaction between solar energy concept and the "habit"ation of the users. Ultimately, it is not only a question of conserving energy, especially by integrating the sun into the design, but also of augmenting the living quality in buildings.

1

Over the years, the foundations for planning a building design that takes the passive use of solar energy into account have grown ever more precise and increased planning stability. At the same time, this development not only served to overcome the arguments and prejudices against energy-saving measures, it also revealed the degree of responsibility residing in the hands of the planner. Energy-efficient architecture – in the context of taking a conscious look at the ecological situation and the constructional and technological possibilities – has become a matter of ethical duty.

Another decisive factor in this development was the growing sensitivity among clients with regard to the necessity of energy conservation. Energy-conscious building rose to the top on an international level. Renowned architects gave it prestige by choosing this approach as their leitmotif – with a corresponding multiplying effect.

The low-energy house became a universal standard that also received the stamp of approval from an economic perspective. Through legislation (e.g. the German energy-conservation act), this standard has now become binding. The new goal is to create the passive energy house, simply called passive house. Promotions and subsidy programs for energy-conserving building have been amended in recent years to reflect this goal. For example, the Kreditanstalt für Wiederaufbau (KfW, or credit bureau for reconstruction) has raised its subsidy program from low-energy houses to the standards of passive houses.

Similar to the debates on the low-energy house a decade ago, today's discussions are passionately concerned with the definitions, building techniques, building materials as well as the limitations and potentials of this new standard. More clearly defined parameters and simpler evaluation methods have improved the conditions under which architects can explore this topic. The basic rules of planning a passive house are unambiguous. Unlike the low-energy house, where deviations from energy-conscious planning could be compensated for by technical means or increased insulation, the compact building skin is an elemental component for this new standard. Architecture is thus called upon to adhere to a stricter discipline with regard to form. The question arises whether one should interpret this circumstance as a hindrance to creative expression or as a virtue that benefits both form and planning.

In building tasks, energy-conservation begins with the decision to build or not to build, followed firstly by decisions regarding building materials and only then by decisions regarding building methods. For the latter, the standard reference literature already contains planning methods and established rules of thumb as well as a selection of newly evolving technical means with which (nearly) every building task can be mastered. It is the first two decisions that represent the greatest savings potential. Opportunities missed at these preliminary stages can only be compensated for at tremendous economic and ecological expense.

"The difficulty does not lie in making things but in creating the conditions under which one can do without those things."(1) Anything that is built or employed for building should be evaluated according to its consumption value and derive its right to exist solely on that basis. Sustainability in a building task is based on necessity. Necessity, in this context, is also understood as the opposite of optional and arbitrary. From this perspective, energy-efficient planning and design cannot stop short at making formal decisions in favor of compact building form or employing specific materials and technologies. On the contrary, it encompasses all stages and areas of the design process. Since priorities must be established at all levels, it is essential to clearly define the goal in advance.

Energy-efficient Housing

Housing is a popular sector for the development of sustainable forms of building. The purpose of a residential building is to house human beings. Providing shelter from the inconveniences and fluctuations of the outdoor climate, housing is essential for life to unfold and flourish in the first place.

However, the shortage of housing and the speculation that arises from it, often lead to

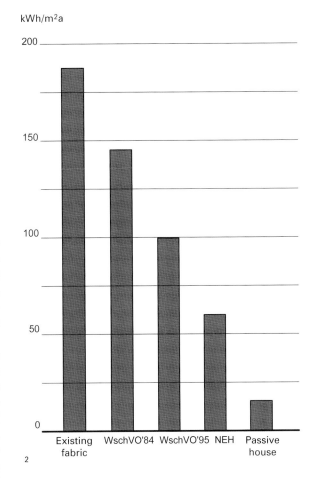

kWh/m²a

2

3

2 Annual heating requirements in the existing fabric based on applicable standards

3 Housing development in Kriens, Switzerland, Lischer, 2001 (see p. 44). Compact building forms minimize heat transmission losses.

(1) Constantin Brancusi (1876–1957)

89

4

4 Halen housing develop-
ment near Bern, Atelier
5, 1955/1961. Narrow
and deep row houses
with one or two narrow
rooms across the entire
width.

5 Housing development
in Passau-Neustift,
H. Schröder and
S. Widmann, 1989.
Narrow and deep row
houses with a single
room across the entire
width.

6 Floor plan design based
on room proportions

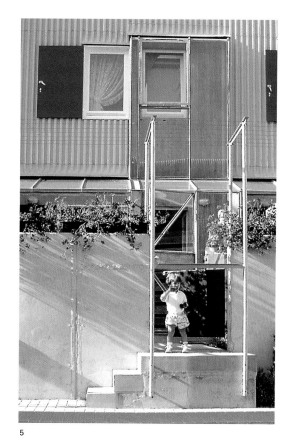

5

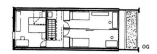

SIEDLUNG HALEN
BERN, ATELIER 5

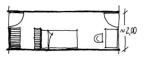
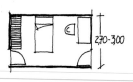

SIEDLUNG RÖTHENBACH
METRON AG

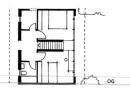
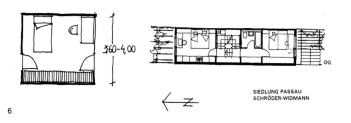

SIEDLUNG PASSAU
SCHRÖDER-WIDMANN

6

compromises in quality over quantity, even though the properties in terms of building physics of housing play such a vital role in climate adaptation and are generally influenced by this development.

Energy-efficient architecture calls for a careful balance between energy conservation and energy gain. The former is chiefly related to compactness and the homogeneous insulation of the building skin, while the latter is best expressed through the passive use of solar energy. From a planning perspective, the greatest influence is on building proportion and orientation.

The Individual Room

The development of these factors is dependent on building typology. The analysis of building typology begins with a study of the fundamental unit of a building: in office buildings, the individual office, in schools, the classroom, etc. Organization principles are then introduced on this basis. In housing, this unit is the individual room. In relation to energy, the proportions of the individual single room and the ratio of room depth to facade are relevant.

Narrow, long rooms are better for the energy balance of a building. Given a high ratio of glazing in the facade, this approach promotes good utilization of solar heat. In buildings of identical width, narrow room proportions allow for a floor plan in which several rooms face south, thereby increasing the use and occupation of the south side of a building.

But room proportions should be based on use and furnishing options. Here wider rooms are preferable, because they allow for different uses and furnishing alternatives. Over the long term, neutral rooms allow for a greater adaptability of the building to the changing requirements of family- and living structures.

Ultimately, this flexibility plays a role in the energy balance as well. Fully utilizing the living area increases the lifecycle of the building. Conversion and refurbishment can be avoided or, if necessary, executed in a simple fashion and, hence, at a low expenditure of energy.

7

Building Proportions

If we study building proportions on the example of a row house typology with south orientation, the compactness of the building is not only determined by the breadth and depth of the units within, but also by the overall height.

The width of a row house is chiefly dependent on the number of individual rooms and living areas and on the arrangement of ancillary rooms and internal circulation. Based on the standard arrangement of one to three adjoining rooms, the possible house width ranges from 4 to 9 m.

The depth of the building is determined by the placement of living areas on one or two sides. This translates into the following options:

– living areas on the south side – ancillary rooms/internal circulation on the north side: this corresponds to the typical layout for solar buildings, although the building depth is decreased;

– living areas on the south side – internal access/circulation in the center – ancillary room/additional living areas on the north side: this results in a greater building depth; to utilize the south orientation, the spatial zones on the south side should be deeper than those on the north side;

– living areas on the south side – internal access/circulation and ancillary rooms in the center – additional living areas on the north side: allows for very deep plans; however, this also results in an equal number of rooms facing north as the number of rooms with south orientation.

One-sided arrangement of living areas is suitable for small row houses with three to four rooms. With larger units, the house becomes too wide, and hence less compact, or the height has to be increased to more than two stories.

Conversely, two-sided room disposition creates large units with four to six rooms even in a two-story house. Another story creates either very large units (possible with in-law apartment) or a significant reduction in building width (single-room width), which means that the houses have very narrow yards.

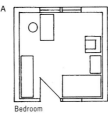

A

Bedroom

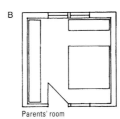

B

Parents' room

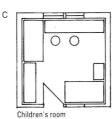

C

Children's room

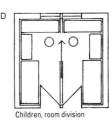

D

Children, room division

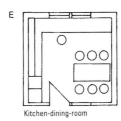

E

Kitchen-dining-room

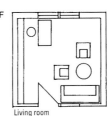

F

Living room

8

6,00 - 9,00

9,00 - 11,00

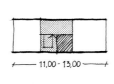

11,00 - 13,00

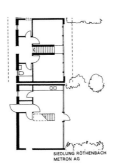

SIEDLUNG RÖTHENBACH
METRON AG

SIEDLUNG HALEN
BERN, ATELIER 5

SIEDLUNG PASSAU
SCHRÖDER-WIDMANN

9

7 Housing development in Röthenbach a. d. Pegnitz-Steinberg, Metron Architektur, 1990. Wide and shallow row houses with two rooms per width.

8 Neutral rooms. Alternative furnishing plans (from: Peter Faller: *Der Wohngrundriss 1920–1990,* Stuttgart 2002)

9 Building depth – internal zoning

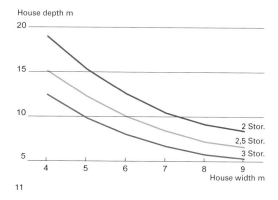

10 Development of the
building height

11 Influence of building
width and number of
floors in a row house
(center of row house for
a constant gross floor
area of 150 m²) on
building depth.

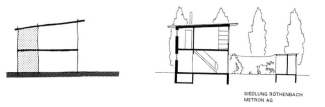

SIEDLUNG RÖTHENBACH
METRON AG

SIEDLUNG HALEN
BERN, ATELIER 5

SIEDLUNG PASSAU
SCHRÖDER-WIDMANN

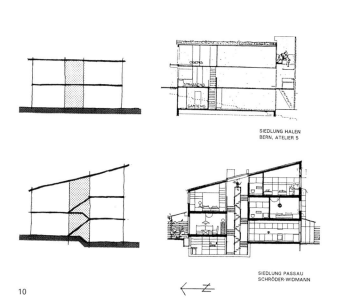

10

←Z

width of house increases, the height greatly
influences the resulting depth. In very narrow
houses, the low number of stories translates
into a building depth that is virtually imprac-
ticable. In very wide houses, this dynamic is
reversed.

If one calculates the S/V-ratio as the width
increases, the number of stories plays a far
less significant role. The principal effect lies
in the building width. Wide plans result is an
S/V ratio that is 50 percent greater than that
of narrow houses. This also translates into a
50 percent increase in heat transmission losses for otherwise identical structures, or in
other words, a need for more insulation in
order to achieve the same values for heat
transmission losses. Moreover, an increase
of 50 percent in the building skin also raises
the building costs and results in a higher consumption of primary energy for construction
and manufacture. Small house widths promote compactness and also allow for private,
albeit narrow, open spaces for a greater
number of units. External access-, supply-
and disposal routes are also reduced by this
means.

Building proportion in all its variations can be
studied in a manner similar to the example
given here for other house typologies.

Orientation
It is interesting to explore building proportion
in the context of orientation. The classic rule of
solar architecture is that living rooms should
be placed on the south side and ancillary rooms
on the north side in all buildings with a north/
south orientation. Although this results in a
diminished building depth and hence less
compact volume, it does improve the use of
solar energy.
Houses with east/west orientation, on the
other hand, should feature deeper plans
because the potential solar gain is lower by
comparison to south orientation. Greater
compactness and minimized heat transmission losses then compensate for the diminished solar incidence.

Split-level plans and roof shape are two possible ways of responding to site differentiation
and creating a greater number of south-facing
rooms. In 2.5 or 3-story units, split-level plans
are especially suitable for creating better linkages between the various areas. Deep plans are
also divided in a more favorable manner by this
means.
A shed roof not only increases the south face, it
also reduces the shading depth on the north
side and thus the distance between the rows.
The formal consequences of creating row housing with shed roof, as well as the characteristics
of the interstitial spaces with varying boundary
heights, require a great degree of care in planning and design.

The relationships between these parameters
can be clearly illustrated (see figures 11 and
12), when the height, width and depth at the
center of a row house are varied – ideally
without altering the total floor area. As the

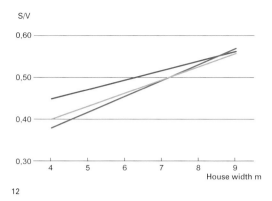

S/V

0,60

0,50

0,40

0,30

    4   5   6   7   8   9
                    House width m

12

This orientation fundamentally allows solar radiation to penetrate the house from both sides. Hence the living areas can be oriented to two sides, with the ancillary rooms arranged along the middle. This translates into a tremendous building depth, that is, a highly compact volume. The qualitative difference between the morning and evening sun should, however, be taken into consideration in the allocation of the living areas.

A careful study of floor plans shows that a third internal zone that faces north is quite feasible when combined with a north/south orientation. This zone could accommodate rooms that do not necessarily require direct sunshine (e.g., parents' bedroom, study) or others that are spatially linked to the south-facing zone (e.g., open-plan dining and living room). As regards the south-facing rooms, deep, narrow layouts are preferable. This allows for generously glazed facades without running the risk of overheating.

This approach to planning creates greater openness in the floor plan design. Lighting from two sides and contact with the outside are also made possible, greatly enhancing the spatial quality of a living unit.

In other words, the south orientation of a building has no adverse effect on designing deeper, more compact buildings. Small deviations from an orientation that is due south also result in interesting planning questions without having any noticeable impact on solar gain. By rotating the principle alignment to the southwest, the sun can penetrate into the building on this side into the evening hours in summer. This has an influence not only on the quality of the interior space but also on the quality of the exterior space that precedes it. The north facade is correspondingly rotated to the northeast with the result that the rooms on this side (e.g., kitchen, parents' bedroom) benefit from the morning sun in summer and during the transitional seasons.

Different concepts are frequently mixed up in the context of working with orientation. It is important here to distinguish clearly between

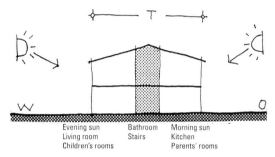

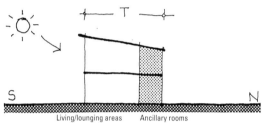

Evening sun   Bathroom   Morning sun
Living room   Stairs   Kitchen
Children's rooms   Parents' rooms

W   O

Living/lounging areas   Ancillary rooms

S   N

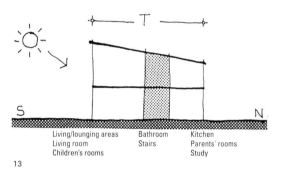

Living/lounging areas   Bathroom   Kitchen
Living room   Stairs   Parents' rooms
Children's rooms   Study

S   N

13

14

12 same as 11: influence on compactness (S/V ratio)

13 Principles of internal zoning depending on building orientation

14 Looren housing development in Affoltern am Albis, Metron Architektur, 1998 (see p. 50). Front-to-back kitchen-dining-living area.

15 Competition "Wohnen 2000," Essen, Stender, Söldner, Gonzalo. Long plans with front-to-back kitchen-dining-living area.

16 Office and apartment building in Wiesbaden, A-Z Architekten, 2002 (see p. 68). The large building depth compensates for the disadvantages of an E-W orientation. The living areas receive light from two sides.

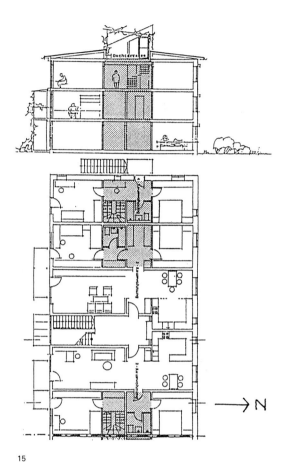

15

16

lighting, solar use for heating and solar incidence in relationship to spatial quality. Lighting from all four cardinal directions is possible. In some cases (work areas, artist's studio), a northern orientation is preferable because it offers an even distribution of natural light without the risk of overheating or glare resulting from direct solar incidence.

A differentiation is made between diffuse and direct solar radiation with regard to the use of solar energy. The diffuse component is evenly distributed across all cardinal directions, resulting in a small amount of solar gain also being achieved on the north side. When it comes to the passive use of solar energy for heating, direct radiation is the most significant variable, because of its intensity, and it generates the highest value on the south side. This value quickly drops with any deviation towards the east or the west.

The availability of solar energy in cases with east/west orientation should also be studied in conjunction with temperature curves. Both sides receive approximately the same intensity of radiation. However, outside temperatures are lower before noon than in the afternoon. Consequently, the energy requirements are higher in the room before noon and this stands in direct correlation to the utilization factor of the solar energy potential. Despite these variables, a west orientation is generally preferred for living areas because of the quality this orientation offers and the time of occupation by the inhabitants (usually in the afternoons).

Another factor should be taken into consideration when studying solar incidence as a contribution to improving the spatial quality: this is the solar altitude over the course of a day. In winter, the sun rises in the southeast, reaches its highest altitude (and hence its highest intensity of radiation) in the south at noon and sets in the southwest. In other words, the solar radiation will fall onto an east/west facade at an angle that grows increasingly more shallow as noon approaches, which means that sunshine cannot penetrate as deeply into the interior. If this angle is less than 15°, the bulk of the solar radiation is reflected off the glass pane. The greater the distance in time is from the noon hour, the larger the angle of inci-

17

18

19

dence and the lower the solar altitude. Shading from parallel rows of buildings is then increased.

Solar Facades

Early low-energy houses were distinguished from conventional buildings by the largest possible opening of the facade facing the sun. Since energy requirements were still relatively high in these buildings, the solar energy gained from large window areas could be utilized with a high quotient of efficiency. Energy requirements decreased as the constructional and ventilation properties of buildings improved, and the effective window area diminished accordingly. From an energy perspective, fully glazed facades are rarely ideal. Full glazing also goes hand in hand with the risk of overheating in summer. The rule of thumb proposed in the relevant literature is that the maximum glazing ratio on a south facade should not exceed 50 percent of the total area.

The decisive factor for the success of passive solar energy strategies is less the size than the harmony in design and function with the architectural concept of the building. The strategies in their entirety should never restrict the utility of living areas, but send a clear message as a result of their visible effect. This increases acceptance among users and promotes energy-conscious behavior.

The energy exchange between a building and its environment is characterized by a continual crossing of the thermal boundaries between interior and exterior. This unique interior-exterior relationship occurs in various ways, most of which are barely noticeable.

While the cold air draft from an open ventilation flap renders the heat exchange resulting from ventilation perceptible, it does not make users aware of the overall effect on the energy balance. A cold glass pane, for example, is a tangible manifestation of the energy transfer through the building skin. However, a sensory experience of the totality of this process – rendered visible in an infrared image, for example – is not possible.

When sun flows into an interior, we recognize the influx of energy in a more conscious manner. This energy is more than warmth and can

17   Dianas Have housing complex, Denmark, Tegnestuen Vandkunsten, 1992. Spatial accent provided by a north-facing skylight.

18   Housing complex in Eching near Munich, R. Tobey, 1988. Living room with fully glazed south facade.

19   Passive house development Höcklistein in Jona near Rapperswil, Switzerland, Roos Architekten, 2002. The optimized glazing ratio in a south facade is reduced in the passive house standard.

20

21

22

23

20 House in Amaicha,
   Argentina. The bright
   sun accentuates the
   coolness of the shaded
   area.

21 Mashrabiya in Cairo,
   Egypt. The window as a
   filter to the outside
   world

22 Window in Prague. The
   complex demands
   placed on the window
   are expressed in its
   design.

23 Wohntraube housing
   development in
   Veitshöchheim,
   Tegnestuen
   Vandkunsten, 1989.
   Spatial effect of solar
   radiation

(2) Otto F. Bollnow: Mensch
   und Raum, Stuttgart
   1989

be perceived in a variety of ways: simply looking at a surface bathed in sun reveals the presence of this flow of energy. Conversely, the coolness provided by shade in summer is intensified as a pleasurable experience in contrast to the heat of the sun.

Incident sunlight penetrates a room and connects it to the outside world. Solar incidence thus expands our range of perception because it mediates between inside and outside.

"By virtue of the window, the small living space is set into the context of the larger world, and the window makes it possible to orient oneself within this world. Through the window, one looks out into the open, seeing the sky and the horizon (or at least some piece of the outside world in which the horizon, albeit not visible, is nevertheless invisibly inferred). The window thus renders the human interior space open and clear." (2)

Different elements, not just the building skin, but also others that lie in front of or behind the dividing line we call facade, articulate the relationship between interior and exterior. When we look at the principles of passive solar use from this perspective, it is surprising how complex a window is, although it is widely regarded as the simplest system employed for solar energy gain.

The different requirements which a window is meant to fulfill, (light, air, sun, all manner of visual contact – from the outside in, the inside out and across the length or breadth – as well as

the ability to accentuate a space) give this element an infinite variety.

A window can fulfill one or several of these requirements. It can be a simple, modest element or a complex configuration of parts, the totality of which meets different demands. The window is more than simply a surface. In the form of multi-layered facades or in combination with control features (shading, light-deflection, etc.) it can extend toward the inside or the outside. Thus the window adapts to the spatial context and reacts to the changing conditions in the interior or the exterior. A differentiated treatment of windows is possible and necessary if inhabitants are to understand and experience their functions (also with regard to energy management).

"People have often tried to enhance the privacy of the window with window coverings and net curtains, although the modern style of living is characterized by opening the house more pronouncedly to the outside world through large glass areas. Conversely: when people are exposed in a brightly lit room at night to the eyes of a stranger, who may be looking in from the outside without being noticed, then they feel unsafe and like to draw the curtains and close the shutters."(3)

24

25

26

27

The perception of the transition between inside and outside is more difficult on solar walls. The warmth of the sun flows through the transparent or translucent exterior surface and is captured on the wall behind it. This process cannot be tracked from the inside nor can it be coupled with a specific spatial effect.

By virtue of the glazing on the outside, solar walls are similar to windows in appearance. This impression is contradicted on the inside, however, because the wall merges with the other, closed areas. Ultimately, its function as a solar element is entirely a matter of thermodynamic principles. As Bruno Schindler puts it: "Solar architecture is a shirt, not a medal. It is not an accessory; it is both skin and dress. It is something totally enveloping, something ephemeral, easily changeable, far from thermodynamic equilibrium, it is a stage for self-organizing shapes. Solar architecture works through the deep lustre of its surface."(4)

Both systems can complement one another perfectly by carefully harmonizing the dimension, the energy effect as well as the structural and aesthetic realization.

Threshold Spaces

In a greenhouse or conservatory, the interior penetrates the exterior. The architectural effect of a conservatory lies first and foremost in the multiplicity of the interior/exterior relationships that can unfold in such a space.

In practice, the use of glass-enclosed spaces with low temperature requirements as buffer spaces has proven ineffective in terms of heat protection, above all because their effectiveness is greatly dependent upon the user. Incorrect use can easily convert this component from energy contributor to energy guzzler. A conservatory can only achieve a positive energy balance as a buffer space and sun trap if it is utilized as an unheated space. And in most cases the cost that is involved to achieve this is simply too great.

A poll on the use of attached conservatories in the U.K. revealed that 91 percent of these spaces were heated directly or indirectly (by being open to a heated room). One third were heated up to 10° C, primarily to protect plants against frost. The remaining two thirds were heated to over 16° C for use as extended living areas. Quality conservatories with double-glazing were heated twice as long as those with single glazing. (5)

The passive house standard resulted in a pronounced shift in the relationship between interior and exterior. What emerged was a so-called "box architecture." The reasons for this development lie in the search for more clarity in defining the thermal separation between heated and unheated space. A simple volume achieves both greater compactness and a simplification in the implementation of this thermal separation. The required and more stringent standards for ther-

24 Tinggården housing development in Herfølge, Denmark, Tegnestuen Vandkunsten. The window as a hole in the wall

25 same as 24: The window as a differentiated element

26 House in Planegg, Demmel + Mühlbauer. The solar wall is similar to the window surface on the exterior, but indistinguishable on the inside.

27 same as 26: interior

(3) Otto F. Bollnow: Mensch und Raum, Stuttgart 1989

(4) Bruno Schindler: "From Solar Accessories to Solar Architecture," in: Solar Energy in Architecture and Urban Planning, ed. by Sir N. Foster & H. Scheer, Florence, 1993

28

mal insulation can thus be realized in a more economic fashion. Increasing the area that loses heat makes it necessary to improve the quality of insulation in order to maintain the energy balance at a constant level.

Many components that tend to contribute to the formation of transitions and thresholds, such as projecting roofs, balconies, covered patios, patio walls, etc., have a negative impact on the energy balance in winter due to their shading effect and are therefore avoided in passive house design.

No doubt, the calming effect this has on the formal vocabulary of the built environment has its advantages. Out of necessity, traditional architecture followed a similar path in formal development. But the building skin should not be reduced to a mere thermal boundary between interior and exterior space. The design of threshold zones requires careful planning. The effects these zones have on the energy balance must be studied and optimized.

Recent developments in materials and technologies (thermal glazing with high insulation values, vacuum insulation) can inspire new ideas in building skin design. However, they should not be seen as an invitation to simply abandon the formal canon of compact energy-conserving architecture; instead, they should serve to efficiently expand the vocabulary and variety in the dialogue with the environment. The goal of this development must be to improve the quality of living, whereby contact with the outside and its potential uses should not be underestimated.

28 Housing development in Passau-Neustift, H. Schröder and S. Widmann, 1989. Conservatories as vestibules with warm-air shaft in the upper floors.

29 Guesthouse in youth education center in Windberg, Thomas Herzog, 1992. Solar walls and glazed areas complement one another in function and design.

30 "Wohnen 2000," IGA Stuttgart '93, E. Muszynska et. al. Conservatory as thermal transition space realized in the simplest fashion.

31 Nachtgärtle housing development in Fussach, Vorarlberg, Juen, 1984. Conservatory as a shared access space.

(5) T. Oreszczyn: "The energy duality of conservatories: a survey of conservatory use," in: Solar Energy in Architecture and Urban Planning, op. cit.

29

30

31

32

33   34

Utilization and Energy Balance
Energy-efficient building began with the single-family, detached house. Even today, the relevant legislative guidelines seem to take this image as their leitmotif for terms and requirements. However, in a changing society the idea of the "house" must be fundamentally re-evaluated, and not only in relation to energy use and conservation: it should be expanded to encompass building, neighborhood and city, in order to establish the right context for the efforts and possibilities of energy-conscious architecture. Optimizing individual components or even single buildings cannot be the ultimate goal.

Housing should respond to the changes and variety in urban lifestyles. The different stages of life, life situations and habits as well as the special needs of individual groups should be taken into consideration. A built structure that is open and adaptable seems desirable as an object for different and ever-changing users.

"Conquer the earth, God said to the architect with a wink. It is damn uninhabitable here! In the Mediterranean, they live in front of the house, in the lane or on the piazza. There is no living space in the poorer houses and the richer ones are cold with ostentation or due to a lack of furnishings.
In regions where it often rains and is cold, people like to live indoors.
When houses are far apart, people like to meet in their apartments.
The Viennese lives in the coffeehouse.
Ah – you live in Neukölln, what do you do with your living space?
TIDYING UP, TIDYING UP." (6)

What we really need is a redefinition of the culture of living. Societal individualization has translated into a growth in apartments for singles or childless couples in the cities. However, small apartments could contain the potential of growing into larger units through addition. To improve the quality of life in the city, the variety and hence the available living space for families should be supported and promoted. As the family matures, it would be desirable that the space could be divided into independ-

32 Conservatory in Madrid

33 Office and apartment building in Schwarzach, Lenz + Kaufmann, 1999 (see p. 122). Compact building form with roof patios as allocated outdoor areas.

34 Looren housing complex in Affoltern am Albis, Metron Architektur, 1998. (see p. 50). Despite the shading they create, the balconies contribute greatly to the quality of the outdoor area.

37

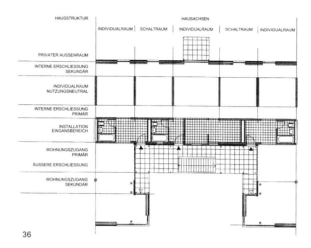

36

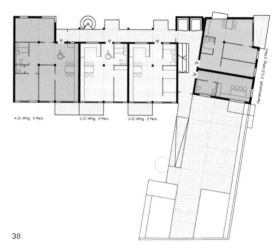

38

35

ent units to ensure that no space remains underutilized.

The energy balance of a building is based on the energy consumed per square meter. It would be far more interesting, however, to shift this reference plane from area to people. Energy consumption per person would include the use of the building and reward area-saving planning strategies. In less than half a century, the living area used per person has more than doubled in Germany. Building in an area-saving manner is the first step not only toward cost efficiency but toward energy conservation. A square meter that is never built does not consume energy. Economic floor plans that are carefully laid out represent a tremendous energy savings potential. Openness in the floor plan makes it possible to develop space using the appropriate means. Open floor plans are also advantageous for heat distribution, for example through incident sunlight.

Unheated rooms or spaces for temporary use (guest rooms, hobby rooms that are only used from time to time, workshops, etc.) should be set apart from the heated core of the house. Creating rooms that are available for shared use by a community is a viable alternative for these areas, making it possible to achieve a balanced ratio between effort and use.

Dense housing developments or urban situations offer a suitable framework for the creation of such usage structures. Habitation is thus invested with a more public character. The individual component is woven into the social fabric, strengthening the collective sense of responsibility and meaning for the well-being of the community. It goes without saying that this should be the fundamental motivation for energy-conscious attitudes toward housing.

40

39

41

39 Housing development
in Puchheim, Munich,
M. Kovatsch, 1989.
Community hall

40 Roof conversion in
Munich with atrium
above stairwell,
F. Dirtheuer

41 Exemplary ecological
renovation on Pariser
Strasse in Munich, Per
Krusche, Arche Nova,
1989

(7) *Günther Moewes:
Weder Hütten noch
Paläste, Basel 1995,
p. 28*

Energy-efficient Refurbishment

Conversion versus new Construction:
Advantages

Optimizing the energy balance of new buildings is extremely important for the future because these structures will be in use for several decades. However, if we look at the current situation, then the truly significant energy-saving potentials lie in the refurbishment of existing fabrics. Postwar buildings, that is buildings that have not yet fulfilled their anticipated lifecycle, are characterized by energy requirements that are much higher than those defined by the new standards.

Upgrading the energy behavior of a building not only lowers the energy requirements, it also lengthens the building's lifecycle. The energy consumed for manufacture and demolition at a later point can be amortized over a longer period of use. Last but not least, upgrading the energy behavior also results in a noticeable improvement in comfort.

Urban land for development is growing increasingly scarce and the expansion of urban boundaries is not a desirable solution due to the familiar negative consequences (commuter traffic, ground sealing, infrastructure, etc.). In future, renewing the existing fabric will therefore gain in importance.

"All new buildings increase the building volume and hence the energy requirements (...). Fundamentally, energy requirements can only be decreased by avoiding new development and implementing strategies for old buildings or straightforward replacement buildings." (7)

Renewal by means of demolishing old fabrics and replacing them with new buildings can only be justified from an economic point of view if this results in a more effective use of the built area and in higher density. Even without demolition, the addition of new stories or density augmentation of existing structures is a strategy that makes better use of the developed land and also offers energy savings.

Upgrading the energy behavior of buildings is the best recycling option in the building sector, because the final product is the entire building, which is made available for re-use. Primary energy costs for demolition and for new construction can thus be avoided.

From the perspective of energy-efficiency and ecology, building in the existing fabric aims to achieve the following goals:

– conversion instead of new construction;

– increasing the lifecycle of materials by utilizing existing building fabric;

– material savings as well as prevention of developing and sealing even more ground;

– improving the energy balance of the existing fabric and reducing the emission of pollutants.

101

42

43

Suitability for Refurbishment

The principal criteria for building in the existing fabric are the suitability for refurbishment and the sense of doing so in each case. Suitability for refurbishment relates to the substance of the building as such. When planning for building in the existing fabric, an individual list of criteria must be drafted and evaluated for each project. These criteria include the urban context, the existing structural parameters and the suitability of the building fabric.

Aside from the condition of the existing fabric, there are additional aspects which must be taken into consideration for any conversion project. These determine whether or not it makes sense to go ahead with refurbishment or conversion:

– proof of economic viability by comparison to new construction;

– functional suitability;

– aspects related to the conservation of historic buildings;

– ecological and energy-consumption parameters.

The last item in this list is determined first and foremost by the potentials for energy and resource conservation. To evaluate this aspect, one should compare all viable alternatives – conversion, replacement through a new building on the same site (demolition and new construction) or new development at another site.

44

42 Industrial buildings converted into sports complex in Madrid, Oscar Tusquets Blanca, 2004, interior

43 same as 42: exterior

44 Conversion of the former Zeisehallen in Hamburg into a cultural and entertainment center, Medium, Jentz, Popp, Wiesner, 1996

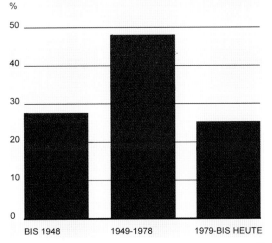

45

However, the refurbishment of a building should also be studied with a view to redefining building use. Reorganizing the function within an existing fabric, if possible accompanied by increasing the density, results in better use of urban districts with existing infrastructure and is therefore the most sensible building strategy from an ecological perspective, namely the avoidance of new development in the first place.

Although there are specific building characteristics for different periods for which tried and tested solutions have been developed, there are no universal rules. Insulating the building skin, replacing old windows and retrofitting heating systems to the latest standards in technology are frequently the first steps. Choosing among these measures is only possible on the basis of an energy-balance study and evaluation.

When we take the postwar building boom that lasted into the 1970s into consideration, the tremendous potential that lies in refurbishment is self-explanatory. These buildings have barely reached the mid-point of their lifecycles, and yet they consume five times more energy than a new building constructed in accordance with today's standards and more than ten times the energy of a passive house. From the perspective of energy consumption, an estimated 24 million apartments are in need of refurbishment in the Federal Republic of Germany, that is, buildings that consume more than 150–200 kWh/m²a. Seventy-five percent of the buildings were created prior to the first heat protection act (1977). Depending on their condition, savings of thirty to seventy percent can be achieved in terms of technology and economy. Yet many of these buildings are demolished due to poor energy quotients and replaced with new structures with the result that the primary energy that was initially consumed to construct them is never fully amortized.

The motivation for refurbishing a building is rarely founded in improving the energy-related properties alone. In addition to lowering energy costs, other goals come into play, for example, the repair to structural damage (above all dampness as a result of thermal bridges and leaks), the replacement of materials that represent

46

47   48

45 Student residence in Wuppertal, Müller, Schlüter, 2000/2003. The rooms were expanded as part of the upgrade to passive house standard.

46 same as 45

47 Percentage of apartments in the existing fabric according to building age. Three quarters of all the apartments were constructed prior to the first heat protection act. Source: statistical yearbooks

48 Roof covering over courtyard at the Museum für hamburgische Geschichte in Hamburg, von Gerkan, Marg and Partner, 1989. As an unheated buffer zone, this area expands the uses of the museum and reduces heat losses.

103

49

50

51

health hazards (paint, asbestos) or the desire to upgrade equipment to new standards. Adapting the use to new requirements and improving comfort are the principal visible consequences of an overall refurbishment.

There is no wholesale definition of the scope and breadth of refurbishments. Instead, the measures and energy-saving potentials must be determined based on an analysis of the existing fabric. Different constructional and technical solutions can be applied in accordance with the individual components of the energy balance.

Thermal Insulation

The thermal properties of building skins in postwar buildings are sometimes poorer than those of earlier buildings. A one-sided, one might even say superficial approach to opti-mizing costefficiency and the proliferation of skeleton construction resulted in walls that were increasingly thin without any accom-panying improvement to the insulating capac-ity of the materials. Even new double-pane thermal glazing has a poorer U-value than the old "box-type" windows.

The building components must be treated in a differentiated manner to improve the thermal insulation. Roofs are usually recovered or even raised, whereby the effort required for improved thermal insulation, taken in isolation, is rela-tively low. An additional layer of thermal insula-tion on the underside of the basement ceiling is generally speaking inexpensive, efficient and simple – unless it diminishes the utility of the basement rooms by reducing the room height to unacceptable levels. In buildings without basements, retrofitting with thermal insulation presents a variety of complications even when floor coverings are renewed. The existing clear room height, doorway clearance and threshold- and barrier-free connection to other areas must be taken into consideration.

There are two principal methods of adding thermal insulation to exterior walls: the most common method is to install external thermal insulation in the form of a composite thermal insulation system or behind suspended facade

52

cladding with a ventilation cavity. In this case, the thermal insulation layer is ideally placed in terms of building physics and construction. With external insulation, the space benefits from the wall as a storage mass, which balances temperature fluctuations in the interior space.

Thermal insulation installed on the inside, conversely, has a negative impact on the storage mass and on the internal climate. Constructional issues (humidity control, dew point) also dictate that it is only a viable option for cases where the appearance of a building prohibits the use of external insulation (e.g., exposed masonry, articulated facades or the conservation of historic buildings). The joints to interior walls and ceilings must be carefully planned in order to avoid thermal bridges, whereby continuous installation of the required vapor barriers is an important factor. Otherwise, one should choose vapor-proof thermal insulation systems.

Most refurbishments require the replacement of windows. If this measure is combined with the addition of a thermal insulation layer on the exterior wall, it is vital to prevent the formation of thermal bridges at the joints. Windows should therefore be installed flush with the thermal insulation; another alternative is to carry the insulation across the windowsill. Special attention must be given to thermal bridges in concrete components in reinforced steel skeleton structures with bands of windows.

Improving the thermal insulation properties of the building skin goes hand in hand with an increase in the surface temperature in the interior space. This translates into structural advantages (avoidance of condensation) and also improves comfort.

Ventilation

Unregulated window ventilation leads to uneven, uncontrolled air exchange combined with correspondingly high heat losses. Heat transmission losses are diminished by retrofitting the building skin to meet higher energy-efficient standards; the manner in which heat loss from ventilation is treated is significant in this context.

The efficient and economic operation of a controlled ventilation system, for example by

53

54

55

52 Energy-efficiency renovation and redesign of a 1970s kindergarten in Lochham, Pollok + Gonzalo, 2003. The concrete crosswalls required internal insulation of the thermal bridges.

53 same as 52

54 Conversion of a hall erected for EXPO Seville for use by the university, SAMA, J. López de Asiaín, 1996. Minimal use of air-conditioning due to natural lighting and sun protection.

55 same as 54: Light deflection systems in front of the windows.

56

57

provide not only an efficient use of energy that meets comfort requirements; they also allow for subsequent monitoring and, if necessary, adjustments to the anticipated system criteria. Furthermore, these systems permit consumption-based meter readings for individual users, instant malfunction notification and automated self-monitoring.

In the context of economic viability studies, the refurbishment strategies for saving and gaining energy can be divided into two groups: the first group includes measures that are necessary from a technical perspective and/or due to legal stipulations, for example:
– insulation of building components that have to be renewed;
– window upgrades;
– heating system upgrades.
The most favorable implementation must be selected from a variety of different alternatives. The need for an efficiency calculation is obviated if the renewal or replacement of any of these elements is dictated by codes and regulations such as the energy-conservation bill.
The second group comprises measures that are technically possible and correspond to the latest state of technology but are justified on the basis of savings in operating costs, for example:
– measures to utilize renewal resources (e.g., solar collectors for water heating, photovoltaic systems);
– controlled ventilation with heat-recovery;
– temperature controls for individual rooms with consumption meters.
An efficiency study with a comparison of investment and amortization is required to justify the implementation of these measures. However, low energy costs sometimes lead to very long amortization periods. To reach a decision it is therefore necessary to combine the objective cost-benefit analysis with a consideration of other aspects, such as creating a safeguard against rising energy costs, increasing the value of an energy-efficient building and, above all, responsible consideration of environmental issues.

means of ventilation ducts, requires a building skin that is sufficiently airtight. When new windows are installed, sealed and airtight joints are especially important. The sealing of construction joints, above all along the seams of different building components and around penetrations (e.g., chimneys) deserves particular attention.

Low room heights or other unusual characteristics in the building form can present a challenge for the installation of ventilation ducts. Here it is usually very difficult to install a central ventilation system. The distribution of the ventilation system across decentralized units allows for simpler duct systems running along shorter distances with smaller cross sections.

Heating Systems

One of the most important measures to reduce the heating energy when refurbishing a building is to renew the heating system. Depending on the age of the building, the whole heating installation may have to be redesigned.

The selection of a new heating system should be based on an analysis of all factors contributing to the energy balance, in the same way as for new buildings (solar gain, temperature requirements, controlled ventilation, internal heat gains). Tremendous energy-saving potentials lie in a precise determination of the heat consumption and in the regulation of individual room temperatures. Modern regulating systems

56 Renovation on the Sonnenäckerweg in Freiburg, Rolf Disch 1989. Translucent insulation on the solid old walls shifts their energy balance into the positive range and characterizes the appearance of the renovated development.

57 same as 56

58

Energy-efficient Commercial Buildings

Requirements

Energy-efficient design is far more complex for commercial buildings than for housing because of the functions the former must fulfill. The term commercial building encompasses a multitude of building types with differing functions and correspondingly differing requirements in terms of the energy balance. The individual aspects that determine the energy balance must be seen in the context of the overall result. The optimized use of a high internal heating load, the avoidance of overheating, sun- and glare protection as well as natural lighting are but some of the additionally relevant factors for the energy balance. Depending on the function of a building or building component, each of these factors may assume a different degree of importance.

Owing to this circumstance, rules of thumb and global solutions do not apply. At the same time, this opens up a challenging scope for the creative exploration of energy-conserving measures.

Changing organizational principles and structures as well as neutral floor plans are even more important here than in housing. These aspects ensure flexibility in the face of changing requirements without great expenditure in energy and can improve the lifecycle of a building. Grid plans, modulated facade structures and light-weight internal division are preferred for this purpose. The same principles apply to the refurbishment of existing structures. Most existing office buildings are less than thirty years old. They usually fail to meet comfort requirements despite exorbitant energy consumption. In summer especially, these buildings tend to depend on air conditioning systems with high energy consumption rates.

59

60

Energy Balance

The goal of energy-efficient planning is to achieve a balance between energy gains and energy losses. Imbalances mean the loss of thermal comfort in the interior space and the need for additional regulatory measures (e.g., sun protection, more effective thermal insulation). If these do not suffice, then the balance must be achieved at the cost of additional energy (heating or cooling).

The energy balance can be influenced through planning, construction and technology. The sequence in this enumeration reflects the complexity and effort required for solutions in each of these fields: planning solutions are often the simplest and technological solutions the most elaborate with a view to achieving the same effect.

The compactness and thermal insulation quality of the building skin determines the level of heat transmission losses. Commercial buildings tend to be compact for economic reasons. However, the possibility for an even distribution of natural lighting in summer and natural ventilation must be taken into consideration. Differentiated zoning of internal spaces according to lighting requirements does allow for deep, compact volumes.

In comparison to housing, the work conditions in commercial buildings or the concentration of occupants tend to call for a much higher air change frequency and hence greater ventilation

58 Office building in Sursee, Switzerland, Scheitlin Syfrig + Partner, 2002. Compact building skin as a basis for energy-efficient design (see p. 128).

59 Office complex in Duisburg, Schuster Architekten, 2002. Compact building. The glazed areas are complemented by solar facade panels on the south side (see p. 134).

60 same as 59: facade detail

62

61

63

64

heat losses. In compact buildings with good thermal insulation, the heat losses resulting from ventilation are higher than those resulting from transmission.

Natural ventilation can lead to extremely high heat losses and also includes the risk of improper use, for example, windows that are left open or, conversely, insufficient ventilation and therefore an unhealthy concentration of toxins or vapor (condensation damage).

Controlled air change offers an efficient solution and makes it possible to utilize the heat from the ventilated air to preheat the supply air. Overheating as a result of internal heat loads (e.g., people, machines) or external influences (e.g., solar heat) is thus compensated because the heat can be distributed more effectively across the entire building.

A well-designed airtight building skin is a prerequisite for a ventilation system. The following constructional design aspects should also be taken into consideration in the interest of optimizing the design of ventilation systems:

– problems arising from air circulation across several stories;

– internal division of rooms that require mechanical ventilation in summer;

– functional integration with the heating system;

– options for natural or summer ventilation.

Traffic noise and emissions diminish the quality of the work environment. To avoid these prob-

lems, windows are often kept closed which makes natural ventilation in summer more difficult.

Double-skin glass facades were developed as a structural response to this challenge. By staggering the openings in the two layers, noise levels are diminished and natural ventilation is nevertheless made possible. In a similar way and despite strong wind impact, operable windows can also be provided in high-rises. The cavity in the double-layer facade can serve as an access area for maintenance and accommodate various control mechanisms, such as sun and glare protection as well as light-deflecting systems in a weather-protected space. Similar to conservatories, double-skin facades have a buffer effect as a temperature-controlling interstitial space and generate heat exchange during ventilation.

This approach is by no means new. Its predecessor is the box-type window, which was developed to improve the poor thermal properties of single glazing and the permeability of windows and window frames. Gerrit Rietveld employed this system in the form of a suspended facade on the Academy of Art in Rotterdam. And Peter Behrens envisioned double-glazing for the windows of his tobacco factory in Linz, Austria, in order to avoid the condensation that would result from the high humidity in the interior.

65

66

67

However, the construction effort required to build a double-skin glass facade is too expensive to justify this approach on the basis of its influence on the energy balance alone, without taking the influence of other factors such as noise or wind pressure into consideration. Similar to glass-enclosed buffer spaces, the thermal processes in this system require careful regulation. Increasingly employed for aesthetic reasons alone, these systems failed to achieve the anticipated effect. On the contrary, overheating, expensive maintenance costs and increased energy requirements are the more likely and frequent outcome.

Commercial buildings have a very high internal heat load. They are more densely occupied and are subject to considerable internal heat gains, chiefly from artificial lighting but also from machines and equipment. The ratio of window area to solid wall required for natural lighting can furthermore increase the heat load through incident solar radiation. And finally, these buildings are used during daytime hours when outside temperatures are higher. In summer, especially, the combination of all these factors can lead to very poor comfort conditions, ultimately resulting in a need for energy-inefficient air conditioning systems. The negative influences can be overcome, however, through relevant planning strategies. These can be divided into two categories:

– strategies to avoid overheating, for example sun protection in summer (and frequently also in winter) and optimizing natural and artificial lighting;
– strategies to extract excess heat, mainly through various forms of natural ventilation but also through a temperature-regulating building mass.

Sun Protection
Incident solar radiation in summer is one of the prime causes of overheating. Sun protection measures are employed to prevent this. The type of sun protection is chiefly dependent on the direction in which the openings face. South-facing windows are most easily protected against the high-altitude summer sun. Skylights as well as glass areas in flat or shallow-incline roofs deserve particular attention because of the high solar altitude in summer. East-west orientation also presents a problem due to the morning and evening sun, which stands perpendicular to the windows.
Depending on window orientation, light incidence and sun protection must be harmonized. Sun protection systems must not interfere with natural lighting. Rather, sun protection measures can block direct sunlight, offer efficient glare protection and simultaneously provide better lighting in the depth of the interior space by means of daylight deflection. The position of the sun changes over the course of the seasons

65 Atenea school in Mairena del Aljarafe, Seville, SAMA, J. Lopez de Asiaín, 1991. Rigid sun protection composed of prefabricated concrete elements.

66 School of architecture in Lyon, France, F-H. Jourda, 1987. 67 same as 66: Stretched textiles as sun protection.

68

69

70

71

and the day. The influence of the sun also differs according to weather. A correct response to these conditions is only possible with sun protection systems that are adaptable to the requirements at any given time. Adjustable systems are not only more elaborate; they also require additional solutions with regard to control and operation (automatic or manual). By contrast, rigid systems call for a precise definition of the times when the sun protection system is needed and must be designed accordingly.

Utilizing the benefits from natural protection provided by trellises, pergolas or trees is usually insufficient; these "systems" can moreover not be regulated in a flexible manner when the need arises.

Natural and Artificial Lighting

The use of daylight is more an architectural than a building-systems challenge. Optimizing the distribution of daylight saves energy and reduces the heat generated by artificial lighting. First and foremost, however, natural lighting is a key factor in the architectural design of a space and promotes the visual comfort of the user.

Many buildings with sufficient daylight in the interior are nevertheless plagued by problems arising from glare, usually in connection with computer-related work. What is needed in these situations is dispersed light or deflection of incident sunlight, which can also improve the distribution of light in the interior. The elements employed to this end should not influence the light quality (especially the color). Daylight intensity diminishes rapidly as the distance from the window increases. Given an average room height and fenestration, the maximum depth of penetration of daylight into a room is 6 m. Light-deflection systems can improve the light distribution in the room without, however, greatly expanding the effectively lit room depth. Greater room depths, which result from a more compact building form, must then be equipped with additional artificial lighting.

68 Office building in Wiesbaden, Herzog + Partner, 2003. Adjustable sun protection also used for light deflection (see p. 146).

69 same as 68: Office interior

70 School complex in Pichling, Austria, Loudon + Habeler, 2003. Classrooms receive light from two sides with the help of skylights in the central corridor (see p. 170).

71 same as 70: Classroom interior

There are, however, some design strategies that make natural lighting in deep interiors possible, for example, skylights, light domes, light wells and atria. Sun protection in summer is vital in connection with these elements.

The ideal goal in the selection of energy-supply systems is to achieve diminished energy use in combination with optimized use of the energy value; in other words, losses incurred through transformation and transfer/distribution should be minimized.

A critical evaluation of the requirements is especially necessary with regard to the use of electrical energy. In addition to the selection of electrical appliances and efficient lighting systems, structural alternatives should be taken into consideration with regard to the consumption of electricity (daylight use, natural ventilation in summer, diminishing mechanical distribution routes).

Electrical consumption for lighting is uppermost on the list for commercial buildings. Tremendous savings are possible in this area. Luminaires and lamps with a high luminous efficiency and a high visual effectiveness coupled with low consumption are preferable. Individual workstation lighting makes it possible to operate with a lower overall luminous intensity and task-oriented lighting, which can be controlled by the user.

Artificial lighting should be conceived as a complement to natural lighting. Light-deflecting systems make it possible to adapt artificial lighting to daylight conditions in order to maintain a certain lighting level. The controls of these systems are also capable of operating zones with different natural luminous intensities. Aside from the technological progress in lamps, luminaires and controls, lighting strategies alone can achieve energy savings potentials of 30 to 50 percent based on correct design and daylight-dependent light deflection.

Ventilation and Cooling
If the temperature in the room is higher than the outside air temperature, the excess heat can be removed through ventilation. This ventilation can be mechanical or natural. Cross-ventilation optimizes natural heat extraction. Openings should be provided on two sides of a

72

73

74

72 Office building in Munich, Henn Architekten, 2003. Offices receive light from two sides through a glazed courtyard (see p. 140)

73 School in Ladakh, Ove Arup, 2001. Deep rooms receive light through high ribbon windows (see p. 188).

74 Office and apartment building in Schwarzach, Vorarlberg, H. Kaufmann, Ch. Lenz, 1999. Natural lighting is complemented by individual lighting at the workstations (see p. 122).

77

75 School complex in Gelsenkirchen, plus+ Bauplanung, Hübner, 2004. Convective ventilation of the hall by means of ventilation shaft (see p. 182)

76 same as 75: Recess hall

77 Office and apartment building in Wiesbaden, A-Z Architekten, 2002. The untreated building mass has an equalizing influence on peak temperatures (see p. 68).

75

76

space for this purpose. In long, compact buildings, the internal zones must be linked for this type of ventilation (e.g., by skylights). The ventilation openings should be placed in such a way that the airflow is directed at areas that generate a lot of heat (e.g., by machines) or at specific building components that absorb heat. Uncomfortable drafts should be avoided at work-surface level.

Convective ventilation is another option: here, warm air is ventilated through the natural effect of warm air rising and replaced with fresh air. This system is especially suitable for high-ceilinged rooms. The greater the difference in height between extracted air and supply air, the greater the air change rate.

The daily temperature fluctuations can also be utilized to cool the building mass through ventilation at night. The building mass is then able to absorb excess heat during the day. The location and shape of windows is highly relevant in connection with directing fresh outside air toward the solidly constructed building components.

The absorption of the internal heating load and the temperature fluctuations in the space are largely dependent on the thermal capacity of the building components. This capacity is provided by heavy, massive elements. The greater the temperature fluctuations are, the more important is the significance of the thermal storage mass. A solid form of construction can absorb peak loads and thus diminish the heating or cooling requirements.

Building Component Activation

Solid building components can also be deliberately warmed or cooled to ensure that they promote thermal balance or compensation in the room. This approach is called "building component activation" and can be realized through passive (e.g., ventilation) or active measures. Natural resources (solar energy, geothermal heat) can also be employed for building component activation.

Office buildings are usually completed in a lighter manner to provide the necessary flexibility. The solid, load-bearing components (floors, ceilings) are frequently obscured by finishing elements (suspended ceilings, installation floors). For building component activation these areas should not be hidden. In the case of unclad, solid building components, the acoustic properties of the hard surfaces must then be compensated through other sound-absorbing measures.

But the challenges presented by commercial buildings should not be reduced to the buildings themselves. On the contrary, the individual buildings must always be regarded in the urban context. Freestanding, commercial buildings are comparable to the single-family house in typology. As a result of the greater volume, they achieve a better ratio of surface to volume and hence a better point of departure for an energy-efficient form of building. Access, ground sealing and supply are negative parameters in freestanding commercial buildings to the same degree as described for detached houses.

Mixed Use

Contrary to the earlier tendency of separating functions and banishing commercial buildings from the city to faceless commercial districts, the current goal is to aim for mixed use. This results in a sensible utilization of existing urban areas and infrastructure, which in turn translates into extraordinary energy savings. Another advantage of mixed use is the synergy that results from the different energy requirements. Commercial buildings consume large amounts of energy. This consumption is concentrated, however, on limited time periods resulting in uneven demands on the supply grid. Commercial buildings have exorbitant requirements for power and processes, whereas the heating requirements are usually covered by internal heat generation. The opposite is the case for residential buildings.

This situation speaks for the use of combined heat and power plants, which generate power for commercial use and make the resulting waste heat available for the heating supply to neighboring residential buildings. In addition to the synergy effect, this also minimizes distribution losses.

A mix of functions in the inner city also makes sense with regard to solar incidence. Shaded areas can be allocated to commercial uses allowing for greater density.

78
79

Energy-efficient Cultural Buildings and Public Institutions: Unique Features

The role of public institutions as models of rational energy use is more significant than the actual energy savings they might achieve.

The unique features related to use are a key criterion for the development of the energy concept. Studies on air quality in school buildings, for example, have shown that natural ventilation on demand cannot guarantee sufficient air change rates with regard to the use of these buildings (SIA, 1992). Lack of concentration and poor student performance are the consequences. Controlled ventilation is advantageous in this case, and not only from the perspective of the energy balance.

Our attention is often focused on new buildings. But it is the existing fabric that is far more significant: the majority of these buildings are over thirty years old and hence in need of refurbishment. Schools and kindergartens from the 1960s and 1970s in particular are notable for the level of repairs they require.

Common characteristics among buildings from that period are severe lines, neutral floor plans and modular construction. These are ideal conditions for energy-conscious refurbishment, both from a structural and from a functional perspective.

Despite their importance, cultural institutions and museums are rarely designed with energy efficiency in mind. These buildings must satisfy a complex set of requirements. They must guarantee an appropriate room climate for visitors and staff and also for the objects on display. Temperature, humidity, lighting, sun protection and visual quality must be harmonized. Energy-efficient design is essential here to diminish the complexity of the building systems and the operating costs associated with such systems.

Museums are frequently housed in historic buildings. Here, energy-conserving refurbishment is at least as important as it is in new buildings. The refurbishment measures must usually correspond to the concerns related to historic conservation. New materials and progress in technical equipment are valuable aids in this regard. Vacuum insulation, for example, provides good thermal insulation at just a few millimeters and is suitable for areas where the

78 Apartment and office building in Munich, Martin Pool, 2004. The apartments occupy the upper floors and receive more sunlight (see p. 62).

79 Energy-efficient renovation and redesign of a 1970s kindergarten in Lochham, Pollok + Gonzalo, 2003. Energy consumption was reduced and natural lighting optimized.

80 Old-age home an Lautertal in Titting, Hans Nickl, 1993. Spatial effect of natural lighting

80

usual constructional strengths are not possible. Thick, solidly constructed walls can generate a positive climate-balancing effect, however, because their thermal mass dampens temperature peaks, thus lessening the load on the heating and cooling systems.

Aside from exhibition spaces, museums and cultural institutions also accommodate a multitude of activities such as shops, restaurants and cafeterias, research facilities, administration, meeting rooms, social facilities, etc. These must be studied separately with regard to their energy requirements. The aforementioned criteria for office buildings apply to many of these areas.

The energy-efficient planning of a building calls for an understanding of the sometimes complex influence of differing factors seen as an integrated system. As numerous examples demonstrate, this opens up unlimited possibilities to the planner of designing the built environment in a creative manner.

81

82

83

81 Art Museum in Riehen, Renzo Piano Building Workshop, 1997/2000.

82 same as 81: Glazed roofs for natural lighting with sun protection (see p. 194)

83 Museo Romano in Merida, Spain, Rafael Moneo, 1984. Deep concrete louvers above the skylights reflect and distribute the light and provide sun protection.

ENERGY-EFFICIENT BUILDING DESIGN: EXAMPLES

Low-energy and Passive House Renovation	Student Residence in Wuppertal	PPP Müller Schlüter	
Flexible Use	Office and Residential Building in Schwarzach	Lenz Kaufmann, Schwarzach	
Passive House as Systems Building	Office and Residential Building in Sursee	Scheitlin-Syfrig + Partner, Lucerne	
Differentiated Facade Design	Office Complex in Duisburg	Schuster Architekten, Düsseldorf	
Natural Ventilation in a High-rise	Office Building in Munich	Henn Architekten, Munich	
Intelligent Shading and Daylight Deflection	Office Complex in Wiesbaden	Thomas Herzog + Partner, Munich	
Sustainable Office Building	Parliament Buildings in London	Hopkins Architects, London	
Integrated Ecology	Offices and Workshops in Weidling	Georg W. Reinberg, Vienna	
Headquarters Building in Passiv House Standard	Commercial Building in Steyr	Walter Unterrainer, Feldkirch	
Low-energy School Ensemble	School Complex in Pichling	Loudon + Habeler, Vienna	
Passiv House Standard for Children	Montessori School in Aufkirchen	Walbrunn Grotz Vallentin Loibl, Bockhorn	
Built Participation	Comprehensive School in Gelsenkirchen	plus + bauplanung, Hübner, Neckartenzlingen	
Response to Extreme Conditions	School Complex in Ladakh	Arup Associates, London	
Adjustable Daylight Technology	Art Museum in Riehen	Renzo Piano Building Workshop, Paris/Genoa	

Low-energy and Passive House Renovation:
Student Residence in Wuppertal

Architects:
1st Construction phase: PPP in partnership with Michael Müller
and Christian Schlüter, Düsseldorf
2nd Construction phase: Architektur Contor Müller Schlüter, Wuppertal

1

Selected data:

Completion:
1st phase: 2000
2nd phase: 2003
NFA: 17,200 m²
GFA: 20,000 m²
GRV: 56,500 m³

Heating energy consumption
1st phase: 68.1 kWh/m²a
2nd phase: 15 kWh/m2a

U-value window
1st phase: 1.56 W/m²K
(frame: 1.6, glazing: 1.1)
g-value: 62 %
2nd phase: 0.82 W/m2K
(frame: 0.75, glazing: 0.7)
g-value: 53 %

Insulation thickness at eaves
1st phase: 18 cm
2nd phase: 28 cm

Insulation thickness at gable
1st phase: 14–19 cm
2nd phase: 25–30 cm

Insulation thickness roof and
lower story to plinth story:
1st phase: 18 cm
2nd phase: 28 cm

With six hundred residential units, the Burse residence, Wuppertal is one of the largest student residences in Germany. Built in 1977, it had become somewhat superannuated; in the end, the facility was plagued not only by functional shortcomings but also by considerable structural defects. These were mostly related to building systems that were completely outdated and a poorly insulated facade in which leaks had developed over time. The functional shortcomings were chiefly related to the fact that access within the large complex was provided by a single elevator and a poorly lit central stairwell. Groups of thirty-two residents had to share wholly inadequate sanitation facilities. The unappealing character of the facility resulted in vacancies in the ensuing years, while the unattractive entrance area with a vast bank of mailboxes invited acts of vandalism. The task was to improve the situation in order to prevent the complex from becoming even more of a social flash point than it already was.

A study commissioned by the architects focused on establishing a comparison between a completely new construction and an alternative solution that would utilize the existing raw structure with partial demolition where necessary. The result came as a surprise: the savings potential of 25 percent made a clear case for the renovation solution. In the design, the key decision consisted in demolishing the desolate core of the complex and replacing it with two new access zones. The renovation of the complex and the residential units was undertaken in two stages, each characterized by differing standards in terms of building physics. Whereas the first construction phase aimed for "low-energy house" quality, the successful implementation of these parameters provided the basis for aiming even higher during the second stage, that is, to realize a "passive house." To this end, it was necessary to carefully calculate the investment costs for a ventilation system and to compare them to anticipated operating costs.

The renovation began with the removal of the decrepit prefabricated facades and emptying the interior of the building. The functions were reorganized within the given load-bearing cross-wall structure. Residential clusters for thirty-two individuals were largely replaced with bachelor units equipped with private showers and a kitchen counter along one wall. A link

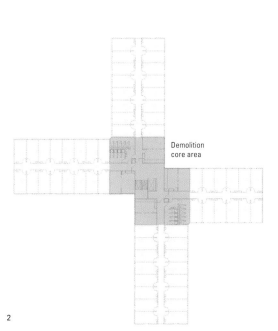

Demolition core area

2

3

4

5

6

to the university computer center is also part of the new, contemporary infrastructure.

Expanding the basic structure by roughly two meters furnished the additional required space. The frame, which was placed in front of the building, could and needed to be utilized for bracing as well, since the previous stabilizing section with elevator and stairwell was to be removed. The communal facilities, which had been located at the center of the complex, had become superfluous. Two fully-glazed new stairwells were inserted into the resulting free space between the two building halves. The fully transparent weather protection creates a visually controlled space with outstanding communicative qualities. Climatically, it is treated as an outdoor space.

A large uninviting complex of buildings that lacked clarity especially in the interior has been transformed into a new, transparent configuration with two clearly structured residential wings with attractive access features.

From the cold stairwells, occupants step into the "warm" living quarters of the building. The two wings were treated differently with regard to insulation standards and the heating and

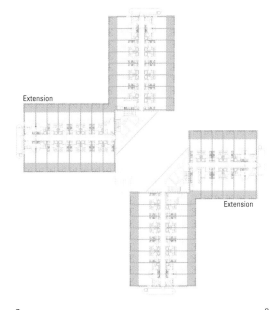

Extension

Extension

7

8

1 View of complex and integration with park

2 Plan of existing fabric

3 Facade of existing fabric

4 Elevator and stairwell of existing fabric

5 Room in existing fabric

6 Room in existing fabric, window side

7 Plan for renovation concept, not to scale: low-energy i.e. passive house standards were achieved despite different orientations with differing conditions for solar radiation.

8 Floor plan of a new bachelor apartment with plumbing unit and cooking counter, not to scale

9

10

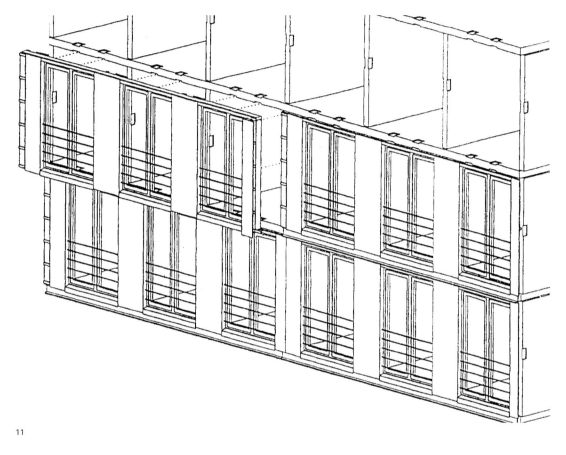

11

ventilation systems. The first wing was realized as a low-energy house, while the second was built to passive-house standards. Implementing two different options for identical uses in one and the same building complex make this project particularly interesting for scientific observation and analysis. Associates from the University of Wuppertal have begun a monitoring process to collect numerous individual data aimed at studying user behavior, on the one hand, and at establishing parameters for potential adjustments to the technical systems. The monitoring process has been scheduled to continue for a period of three years.

Detail solutions include a complete cladding of the compact building volume with a suspended wood panel construction. The facade was prefabricated in 12 m long sections. In addition to the internal and external panels, the highly insulated components also included the window elements with fall protection. This prefab-

rication not only shortened the construction time, it also resulted in recyclable building components that remain fully intact when dismantled. It is worth drawing attention to the considerable improvement in the quality of the construction, particularly since airtight joints play an important role in achieving the energy efficiency that was set as a goal. The number of joints that had to be sealed on site was reduced to a minimum and the target of achieving a low transmission heat loss was met with ease.

At the end of the first heating period, the operator could already document the significant reduction in heating energy requirements for the completed first building section.

Conversely, the airtight facade and the inadequate ventilation practices of individual occupants did lead to difficulties in the building hygiene that were not entirely unexpected. Uncontrolled individual airing (window ventila-

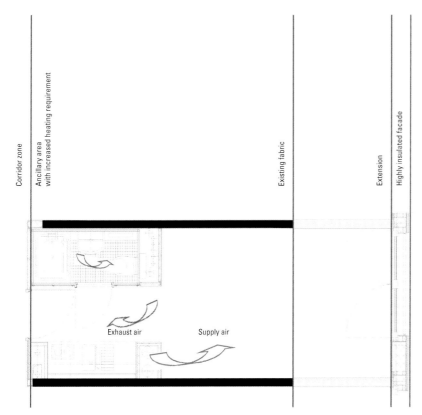

Corridor zone

Ancillary area with increased heating requirement

Existing fabric

Extension

Highly insulated facade

Exhaust air

Supply air

Additional space for the sanitation units of the apartments was created by expanding the basic structure by roughly 2 m beyond the existing fabric.

Each apartment is equipped with a private 3-piece bathroom and a galley kitchen

13

14

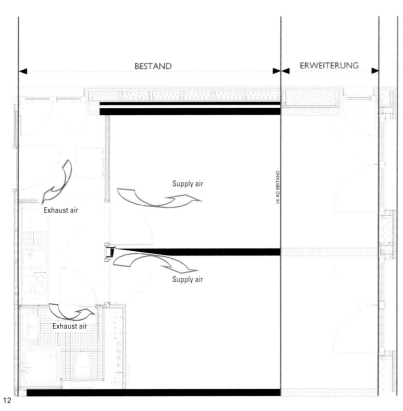

BESTAND

ERWEITERUNG

Exhaust air

Supply air

VK AD BESTAND

Supply air

Supply air

Exhaust air

12

Two units are combined into a double apartment at the gable ends. The kitchen receives natural light through the gable wall.

12 Detail from working drawings, not to scale, indicating the functions of controlled ventilation

13 Elevation of the new access zone with elevator and stairwell as a "cold house," fully glazed for protection from the elements.

14 same as 13: Elevation lit at dusk; open design that promotes communication as a strategy to prevent vandalism.

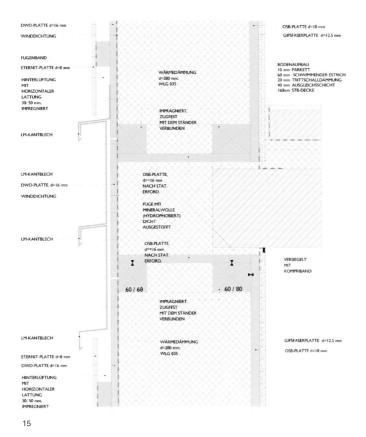

DWD-PLATTE d=16 mm
WINDDICHTUNG
FUGENBAND
ETERNIT-PLATTE d=8 mm
HINTERLÜFTUNG
MIT
HORIZONTALER
LATTUNG
30/ 50 mm,
IMPRÄGNIERT
LM-KANTBLECH

WÄRMEDÄMMUNG
d=280 mm,
WLG 035

IMPRÄGNIERT,
ZUGFEST
MIT DEM STÄNDER
VERBUNDEN

OSB-PLATTE d=18 mm
GIPSFASERPLATTE d=12,5 mm

BODENAUFBAU:
10 mm PARKETT
60 mm SCHWIMMENDER ESTRICH
20 mm TRITTSCHALLDÄMMUNG
40 mm AUSGLEICHSSCHICHT
160mm STB-DECKE

LM-KANTBLECH
DWD-PLATTE d=16 mm
WINDDICHTUNG

OSB-PLATTE,
d=16 mm
NACH STAT.
ERFORD.

FUGE MIT
MINERALWOLLE
(HYDROPHOBIERT)
DICHT
AUSGESTOPFT

LM-KANTBLECH

OSB-PLATTE,
d=16 mm
NACH STAT.
ERFORD.

VERSIEGELT
MIT
KOMPRIBAND

60 / 60   60 / 80

IMPRÄGNIERT,
ZUGFEST
MIT DEM STÄNDER
VERBUNDEN

LM-KANTBLECH

WÄRMEDÄMMUNG
d=280 mm,
WLG 035

GIPSFASERPLATTE d=12,5 mm
OSB-PLATTE d=18 mm

ETERNIT-PLATTE d=8 mm
DWD-PLATTE d=16 mm
HINTERLÜFTUNG
MIT
HORIZONTALER
LATTUNG
30/ 50 mm,
IMPRÄGNIERT

15

16

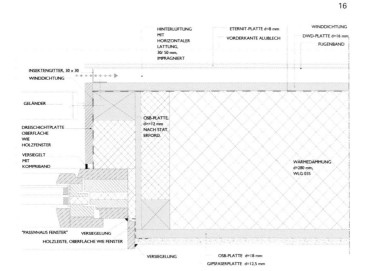

HINTERLÜFTUNG
MIT
HORIZONTALER
LATTUNG,
30/ 50 mm,
IMPRÄGNIERT

ETERNIT-PLATTE d=8 mm
VORDERKANTE ALUBLECH

WINDDICHTUNG
DWD-PLATTE d=16 mm
FUGENBAND

INSEKTENGITTER, 30 x 30
WINDDICHTUNG

GELÄNDER

DREISCHICHTPLATTE
OBERFLÄCHE
WIE
HOLZFENSTER
VERSIEGELT
MIT
KOMPRIBAND

OSB-PLATTE,
d=12 mm
NACH STAT.
ERFORD.

WÄRMEDÄMMUNG
d=280 mm,
WLG 035

"PASSIVHAUS FENSTER"   VERSIEGELUNG
HOLZLEISTE, OBERFLÄCHE WIE FENSTER

VERSIEGELUNG

OSB-PLATTE d=18 mm
GIPSFASERPLATTE d=12,5 mm

15 Vertical section of
facade near ceiling, 2nd
phase with 28-cm-thick
insulation for passive
house standard,
not to scale
Structure, exterior to
interior:
Fibrated cement board,
ventilated cavity in
front of batten grid,
16 mm insulating slab,
waterproof sheeting,
280 mm thermal insula-
tion, 18 mm OSB panel,
12.5 mm gypsum fiber-
board

16 Horizontal section of
facade showing the
integration of a certified
window module of pas-
sive house quality, not
to scale

17 View of facade detail,
2nd phase, without
window vent

tion) can result in unnecessary heat losses. This experience led to the logical decision of designing a ventilation system for the second construction phase that ensures a precisely defined level of air hygiene by centrally controlled air change independent of the students' behavior. The decision was backed by a feasibility study. Taking an efficiency ratio of 80 percent for the heat-recovery system that was part of the plan into consideration, the study proved that the additional investment was balanced out by the lower heating costs: augmenting the insulation standard to passive house level was only logical in this context. The additional costs of roughly 10 percent were in turn incorporated into a detailed financial forecast, which showed that the initiative was sensible in the long term.

The facade design takes the existing fabric into consideration: there is still a tangible sense of the building grid of the original cross-wall construction. Fire-escape balconies in a light steel construction are set in front of the face walls at the ends of the buildings, which are clad in large fibrated cement boards. The facade at the corridor ends is open, allowing daylight to enter – an important orientation guide for the internal circulation. The vertical section on the facing page illustrates the carefully designed transition between components. The interstitial space near the reinforced concrete ceilings was filled with tightly packed water-repellent mineral wool, a measure that ensures a seamless continuation of the high-grade thermal insulation in the facade. Cladding with light sheet metal bent to shape allows for a horizontal structuring of the surface. The horizontal section shows how the certified passive house windows, which are already available in the marketplace, are integrated into the prefabricated facade. Once again, attention was paid to the differentiated profiled sections that are so essential for the design.

Flexible Use:
Office and Residential Building in Schwarzach

Architects:
Christian Lenz, Hermann Kaufmann,
Schwarzach

1

Selected data:

Completion: 1999
NFA: 1,390 m²
GFA: 1,670 m²
GRV: 4,220 m³

Heating energy consump-
tion office: 23 kWh/m²a
Apartments:
10 kWh/m²a

U-value roof:
0.11 W/m²K
U-value exterior wall:
light construction
0.12 W/m²K
U-value floor ground floor/
soil:
0.19 W/m²K
U-value glazing:
0.6 W/m²K

Located on the edge of Schwarzach, a scattered town typical of the Vorarlberg region, a 58-m-long, two-story building stands as an attempt to act against the sprawling development that results from detached single-family houses. The north-south oriented cube, with an office floor and a projecting residential floor floating above it, is moreover characterized by a mix of functions that sets new urban accents in these rural surroundings. An area accommodating athletic facilities now has a spatial completion on the south side.

The plywood-clad volume of the upper story floats above the recessed ground floor. Open external stairwells articulate the north facade, preserving the compact integrity of the heated building volume. The facade openings are designed to reflect orientation and use of the interior spaces in a unique fashion. Floor plans for the apartments are divided into clear zones where ancillary rooms such as kitchen and WC face north, while dining, living and bedrooms face south. A generous patio extends the available living space. This is achieved by means of the staggered arrangement of the stories. Although this design interrupts the ideal compactness of the structure, other advantages such as optimizing insolation in winter and shading for the

ground floor in summer compensate for this factor.

The type of construction chosen for this project offers flexibility in responding to individual preferences with regard to the floor plan. Subsequent changes to the internal divisions can be made without difficulty. The office floor at ground level is characterized by the same flexibility. A system of light dividing walls allows for medium- or long-term adaptation to changing needs, one of the principal aspects of sustainable building.

Offices and apartments are equipped with controlled ventilation while supplementary heating is provided by a gas boiler. The ventilation and heating in the residential units function as follows: fresh air is suctioned via a shaft with a precleaner and then transported through a waterproof network of PVC pipes to roughly 1 m below the ground floor slab – in winter, heat is extracted from the earth at this point – and then carried to each unit through the central fresh-air duct. Depending on the air quality, the fresh air injected into the room is improved by means of natural air ionization.

Each apartment is equipped with a separate, individually controllable microventilation device with heat recovery, fans, filters, air heaters, microprocessor controls and remote con-

2

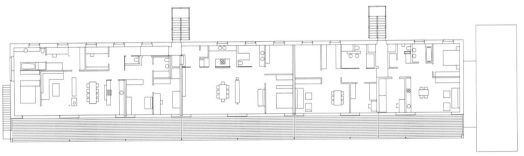

3

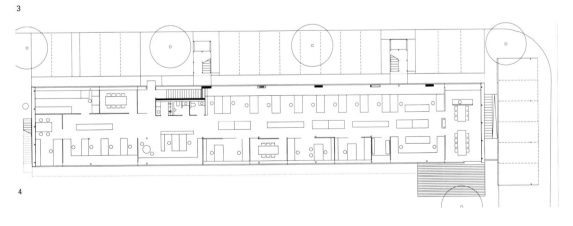

4

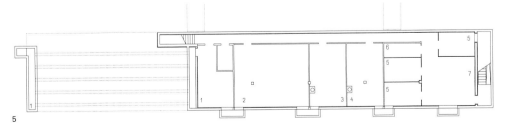

5

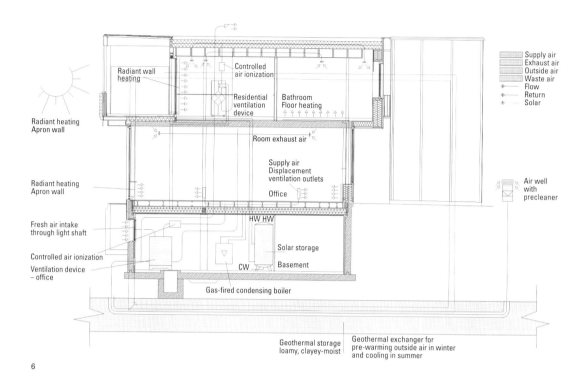

Radiant wall heating

Controlled air ionization

Residential ventilation device

Bathroom Floor heating

Radiant heating Apron wall

Radiant heating Apron wall

Room exhaust air

Supply air Displacement ventilation outlets

Office

Fresh air intake through light shaft

HW HW

Controlled air ionization

Ventilation device – office

CW

Solar storage

Basement

Gas-fired condensing boiler

Geothermal storage loamy, clayey-moist

Geothermal exchanger for pre-warming outside air in winter and cooling in summer

Supply air
Exhaust air
Outside air
Waste air
Flow
Return
Solar

Air well with precleaner

6

7

8

6 Cross section with illustrations of the technological components, schematic diagram of geothermal storage located beneath the building section without a basement, not to scale

7 Southeast elevation

8 West elevation with supply air stela

trol. The ventilation device changes the air volume in the room at a rate of approximately 0.7 times per hour. The fresh air supplied to the device passes through a fine filter and is reheated in the integrated air heater depending on the heating requirement. The air is then injected into the room through an "outlet" set into the ceiling or the wall. Air velocities are kept to a minimum and do not exceed 0.15 m/s in the living areas. In the bathroom, the WC and the kitchen, spent air is suctioned off through mushroom valves. The interior doors are designed not to be airtight to ensure that the supplied air can flow along hallways and corridors toward the extraction position. In the kitchens of the small units, the extraction valve is located near the exhaust hood above the stove. This exhaust itself is designed as a circulating air exhaust. In the large residential units, the exhaust hood functions as an "extraction valve" in the living area.

Since most people prefer room temperatures in the range of 17 to 19°C in the bedroom, the warm supply air can be shut off. An automatic supply air unit ("climate gap") is built into the exterior wall to provide fresh air instead. This "gap" allows for continuous fresh air influx, which can be controlled by a mushroom valve, obviating the need for window ventilation and avoiding unwanted cooling in the room. The automatic air supply unit operates for a range

of external temperatures from approximately 0 to +16°C. Window ventilation can be used when temperatures rise above this range; when below, the valve must be shut off and the supply air vent opened. The spent air is extracted by the ventilation device, fed through a heat exchanger and exhausted at the roof.

The bathrooms are equipped with floor heating. Radiant wall heating on the critical exterior wall areas (near large windows) provides additional heating in the living rooms on cold days. The necessary residual energy for space heating is currently generated by gas combustion, although other energy carriers could also be employed. Each apartment is equipped with a separate heating meter and can be invoiced accordingly. Cold and hot water consumption are also recorded separately for each unit.

Ventilation can be regulated individually in each unit. There is a basic heating level for the apartments, which must be maintained in winter. Overnight, occupants can switch to a reduced air volume, increasing it again during the day.

The room temperature is regulated by remote control with a room sensor. Since the micro air supply system is not designed with a reserve source of power, the ventilation system should not be shut off during the heating period in winter.

9

10

11

9 Assembly of prefabricated wood-panel compo-
nents on site

10 View into the carcass of
the ground floor during
completion. Clearly
visible: the double floor
with installation, the air
vents at the center of
the room, the solid con-
crete ceiling as a future
storage mass and the
modular finishing work
with light dividing
walls.

11 View into the supply air
shaft with connecting
ducts to the geothermal
storage

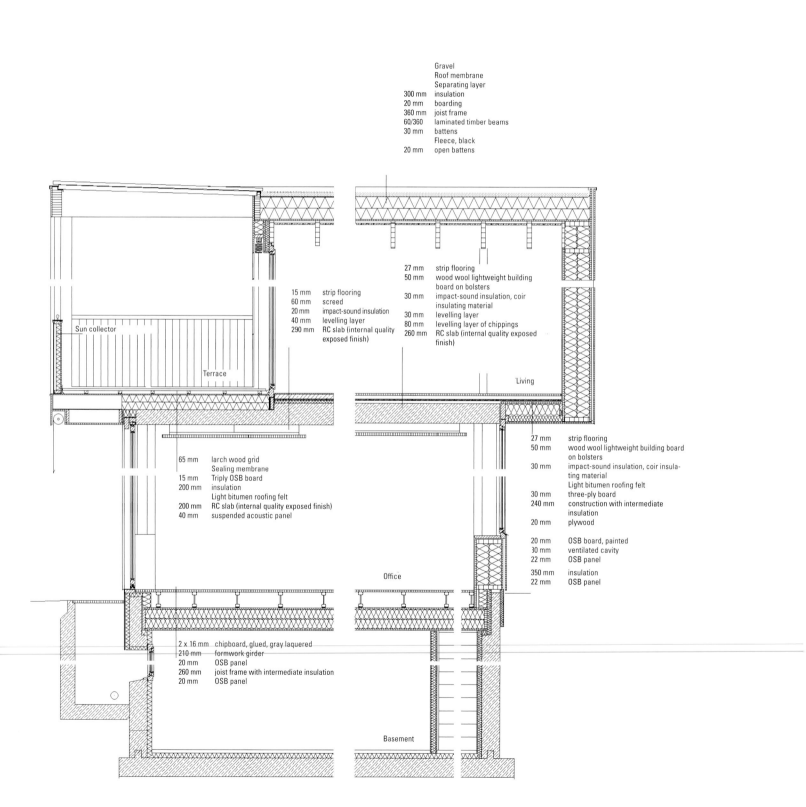

Gravel
Roof membrane
Separating layer
300 mm   insulation
20 mm   boarding
360 mm   joist frame
60/360   laminated timber beams
30 mm   battens
Fleece, black
20 mm   open battens

27 mm   strip flooring
50 mm   wood wool lightweight building
          board on bolsters
30 mm   impact-sound insulation, coir
          insulating material
30 mm   levelling layer
80 mm   levelling layer of chippings
260 mm   RC slab (internal quality exposed
          finish)

15 mm   strip flooring
60 mm   screed
20 mm   impact-sound insulation
40 mm   levelling layer
290 mm   RC slab (internal quality
          exposed finish)

Sun collector

Terrace

Living

27 mm   strip flooring
50 mm   wood wool lightweight building board
          on bolsters
30 mm   impact-sound insulation, coir insula-
          ting material
          Light bitumen roofing felt
30 mm   three-ply board
240 mm   construction with intermediate
          insulation
20 mm   plywood

65 mm   larch wood grid
          Sealing membrane
15 mm   Triply OSB board
200 mm   insulation
          Light bitumen roofing felt
200 mm   RC slab (internal quality exposed finish)
40 mm   suspended acoustic panel

20 mm   OSB board, painted
30 mm   ventilated cavity
22 mm   OSB panel
350 mm   insulation
22 mm   OSB panel

Office

2 x 16 mm   chipboard, glued, gray laquered
210 mm   formwork girder
20 mm   OSB panel
260 mm   joist frame with intermediate insulation
20 mm   OSB panel

Basement

13

A solar system that is integrated into the patio balustrade serves for the hot water processing for apartments and office. In winter, natural gas is used to cover the residual energy requirement.

The office area is heated and ventilated as follows: fresh air is suctioned in through the shared air-intake well equipped with a precleaner. The fresh air supplied to the room is improved by means of natural ionization. The ventilation device functions as a supply/exhaust/circulation-air device with heat recovery, fans, filters and air heaters. The fresh air injected into the ventilation device is filtered once again and reheated as needed in the integrated air heater. It is then supplied to the offices through ducts in the false floor and connected displacement ventilation outlets.

The central earth-air exchanger is used for prewarming the air in winter and cooling in summer. The displacement ventilation system provides heating only to a limited degree and for short periods of time. Spent air is suctioned off at the ceiling.

The suctioned-off air runs through the ventilation device, via a rotating heat exchanger and is vented to the outside. In winter, the air exchange is limited to the basic hygienic amount, while the remainder is processed as circulating air by means of ionization and then returned to the room. In summer, the entire volume of air is transported through the earth heat exchanger for cooling purposes. All offices are equipped with a low-temperature radiant heating system integrated into the apron walls. This system provides a comfortable radiant heat at the work stations and promotes cross ventilation through the displacement ventilation system. Ventilation in the offices can be controlled individually.

High-grade insulation and the detail design of the building skin are prerequisites for the opti-

mized energy balance of the building. The plinth is clad in color-coated OSB panels. The open stairwells are wrapped in textile fabric and are experienced as complete volumes from the outside. From the inside, they simply offer a slightly filtered view of the outside. This is a building where experimentation with materials was a deliberate aspect in design and realization.

The sections on the facing page illustrate the essential details. The timber-constructed, highly insulated double ground floor for ease of installation, maintenance and retrofits is a notable feature. The floor on the upper level, by contrast, has been deliberately executed in concrete to provide a storage mass as a counterbalance and to optimize the acoustic separation between the two stories.

The upper level with 35 cm insulation was built within a few days in as a wood panel construction assembled on site. The roof is composed of narrow Douglas spruce laminated timber beams. It is designed as a non-ventilated flat roof with 45 cm insulation.

14

15

12 Cross-section with all roof, floor and wall structures: the compact building skin with uninterrupted high thermal insulation is a key element. Solar collectors for warm water processing are integrated into the parapet of the patio.

13 North elevation with external stairwells, reduced openings on the upper level and recessed ground floor. Large glazed areas provide ample daylight in the offices.

14 View into office area: untreated magnesite bonded wood fiber panels on the ceiling improve the acoustics without significant reduction to the thermal storage capacity of the concrete floor above.

15 Exhaust air vent

Passive House as Systems Building:
Office and Residential Building in Sursee

Architects:
Scheitlin – Syfrig + Partner, Luzern

1

Selected data:

Completion: 2002
NFA: 5,700 m²
GFA: 5,920 m²
GRV: 20,940 m³

Heating energy consump-
tion 24.4 kWh/m²a

U-value flat roof:
0.19 W/m²K
U-value exterior wall:
0.18 W/m²K
U-value ground floor above
basement:
0.20 W/m²K
U-value ground floor/
exterior:
0.13 W/m²K
U-value window:
1.25 W/m²K

The planning history of this unusual office and residential building goes back eleven years. At the time, the architects won a competition for a project at a challenging urban interface between the new and the old town of Sursee. An old-established cabinet maker's shop had to make way for new uses at this site. The principal design concept survived all subsequent stages of revision. Luigi Snozzi's new town hall and the St. Georgschule, a historic school building that has been placed under a conservation order, dominate the streetscape on the opposite side. The new structure is deliberately modest in expression and it is this quality that draws the eye of alert passers-by. It has closed the gap in the street elevation after the demolition in a completely natural manner. The deliberate reduction in height to three levels on the street front plays a large role as does the unpretentious facade design with a wood cladding varnished in subdued colors. The more animated sections of the building lie to the rear. Here, a public path runs along the fork in the Suhre River, which is once again accessible. It also affords a view into the simple courtyard, which is utilized by the employees during the lunch hour and break times, on

the one hand, and a panoramic vista of the greenbelt along the river with glimpses of the old town beyond, on the other hand. Two two-story studio apartments, which support another two-story residential block, have been erected on the island in the river. Together, they form a block that is nearly square in outline. The closed street front is in contrast to the open face toward the river and the old town. The image of the building is characterized by a varied dialogue with its surroundings.

Since the owner and user of the building, a renowned Swiss wood manufacturer, participated in fine-tuning the program, it seemed logical to realize the building as a prefabricated wood construction. Only the access areas were executed in solid construction for reasons of fire protection on top of the basement, which is at groundwater level and therefore constructed from waterproof concrete.

The wood components went into prefabrication before the foundation work and the construction of the basement from waterproof concrete were complete. Assembly of the four upper

2

3

1 Main elevation facing the suburb

2 Site plan with the town core of Sursee

3 View from courtyard onto greenbelt along the Suhre River and onto the two-story residential structure to the rear with a generous balcony zone

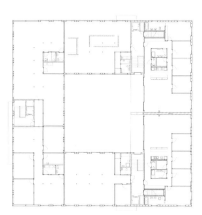

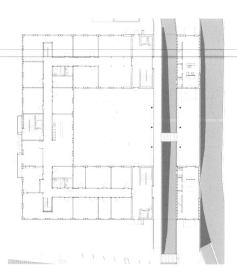

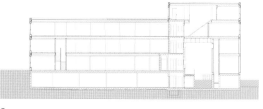

5

4 Floor plans ground
floor to fourth floor.
The bridge structure
over the fork in the
river and the two studio
apartments on the
island is clearly visible
on the ground floor.
The rotation to NE/SW
is advantageous for the
orientation of the apart-
ments.

5 Cross-section indicating
the staggered heights
of the building and the
courtyard location over-
looking the fork in the
Suhre River.

6 Detail from working
drawing of open pas-
sage depicting the
access to the residential
floors and the two-story
studio apartments.

7 View from open pas-
sage toward the east

8 Partial elevation with
open passage

9 Presentation room

10 Cafeteria

11 View from side facing
the old town into court-
yard

floors began in July 2002 and was completed within four weeks. The subsequent finishing work was completed on schedule in December 2002, bringing the total construction time to eight months.

The sustainable plan that took all individual aspects of function, construction, ecology, economy and aesthetics into consideration was very much focused on the energy consumption of the building. The goal was to not only meet legislated minimized requirements, but to explore additional options for optimization beyond this standard. The building skin was designed in a fashion to drastically reduce transmission heat loss and to increase passive solar gains. Excellent thermal insulation values of the individual components played an important role in this context as did the strategy of optimizing the construction of transitions between building components. The prefabricated wood-component construction allowed connecting details to be virtually free of thermal bridges. Only with the installation of the selected wood-aluminum windows into the wood frame structure had a thermal bridge loss coefficient $\Psi_{installation}$ of 0.14 W/mK to be considered. In order to reduce the ventilation heat loss by comparison to the conventional solution with window ventilation, the plan envisioned controlled ventilation with heat recovery, another option of considerably reducing the heating requirements. The residual energy requirement for heating and hot water is supplied by an efficient heat pump system. Two groundwater heat pumps deliver an annual performance capacity of 4. One heat pump can meet the heating energy requirement for outside temperatures of -3°C. The task of the second heat pump is to provide hot water and to meet requirements during peak times when temperatures drop further. Heat is chiefly supplied by floor heating.

The existing energy from solar radiation as well as waste heat from occupants and computers is automatically recorded by thermostats in each room; the floor heating is then adjusted accordingly. It is only as a result of bundling differing strategies that are carefully harmonized that the energy requirements can be minimized as

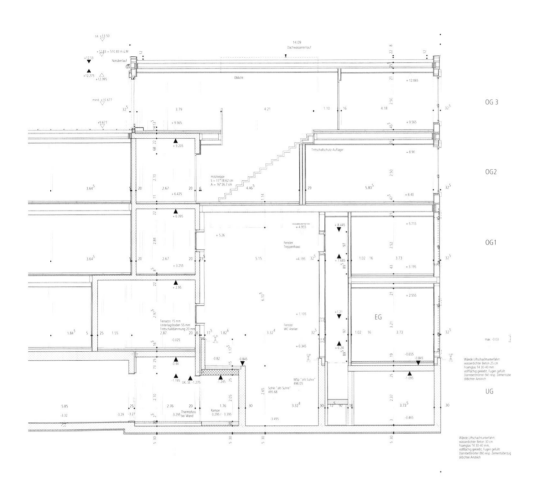

OG 3

OG2

OG1

EG

UG

6

9

10

11

7

8

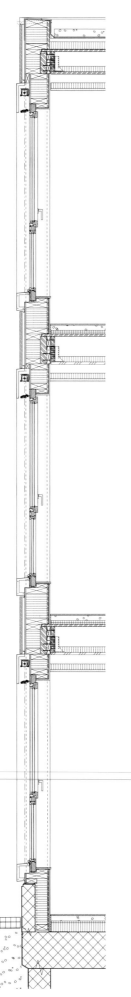

Flat roof from outside:
80 mm extensive planting
or accessible
(70 mm wooden grid)
protective fleece
waterproofing (membrane)
20–60 mm foil laminated PUR
slabs to falls
80 mm (120 mm) foil
laminated rigid PUR slab
10 mm impact sound
insulation where accessible
vapor barrier
25 mm OSB-3
80 x 220 joist frame/
60 mm mineral wool board
25 mm OSB-3
suspended ceiling/
2 x 12.5 mm gypsum
plasterboard, additional
acoustic
ceiling in places

Exterior wall from inside
12.5 mm gypsum
plasterboard wallpapered
vapour barrier/airtight seal
15 mm OSB-3
80 x 240 mm wooden frame/
mineral wool
15 mm gypsum fiber board
waterproof layer
27 mm battening uprights/
ventilation gap
27 mm timber cladding
horizontals

Ceiling from top:
15 mm parquet
55 mm anhydrite screed
separating and sliding layer
impact sound insulation
20 mm mineral wool board
20 mm rigid polyurethane
slab (F 20)
25 mm OSB-3
120 x 280 joist frame/
60 mm mineral wool board
27 mm three-layer laminated
board suspended ceiling/
2 x 12.5 mm gypsum
plasterboard, additional
acoustic ceiling in places

12 Facade section with all
roof, floor and wall
structures, top to
bottom: flat roof struc-
ture, exterior wall structure, standard floor
structure, structure of
floor to basement.

13 Partial north elevation:
anodized aluminum
window frames, clad-
ding with narrow stain-
ed spruce boarding.

12

Ceiling from top:
15 mm parquet
55 mm anhydrite screed
separating and sliding layer
impact sound insulation
20 mm mineral wool board
100 mm foil laminated rigid
polyurethane slab
250–400 mm reinforced
concrete ceiling slab

described above. Various tests (blower-door, thermography, air quality measurement, ongoing measurement of consumption rates) carried out by independent institutions provide the external oversight to ensure that the goals set out in the plan are being met. The data gathered from these tests are taken into consideration for the further development of this building system.

The facade section opposite clearly shows the detail solutions of joining the prefabricated components. In addition to the insulating measures, the plan also explored every means of optimizing sound protection. In the end, the choice fell on a solution with a flexible facing shell composed of two gypsum board panels suspended from the ceilings. Comfort in the building's use is greatly improved by this provision for protection from sound transmitted by air and impact noise, especially when the possibility of future modifications on some of the floors is taken into consideration.

The design of the building skin is notable for the attention that was given to choosing materials according to maintenance requirements and life cycle. Metal appears only at the transition between window and facade. The wide frame takes on the character of a mask and defines the aesthetic appearance of the window openings. The cladding of the remaining surfaces in narrow fir battens is simple and only serves to enhance the effect of the window frames. The visual cohesion of the building volume is strengthened; despite the penetrations and the staggered heights, it is never at risk of falling apart.

Differentiated Facade Design:
Office Complex in Duisburg

Architects:
Schuster Architekten, Düsseldorf

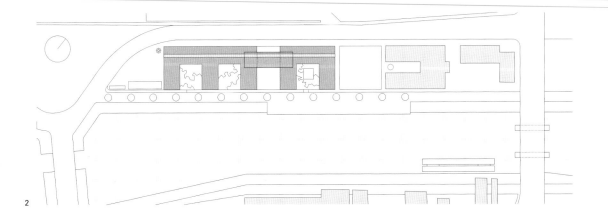

1

Selected data:

Completion: 2002
MUFA: 12,100 m²
GFA: 26,500 m²
GRV: 106,000 m³

Calculated annual heating
requirement:
9 kWh/m²a
U-value flat roof:
0.12 W/m²K

U-value south facade:
0.33 W/m²K without solar
radiation
U-value south facade:
0.05 W/m2K effectively,
with solar radiation
U-value north facade:
0.24 W/m²K
U-value window incl.
frame:
1.4 W/m²K
of which U-value glazing:
1.1 W/m²K

Duisburg is also benefiting from the restructuring of the Ruhr area. The inner harbor is undergoing a transformation from industrial port district to modern service and leisure site. Even today, the quality and identity of the site are defined by the historic warehouses: they are distinctive structures that dominate the character of the harbor.

The new building for Duisburg's central police services (ZPD) offers a contemporary interpretation of this building type. The result is a large, functional house that is compact and exceptionally energy efficient. A response to the unique qualities of the site determined the articulation and divisions of the building and, ultimately, its overall image. The offices open to the south, in the direction of the city and the water. Ancillary rooms and storage areas, on the other hand, were placed along the north side in the direction of the highway. This internal division, which seems only logical, emphasizes not only the clarity and rigor of the entire structure but also firmly anchors the building in the urban context.

The interplay of ecology and building form was the foundation for the entire building planning and design. On the south side, the external image of the complex is defined by a newly developed solar facade. The design reflects the internal uses of the house, resulting in a highly differentiated facade design on the outside. The north facade on the other hand remains closed and impassive. The few significant openings are realized as "green windows" with different themes, investing the facade with focal points and a sense of scale.

The large, multi-story entrance atrium is differentiated in design on both sides of the complex from the other exterior surfaces, signalling the entrance from afar. The interplay of different facade designs is especially legible in this area. The atrium also dominates the internal division of the complex and serves as a central reception area.

An attempt was made to optimize the ecological sustainability of the complex by means of an integrated approach to planning and design. This includes the sensible internal division into

2

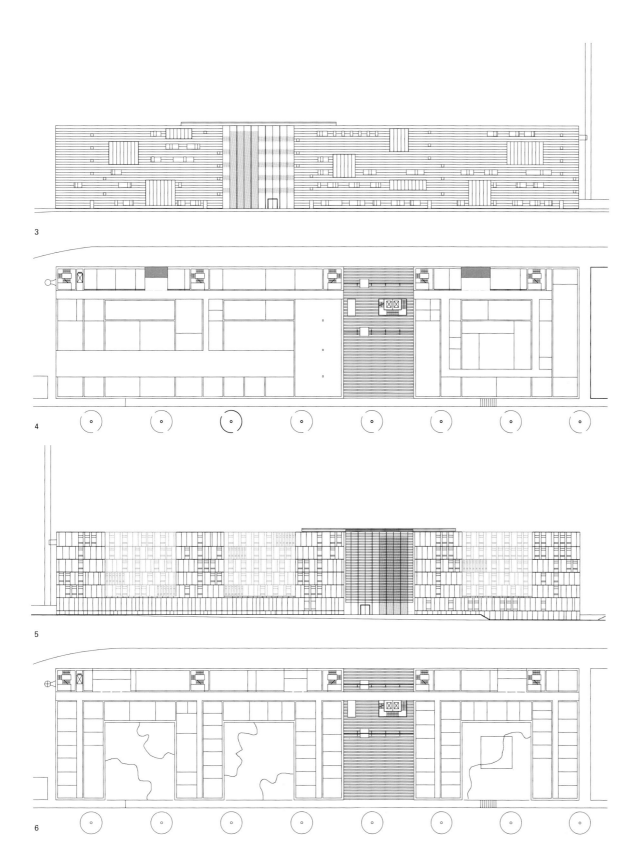

3

4

5

6

1 North elevation

2 Site plan

3 North elevation

4 Floor plan of upper
 story

5 South elevation

6 Ground floor plan
 Plans not to scale

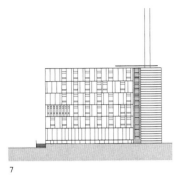

7 Cross section, not to scale

8 South elevation: facade overlooking the harbor

9 View from south east with harbor basin

zones for principal uses and zones for secondary or ancillary uses. The former are oriented to the south, the latter to the north. This makes sense not only from an urban design perspective on the outside, but also in terms of function on the inside. The selection of buildings systems was based on the same focus on simplicity and efficiency.

Passive solar energy is utilized via solar facades on the south side. These facades are composed of panels with glass and honeycomb insulation. The building materials were chosen with a view to minimizing the use of plastics. Natural materials were employed for the interior works.

The innovative ventilation system in the offices operates with displacement ventilation and building component cooling supplemented by the option of individually operable windows. The available storage masses are activated and augment the ventilation comfort. The con-

cept also incorporates heat recovery and natural cooling by means of night-time ventilation. Given the low flow velocities and optimized air movement, the ventilation system only requires 11 percent of the total demand for electricity in comparison with a conventional system. Cooling is provided in three ways: with water drawn from the harbor, night-time cross-ventilation and adsorption chillers. With 9 kWh/m²a, the heating requirements lies 89 percent below the values set forth in the German heat protection act, surpassing even the so-called passive house standard. The regenerative energy concept yields the following gains: the utilization of solar radiation on the entire building generates 111 MWh of heat per annum.

The photovoltaic system generates 32 MWh of electricity per year. Rapeseed oil is used for the combined power and heat plant and peak load boilers, generating 232 MWh of heat per year

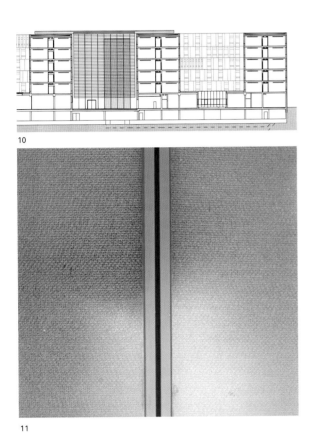

10

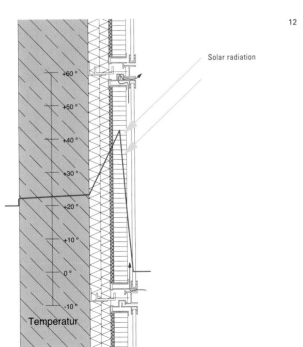

11

12

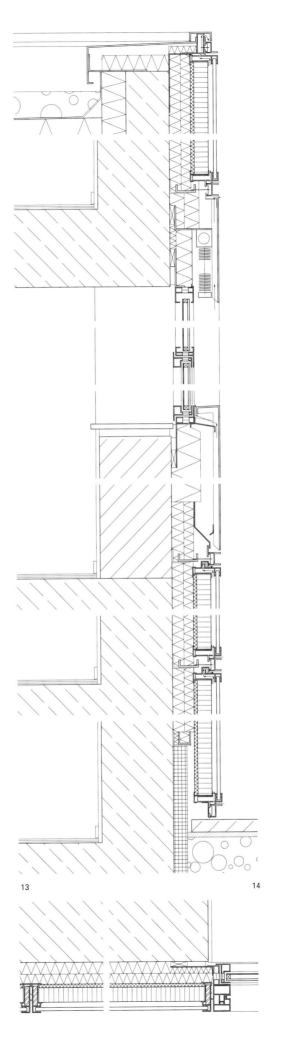

Solar radiation

+60 °
+50 °
+40 °
+30 °
+20 °
+10 °
0 °
-10 °
Temperatur

13

14

10 Partial longitudinal section, not to scale

11 Detail of solar facade panel

12 Solar radiation

13 Vertical section of south facade, from inside to outside:
Reinforced concrete parapet,
90 mm mineral wool,
Solar facade component with 14 mm OSB panel,
60 mm honeycomb board,
22 mm air cavity,
10 mm toughened safety glass on upper story, 13 mm laminated glass on ground floor, not to scale

14 Horizontal section of south facade, with transition to window opening, not to scale.

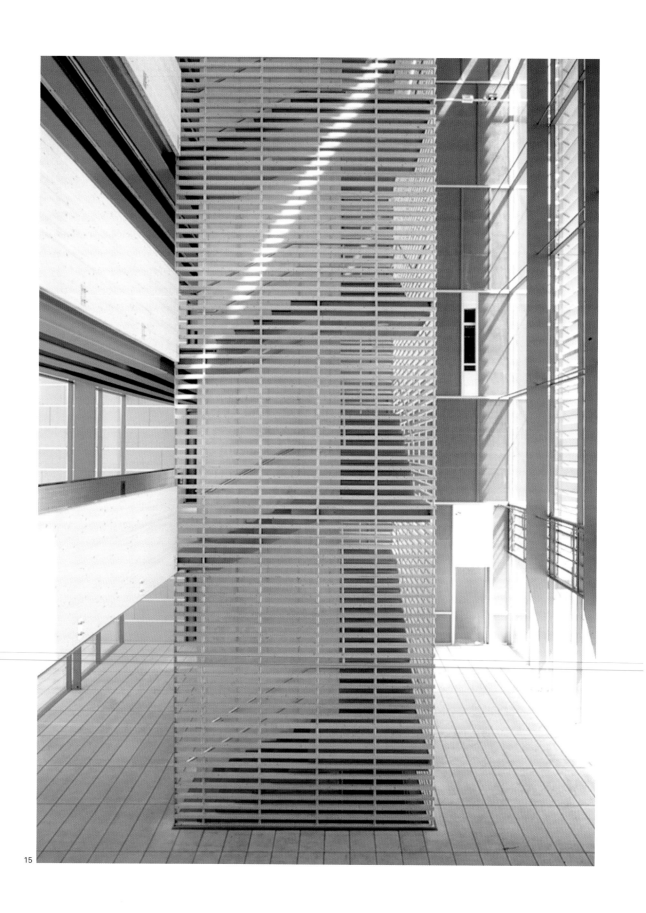

15 View of exposed stair-
well in central entrance
atrium.
Energy-efficient and
ecological building is
by no means incom-
patible with ambitious
design.

15

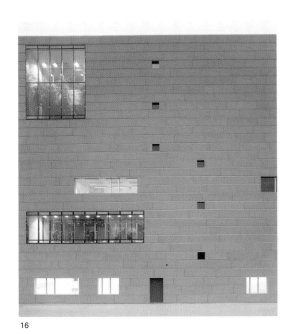

16

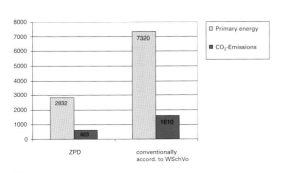

17

and 193 MWh of electricity per year. Together, the regenerative energy sources cover 43 percent of the end energy requirements of the building.

Roof water is collected in a rainwater cistern and utilized for toilet flushing, saving 1,200 m³ of potable water per year. By comparison to a conventional building constructed to the specifications outlined in the heat protection act, the environmental relief corresponds to a CO_2-reduction of 987 t/a.

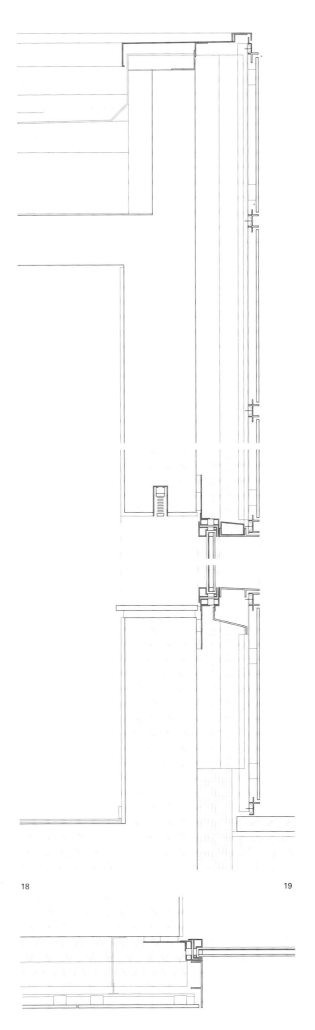

18

19

16 Detail of north facade with "green windows."

17 Comparison of primary energy consumption and CO_2-emissions at the ZPD versus conventional office buildings.

18 Vertical section of north facade, from inside to outside:
Reinforced concrete wall,
200 mm mineral wool,
65 mm air cavity,
12 mm fibrated cement panel on substructure,
not to scale

19 Horizontal section of north facade with transition to window, not to scale

Natural Ventilation in a High-rise: Office Building in Munich

Architects:
Henn Architekten, Munich

Selected data:

Completion: 2003
MUFA: 9,686 m²
GFA: 30,280 m²
GRV: 109,500 m³

Calculated annual heating requirements:
12.10 kWh/m²a
U-value flat roof, planted:
0.28 W/m²K
U-value post-and-beam facade in elongated wing incl. frames
1.3 W/m²K

U-value windows high-rise interior incl. frames:
1.3 W/m²K
of which U-value glazing:
1.2 W/m²K

The Fraunhofer Society undertakes application-oriented research. The decision to gather all central services in one building prompted the launch of an architecture competition from which the firm Henn Architekten emerged as the winners. The location of the new office complex with excellent transportation linkages offers employees direct access to the subway and underground network of the city. Together with the existing institute building, which was completed in 1992, the new construction creates an urban block with a green courtyard as a recreation zone for employees. The new building consists of three sections with differing heights, a two-story low-rise, a five-story elongated wing with atrium and a seventeen-story high-rise as an urban landmark in this heterogeneous environment of intensive commercial and core uses.

A key aspect in the design of the floor plan and the details is the provision of natural lighting and ventilation for all workstations which had been stipulated by the client. In the elongated wing, the planted atrium fulfills the function of a climate buffer. Glazed walls promote communication within the combined office plan and create a surprising and pleasant sense of spaciousness. In the high-rise, pairs of two floors are linked by spiral staircases to form larger functional units. Here too, the combination office serves as the defining organizational model for the floor plan. The offices are grouped around a communication zone with areas for conferences, a tea kitchen, filing cabinets and archives, etc. A guiding principle in the determination of the construction form and the building structure was the possibility of a flexible response to any future office concepts without any structural intervention. A double-skin facade, optimized with the help of numerous adjustments on a 1:1 model, allows for the natural lighting and ventilation in the high-rise.

Various institutes affiliated with the Fraunhofer-Society participated in the development of different innovative building components. While the Institute for Solar Energy Systems (ISE) in Freiburg contributed to the development of the double-skin facade for the high-rise and the development of the overall energy concept, the Institute for Building Physics (IBP)

1

in Stuttgart provided consultation with regard to internal acoustics. In addition to the customized office organization, another institute developed a computer-supported, integrated facility management system for the operation of the complex. A facade-cleaning robot completes the spectrum of interesting but above all innovative new developments for the building.

The following aspects play a key role in the comprehensive energy concept, which was developed in an iterative process: a combined heat and power plant provides the basis for heating and cooling and also covers the basic power demand in parallel operation, whereby the 12-cylinder spark-ignition gas engine also serves as an emergency power plant. A low-temperature gas boiler is available to supply heat during peak times. The two heat genera-

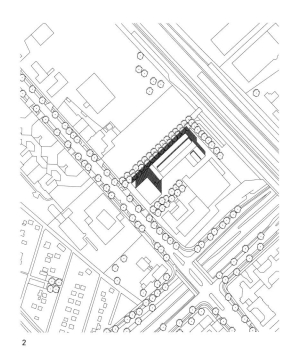

2

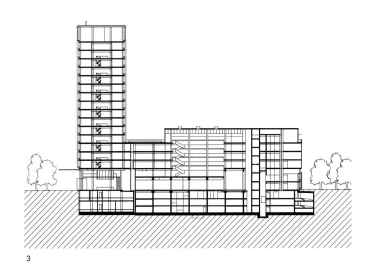

3

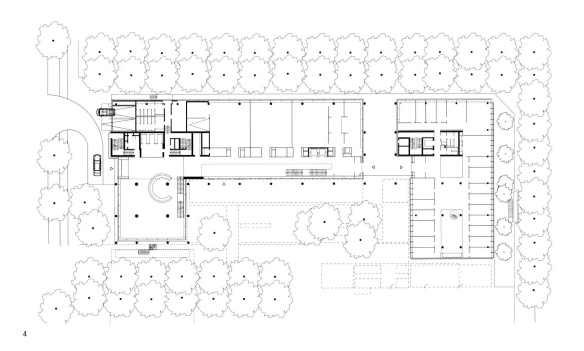

4

1 Entire complex with
  staggered heights,
  low-rise, elongated
  wing and high-rise

2 Site plan

3 Section of high-rise and
  with atrium

4 Ground floor plan with
  entrance lobby, confer-
  ence rooms, cafeteria,
  patent office organized
  as a combination office,
  green courtyard as
  recreation area

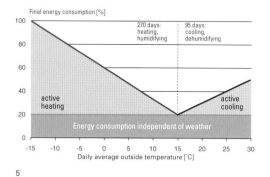

Final energy consumption [%]

270 days: heating, humidifying

95 days: cooling, dehumidifying

active heating

active cooling

Energy consumption independent of weather

Daily average outside temperature [°C]

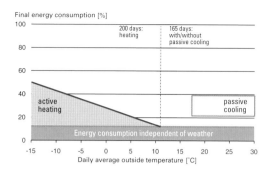

Final energy consumption [%]

200 days: heating

165 days: with/without passive cooling

active heating

passive cooling

Energy consumption independent of weather

Daily average outside temperature [°C]

5

6

7

tors are linked to the heat distribution by a hydraulic switch. Naturally, the CHP also provides heat energy for cold generation in summer. The cold energy is generated via an absorption chiller and is supplied to the kitchen, the cafeteria, the conference room and the core zone of the office floors. The temperature in the offices can be regulated using natural night-time cooling. In winter, the waste heat of the CHP is supplied to the static heating surfaces and the heating vents of the ventilation system. In addition, the basic heating of the building is provided via duct vents integrated into the concrete ceilings. Building component cooling and building component heating operate with low system temperatures. In the entrance hall and the atrium, free ventilation makes use of the large air volumes in these spaces and contributes to a considerable reduction in the necessary effort for technical installations and energy supply. The potential heat gain in the lantern-shaped roof structure

is minimized with optimized ventilation through clerestory windows. Two large fans integrated into the ceiling extract smoke and fumes in the event of fire.

In the high-rise, the passive ventilation concept that was chosen ensures a high degree of comfort combined with optimized energy efficiency at the workstations. This innovative ventilation concept is based on simulation analyses. The sound protection, which is required at this location near a busy urban highway and a railroad line, supported the decision to build a double-skin facade. The outer facade is designed as a modular suspended wall with 12 mm laminated glass, the inner facade is a post-and-beam construction in frame category 1 (refering to the German DIN system). At night, the concrete core activation of the floors provides the necessary cooling. Water is utilized as a heat carrier. The re-cooling plant is located on the roof. Sprinkler tanks can be used as buffer cold storage units

5 Comparison of office building with conventional systems to "slender" office building

6 View into atrium with ceiling opening and lantern-shaped skylight

7 View into atrium with elevator, stairs and plants

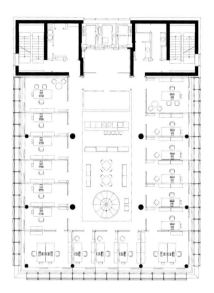

8

9

10

when needed. The natural ambient coolness is sufficient to cool the ceilings into the day.

A model of one office unit with facade was erected on site on a 1:1 scale. This made it possible to optimize the various opening options for natural ventilation in a thorough step-by-step process. In the end, top-hinged sash windows were installed at the lowest possible position on each floor. A series of additional measures serves to reduce the heat input in the supply air volume. Each floor forms a separate air belt. The corners of the high-rise facade were covered in color-neutral sun protection glazing. Lighting at the workstations was optimized by means of daylight simulation. A flat louver divided into two sections reflects light via the ceiling into the depth of the interior from the upper section, while blocking light with the lower section and thus preventing unwanted heat gains. The sun protection feature is controlled by a

central control that responds to the solar altitude. Users can adjust the temperature and the lighting conditions to a large degree and this has proved to be a key aspect in the response to the building services. Each window is additionally equipped with a blind for glare protection. A series of surveys was used to carefully optimize the type of fabric and the color.

Control measurements during the summer heat wave in 2003 confirm the success of the energy concept. Tracer-gas and temperature measurements delivered the tangible proof and demonstrated that the concept was functioning according to plan.
"Although user behaviors (operation of the sun protection features and opening of the sash windows) had a strong influence on the temperatures in summer over a short period, the overall response of the naturally ventilated building is very positive," thus the result of the

8 Office floor plan high-rise story

9 Section of two office units linked by a spiral staircase

10 View into a typical 18 m² office

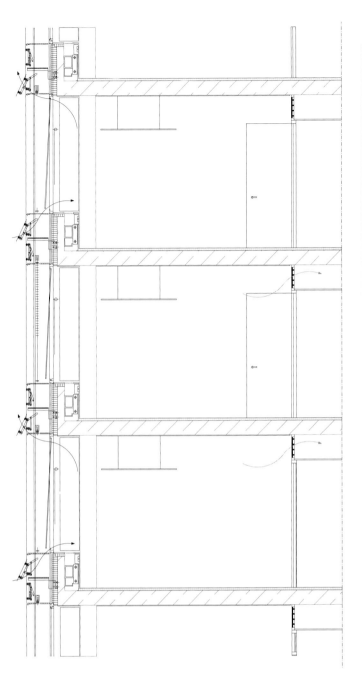

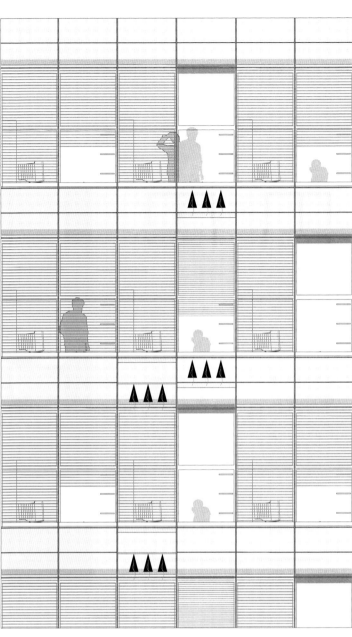

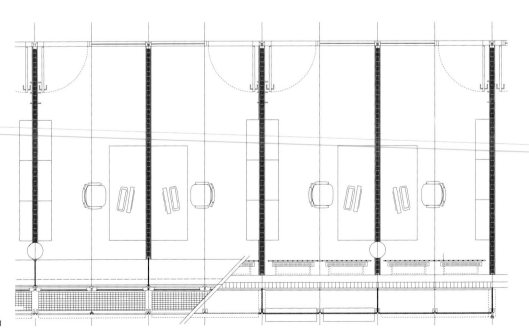

11 Partial section, plan and elevation of facade; the exhaust air vents are clearly marked, not to scale

12 Facade with top-hung sash windows in open position

13 Temperature curve for one week during the heat wave in August 2003 in comparison to plan specifications

14 View into cavity between double-skin facade

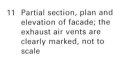

11

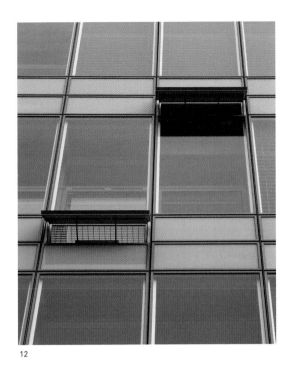

12

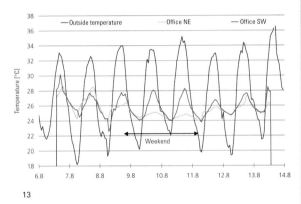

13

investigation. The building meets the planned goals even in real operating conditions. Surveys of the users that accompanied the measurements confirm the positive result. The occupants feel comfortable, justifying the intensive effort in designing a contemporary work environment.

14

145

Intelligent Shading and Daylight Deflection: Office Complex in Wiesbaden

Architects:
Thomas Herzog und Partner, München

1

Selected data:

Completion: 2003
MUFA: 36,250 m²
GFA: 56,150 m²
GRV: 48,798 m³

U-value flat roof:
0.2 W/m²K
U-value glazing:
0.7 0W/m²K

Outstanding economic efficiency in the construction and operation of the buildings in addition to the utilization of environmental energies were the client specifications that defined the design of the office complex. A composite energy system in which heat, power and cooling were coupled was installed to supply energy. Linkages to the existing district heat network guarantee a high degree of efficiency for this system. Two gas-fired CHP plants are employed to generate power and heat, while an absorption chiller generates cold energy from the excess heat.

Taking full advantage of the building code, the large complex was designed as a long connecting building on which four individual office slabs were erected; aside from other advantages, the overall structure allows for natural cross-ventilation. The access cores were located in a manner that allowed the individual use of smaller rental units, and their combination into larger units both in a vertical and in a horizontal direction. The building depth of 12 m and the center-to-center distance of 1.5 m in the facade grid offer flexibility in the floor plan from single or group offices, to combination offices and open-plan uses. Ceiling and floor slabs were thermally activated and designed as storage masses. Hence, the complex does not feature suspended ceilings or double floors. In winter, these solid building components are heated, while heat is extracted from them in summer. Controlled surface temperatures result in a comfortable indoor climate.

The office facades are single-leaf and composed of multiple layers. The wooden facade on the south and north side is partially realized as an insulating panel structure, which incorporates ventilation flaps. Ventilation flaps along the top are closed, half-open or fully open depending on temperature and wind conditions. These flaps provide natural ventilation for the interiors and are designed to ensure the

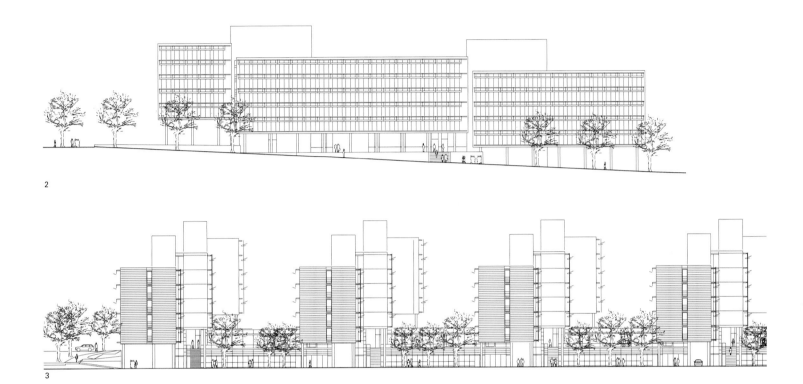

2

3

air change necessary for hygiene. A small convector pre-warms outside air flowing into the
interior in winter. The fixed glazing with triple
insulating glazing with rare-gas filling has excellent insulation properties. The colorless glass
results in a high light transmission factor. One
innovation is the integration of the building
services systems for the offices in the facade. A
wooden box, mounted at table height on the
inside wall, houses the power distribution.
The development of innovative technical components was supported by funds from the
Deutsche Bundesstiftung Umwelt (German
Federal Foundation for the Environment).

The metal surfaces on the facade are another
unique feature. On the north side, they direct
zenith light via the ceilings into the depth of the
room. Moveable components were developed
for the south side: on overcast days, they direct
zenith light to the underside of the ceilings, in
analogy to the system function on the north

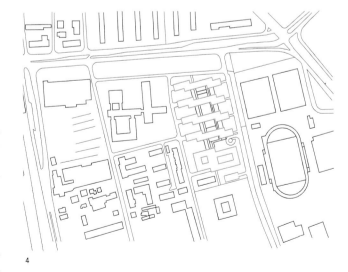

4

1 Staggering of office
  wings, at twilight

2 North elevation of an
  office wing, not to scale

3 West elevation of entire
  complex, not to scale

4 Site plan depicting the
  linkage of the four new
  structures with the
  existing building in the
  context of the sur-
  roundings, not to scale.

147

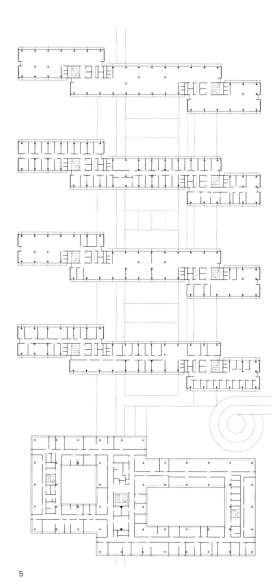

5

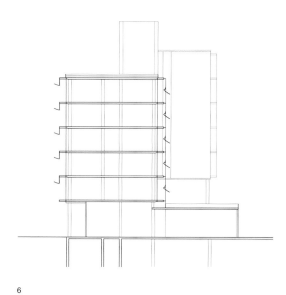

6

7

8

5 Floor plan of second floor. The four new office wings are connected to the existing administration building via two access corridors, not to scale.

6 Cross-section of office slab, not to scale

7 Frontal view of facade axis with the following components: vertical ventilation flap, open (left), closed (right), composed of a frame of laminated spruce, plywood with cherry mahogany veneer, insulation, integrated, adjustable ventilation flaps, lighting strip, wood box (left) with convector, wood box (right) with power supply

8 Diagonal view of facade axis with partially drawn glare protection

9 Detail section of north facade, not to scale

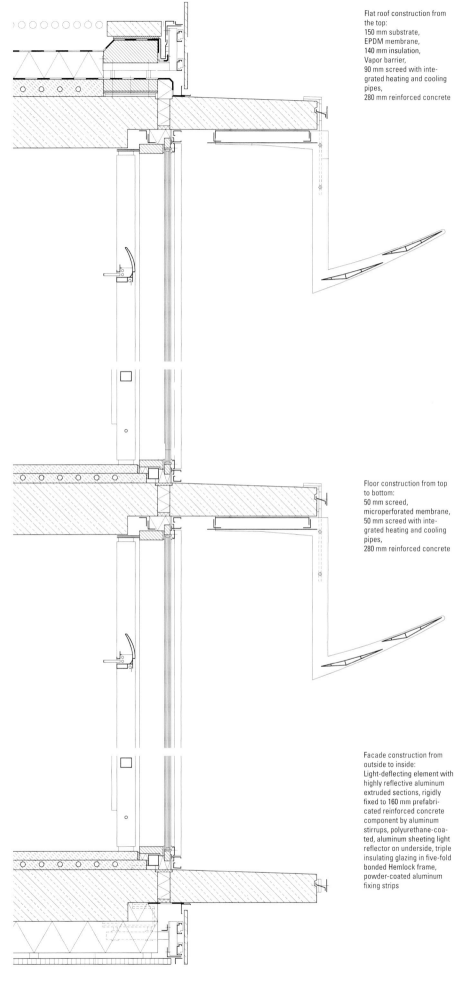

side. On sunny days, the components shift vertically into a sun protection position. Light-deflecting elements folded inward at the top of each component provide maximum shading, while the middle section allows sufficient direct sunlight to penetrate into the room. The lower section consists of a projecting element, which also provides shade. Visual contact with the outside is given beneath this element. The artificial light in the room is directed onto the table surfaces near the windows – indirectly by reflection off the ceiling and directly through a light-dispersing sheet. Deep rooms in the connecting slab, for example the restaurant, receive natural light via clerestory windows, which have been developed especially to optimize the supply of daylight.

The individual controls in the office areas are an important aspect of the systems concept for this complex. In an energy-conserving manner, they are in a constant "stand-by" state, ready to operate when needed. "Ready-state" is only activated when the user is present. Upon entering, the controlled natural ventilation coupled with the convector and the artificial light, which complements the daylighting with the help of control sensors, is activated.

Another important ecological balancing measure is the dense, differentiated planting scheme on the roofs. Rainwater is collected, stored in cisterns and used for artificial irrigation of the roof areas. The natural ventilation of the open underground garage obviates the need for mechanical ventilation, sprinkler systems and smoke detectors. All rooms, even the archival and storage areas in the depth of the building, offer views onto verdant atria. Th. H.

Flat roof construction from the top:
150 mm substrate,
EPDM membrane,
140 mm insulation,
Vapor barrier,
90 mm screed with integrated heating and cooling pipes,
280 mm reinforced concrete

Floor construction from top to bottom:
50 mm screed,
microperforated membrane,
50 mm screed with integrated heating and cooling pipes,
280 mm reinforced concrete

Facade construction from outside to inside:
Light-deflecting element with highly reflective aluminum extruded sections, rigidly fixed to 160 mm prefabricated reinforced concrete component by aluminum stirrups, polyurethane-coated, aluminum sheeting light reflector on underside, triple insulating glazing in five-fold bonded Hemlock frame, powder-coated aluminum fixing strips

9

149

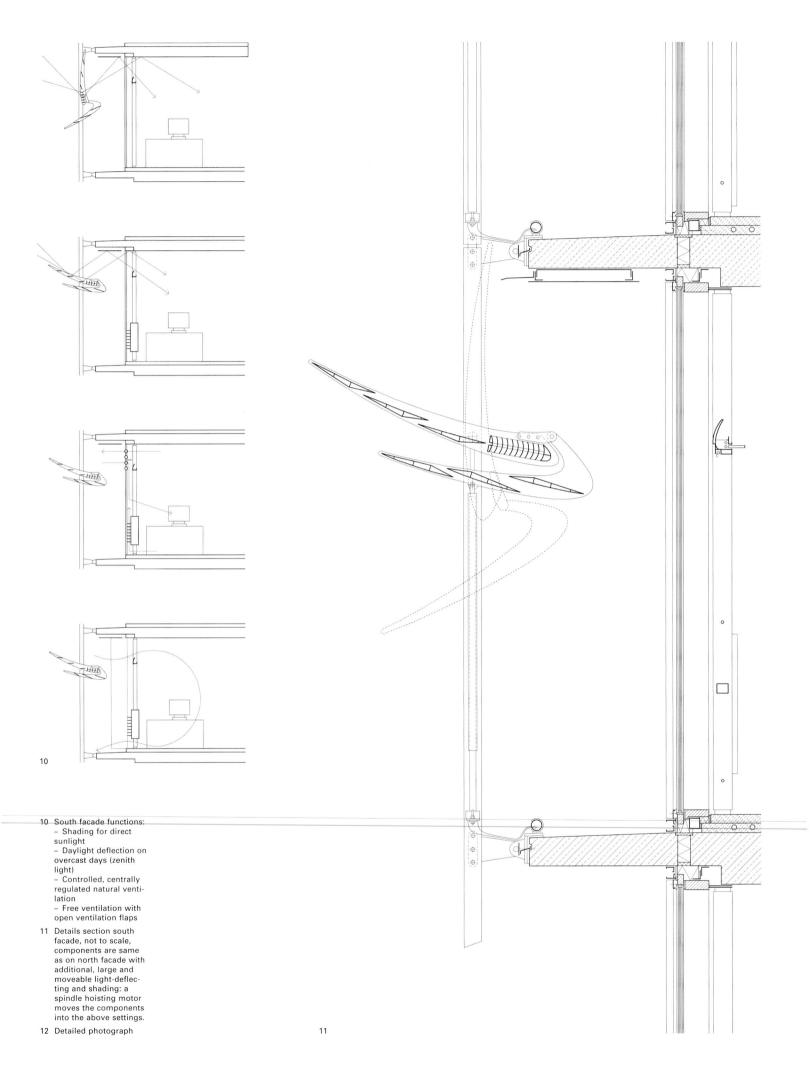

10 South facade functions:
  – Shading for direct
  sunlight
  – Daylight deflection on
  overcast days (zenith
  light)
  – Controlled, centrally
  regulated natural ventilation
  – Free ventilation with
  open ventilation flaps

11 Details section south
  facade, not to scale,
  components are same
  as on north facade with
  additional, large and
  moveable light-deflec-
  ting and shading: a
  spindle hoisting motor
  moves the components
  into the above settings.

12 Detailed photograph

10

11

Sustainable Office Building:
Parliament Buildings in London

Architects:
Hopkins Architects, London

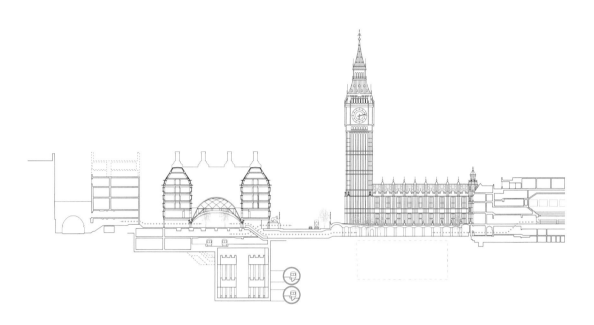

1

Selected data:

Completion: 2000
NFA: 22,811 m²

Calculated energy con-
sumption:
90 kWh/m²a

U-value roof:
0.25 W/m²K
U-value exterior wall:
0.27 W/m²K
U-value window:
0.15 W/m²K

At a unique prominent location in the center of London on the banks of the Thames, in the immediate vicinity of Westminster Palace (architect C. Barry with A.W.N. Pugin) and the former Scotland Yard building (architect Norman Shaw), the complex task was to erect a new building for 210 members of parliament and their staff. For the planning architects the task was made even more challenging by the fact that an underground station where two lines intersect had to be integrated below ground. Despite the complexity of the brief, the planning team composed of Hopkins Architects and engineers from Arup set themselves the ambitious goal of designing and realizing an energy-efficient and sustainable building. The "Joule II" program of the European Commission made it possible to execute the planning and design within the framework of a research project. Reducing energy consumption for construction and operation and the use of renewable energy resources were priorities in the deliberations. A sustainable building, according to Hopkins and his colleagues, should also offer high quality in terms of use and have outstanding aesthetic standards. The form that emerged from this process did not meet with unanimous praise in the eyes of the public and the media, on the contrary. However, Peter Davey's analysis in *Architectural Review*, entitled "Commons Sense," demonstrated that the neighboring buildings had faced similar controversy in their day. The initial storm has long since abated and the high quality of use has accelerated habituation. The courageous and distinctly shaped ventilation stacks give the massive block structure and scale. Reflecting similar motifs in the neighboring buildings, the block is successfully integrated into the famous silhouette of the buildings on the Thames. In his Houses of Parliament, Pugin too had cleverly integrated the necessary ventilation features in turrets in the Gothic Revival style. The monumental chimneys of the Scotland Yard building are similarly distinctive. Numerous, elaborately equipped working models were used to finalize the building form in all its details and the surface structure. No detail, no matter how small, was left to chance.

The offices for the members of parliament and their staff are arranged around a central courtyard with a glass roof. In contrast to the rooms overlooking the tranquil courtyard, the rooms facing the street feature oriels; on this side the windows cannot be opened for reasons of security and sound protection.

2

The building is supplied and ventilated with 100 percent fresh air, which is suctioned in at the base of the tall ventilation stacks and pre-warmed in rotating heat exchangers running counter current to the centrally extracted spent air. Below the roof, the supply air to the offices is processed and heated or cooled. Distribution to the individual floors is effected from the inner side of the facade. Finally, fresh air is supplied to each office from the corridor via the double floor by displacement. A cleverly designed built-in component at the window optimizes the ingress of daylight into the interior and integrates the artificial lighting, which incorporates downward spot lights for reading as well as indirect radiant light directed toward the curved ceiling to provide even lighting throughout the room. The high daylight ratio makes it possible to reduce the need for artificial lighting and to conserve energy. The ventilation openings for spent air are located in the upper section of the window embrasure. The ceiling, which is prefabricated and composed of high-quality exposed concrete, furnished the necessary storage mass for balancing the internal temperature. There are sufficient storage masses throughout the interior of the building in the form of exposed columns, arches, ceil-

ings and partitions – all composed of prefabricated white exposed concrete components. In summer, the building is flushed with fresh air and naturally cooled at night. The heat loads that have accumulated over the course of the day are evacuated. Spent air is extracted on the outside at the facade, on both sides of the solid sandstone columns. The material chosen for the visible air ducts, the roof surface and the ventilation stacks is an aluminum and bronze alloy, which required extensive exploration of casting and extrusion processes, weld joints and suitable patina processes. The windows are triple-glazed and function as absorbers in winter. Dark-tinted blinds absorb solar heat.

The heat gained by this means is channelled to the ventilation cycle via the outgoing air. In summer, the supply air, which is pre-cooled with groundwater, can be directed at the windows. This building does not include any conventional cooling or air-conditioning units.

A unique feature in the sanitation system is that the groundwater used for cooling is then utilized as gray water for toilet flushing. Other measures round out the strategy of minimizing potable water consumption.

The courtyard, in which large tree thrive beneath a glass roof, serves as a communication and

1 Section of block with underground station below grade, not to scale

2 View from the Thames: Houses of Parliament with Big Ben, parliament buildings: Portcullis House, formerly Scotland Yard

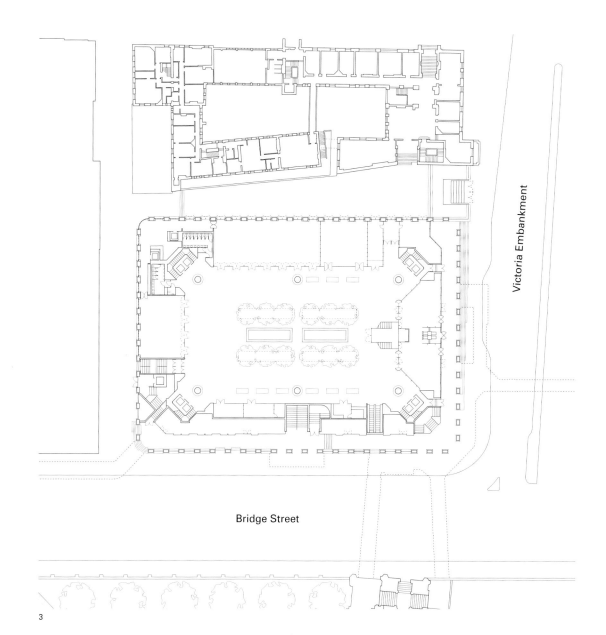

Victoria Embankment

Bridge Street

3

4

relaxation area. The filigree load-bearing structure composed of American oak, stainless steel structural joints and glass, invest the space with an atmosphere that is both friendly and elegant, offering an unobstructed view to the offices above. The differentiated design of the facade is also effective when seen up close. There should be little difficulty in surpassing the projected lifecycle of the building of 120 years.

3 Plan at street level with
  courtyard
4 View of facade from
  courtyard
5 Facade detail: courtyard
  above glass roof

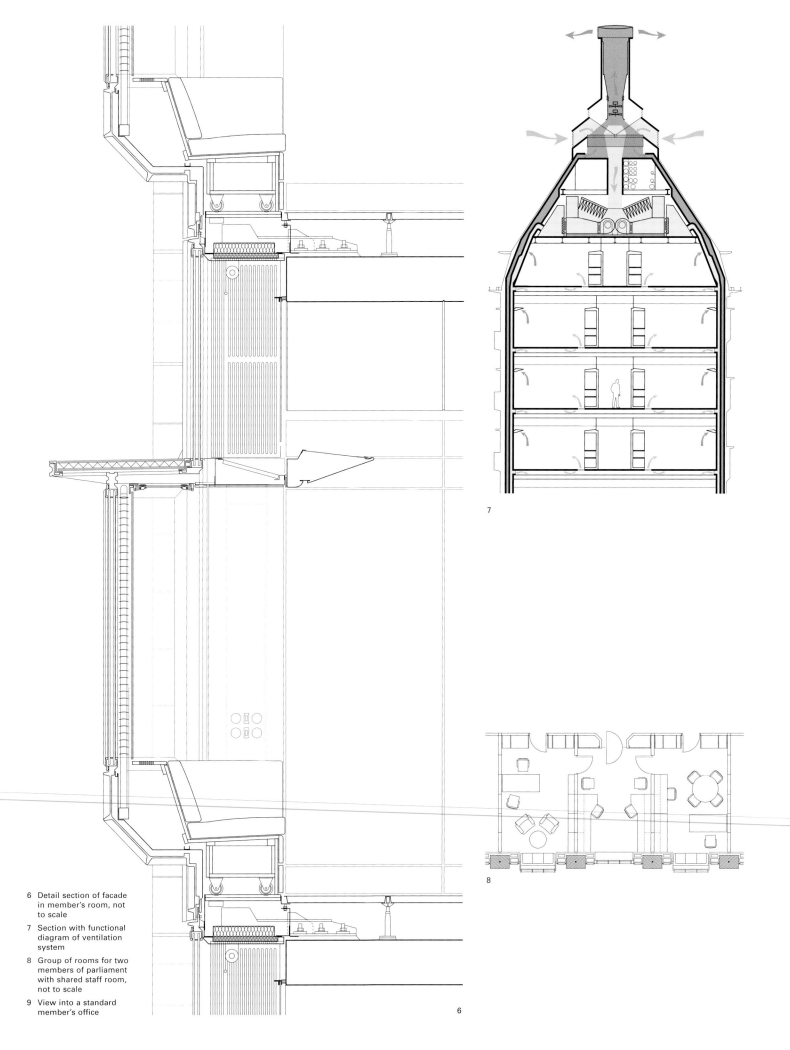

6 Detail section of facade
in member's room, not
to scale

7 Section with functional
diagram of ventilation
system

8 Group of rooms for two
members of parliament
with shared staff room,
not to scale

9 View into a standard
member's office

7

8

6

9

Integrated Ecology:
Offices and Workshops in Weidling

Architects:
Georg W. Reinberg, Wien

1

Selected data:

Completion: 2003
NFA office: 419 m²
GFA office: 499 m²
GFA total: 961 m²
GRV: 2,579 m³
(office and workshop)

Heating energy
requirement:
19.4 kWh/m²a

U-value roof:
0.11 W/m²K

U-value exterior wall:
0.18 W/m²K
U-value ground floor/soil:
0.19 W/m²K
U-value glazing:
0.7 W/m²K

A company that began as a landscaping firm has today evolved into a specialist in the installation of swimming ponds and biotopes for wastewater treatment. A limited competition was held for the expansion of the production and administration building. The winner of the competition made clever use of the advantages of the site, characterized by an attractive landscape and natural bodies of water. The new buildings are placed transverse to the valley; together with the treed mountain slopes, they create a spatial frame around the large water surface. The administration wing lies directly adjacent to the existing pond. The glazed south facade mediates between exterior and interior. Access and internal circulation functions are cleverly linked to effective shading, on the one hand, and the utilization of solar energy gains on the other. Access is provided along the water on the narrow west side of the building. A generous reception area gives clients access to the two-story consultation zone. Workshops and warehouse are linked to the north by an open covered corridor. Traffic access to this zone is clearly separated from the client area.

The grounds are an essential aspect in the contact with potential clients. Here, the range of services provided by the company can be demonstrated in a tangible fashion. Key technical components are a pond membrane and a system for enriching water with CO_2. Visitors can follow a path leading through the grounds and over footbridges close to the water surface to familiarize themselves with different types of biotopes. The carefully devised water concept emphasizes and dominates the landscape design. The existing pond offers a view of the vegetation along the edge, which has been allowed to establish itself over a long period. Naturally, the large body of water is also suitable for swimming. Footbridges divide the adjacent areas with different plant species. Sewage and wastewater are treated and clarified in a biotope treatment plant on the southeast side. Roof drainage is collected in a seepage pit located between the buildings and integrated into the landscape design in a natural manner.

Lengthwise, the office wing is divided by a concrete-storage wall core and is otherwise composed of a highly insulated timber construction with plywood boarding. The south facade is dominated by glass and wood.

To optimize the energy-efficient operation of the complex, thermal building simulation was employed during the planning and design stage. These studies led to the development of sustainable solutions for heating, shading, a

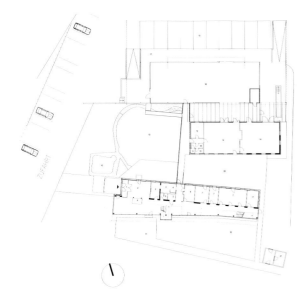

2

3

4

1 South elevation

2 Site plant showing the arrangement of the following elements: administration building overlooking the swimming pond, workshops, warehouse, access, not to scale

3 View into two-story access and circulation zone

4 North elevation with pond and connection to

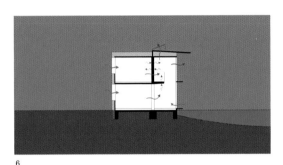

5

9

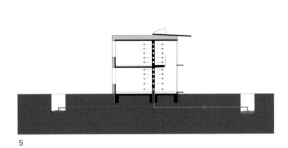

6

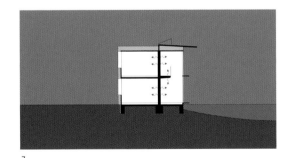

7

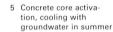

8

5 Concrete core activation, cooling with groundwater in summer

6 Example of ventilation on a summer's night

7 Example of the storage wall as a heating component on a winter's night

8 Clear, sunny day in winter

9 Appearance of building at night

10 Detail of south facade with collector installation. Shading is provided by the roof overhang and, when needed, by fabric banners suspended in front of the lower part of the facade.

11 Ventilation diagram

12 Offices with exposed ventilation ducts

13 Diagram of rainwater and wastewater management in the grounds

solar thermal installation and the necessary ventilation concept. They focused on exploring the interplay of all key characteristics relevant to energy consumption and comfort in the building. The evaluations of the simulation tests yielded the following results: given the appropriate construction, the building cools gradually, enough, in fact, to survive a ten-day interruption in supplementary heating without incurring any damage from frost. This is achieved by means of a 20 cm insulation layer in the exterior walls and a 30 cm layer in the roof area in combination with triple insulation glazing. Heating is provided by a 16 m² collector area integrated into the south facade and a wood-fired boiler combined with two buffer storage tanks with a capacity of 1,500 l each. The partially solar heating system functions without user input and balances the temperature in the offices even during the Christmas break.

Fresh air is supplied to the offices and suctioned off by way of the access hall in the WC and the staff kitchen. A 7-10 mm wide joint below the doors allows air to flow from the offices into the circulation area. Three earth ducts and a controllable heat-recovery system ensure comfort in summer and provide a balanced energy concept. The shading system has been optimized and designed to operate in harmony with the air-cooling components and the well-water cooling system. This made it possible to design the shading in a transparent manner and permitted an unobstructed view of the attractive swimming pond at all times. The corridor, by contrast, requires intensive constant cooling at night in summer. The central storage wall can be cooled with the available groundwater with-

10

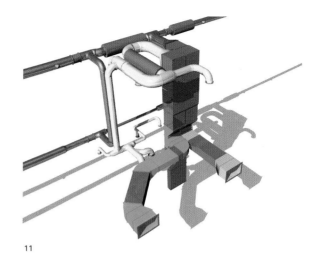

11

out any need for elaborate technical systems. The positive influence on the summer climate is tangible: internal temperatures never exceeded 26° C even during the heat wave in the summer of 2003. Computer simulation demonstrated that optimized insulation in winter and a high degree of comfort in summer were by no means mutually exclusive. At the same time, no effort was spared to minimize the need for technical systems. Existing features, such as the extraction fans at wood-processing machines and well-water distribution for pond management, were seamlessly integrated into the ecology building systems concept.

The construction concept reflects the energy concept. Aside from the long continuous concrete wall, which can be utilized for heating and cooling under the guise of concrete core activation, the remaining structure is built of plywood. Roof and facade are highly insulated with rock wool and airtight. Every aspect of function and aesthetics has been fully realized in this building.

12

13

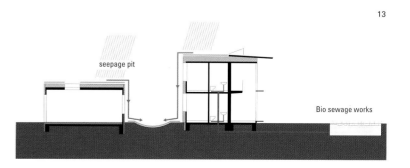

seepage pit

Bio sewage works

14 Cross-section, not to
scale

15 Detail sections of north
facade with vertical sec-
tion through exterior
door and horizontal
section of window, as
well as a vertical sec-
tion of the south facade
with wood deck above
adjacent water surface.

Construction of north
facade, from outside to
inside:
3.5 cm larch battening,
4/5 staggered wood
battening,
3 cm ventilation cavity,
UV-resistant membrane
as wind barrier,
20 cm rock wool
between wooden posts,
9.8 cm thick wood
panel,
1 cm reed mat,
1.5 cm heating vent,
1 cm clay rendering,
not to scale

16 West elevation with
main entrance

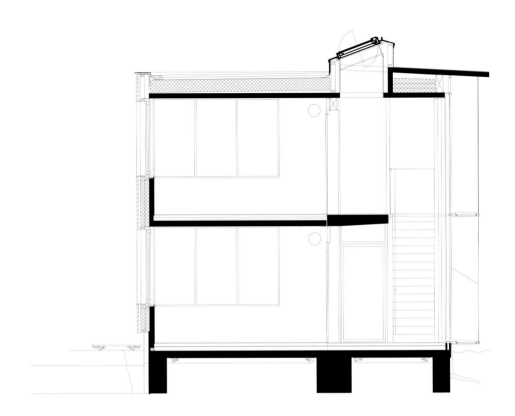

14

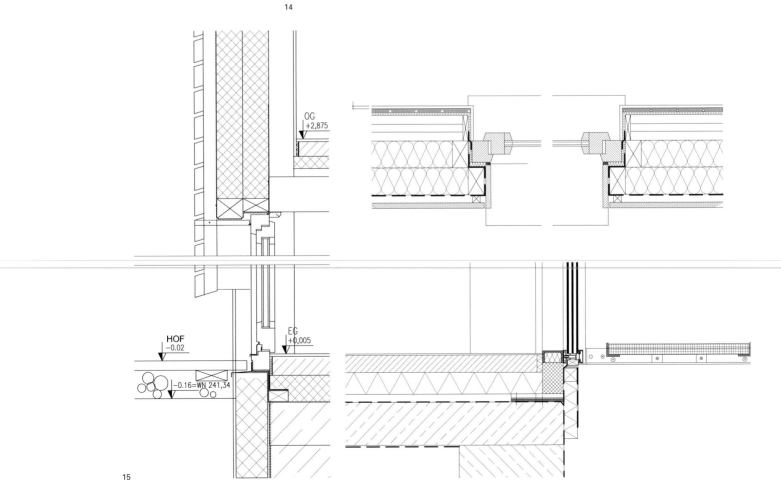

15

Headquarters Building in Passive House Standard:
Commercial Building in Steyr

Architect:
Walter Unterrainer, Feldkirch

1

Selected data:

Completion: 2002
Total office area: 1,042 m²
GRV office: 4,015 m³
Total warehouse area:
572 m²
GRV warehouse: 2,630 m³

Heating energy requirement
14 kWh/m²a

U-value flat roof:
0.10 W/m²K
U-value exterior wall:
Light construction
0.12 W/m²K
U-value floor slab:
0.20 W/m²K
U-value basement ceiling:
0.20 W/m²K
U-value glazing south and
west:
0.5 W/m²K

U-value glazing north and
east:
0.9 W/m²K
U-value window:
0.82 W/m²K

The client is an established plumbing firm in Steyr with some seventy employees. For some years the firm has been a regional leader in energy-efficient building systems. The new headquarters building, built to passive house standard specifications, is a visible expression of the company's philosophy demonstrated in the building skin and the exposed, ecologically conscious building systems.

The urban situation of this commercial building is full of contradictions and complications. The entire commercial district is hidden behind a 3-m-high embankment for noise protection and can be accessed only via a complicated network of service roads. In placement and proportion, the building stands in direct reference to a neighboring quadrangle, which is a listed building and will be converted to a new use in the coming years.

The brief was to erect a cost-efficient, practical and flexible office building to be completed in a short period and meet a high standard of ecological excellence. The solution was achieved through a synthesis of functional planning, energy efficiency by means of passive house technology and accelerated construction through prefabrication. In all this, no compromise was made with regard to the spatial and architectural quality or to maintaining the appropriate image and aesthetics in the details.

The building is divided into a two-story retail- and office area and a single-story, high-ceilinged warehouse and workshop area. The two areas are separated by a green courtyard, oriented toward the retail area, with an inviting staircase leading up to the roof of the warehouse, which is also used as a retail area. A wide range of collectors and photovoltaic components are installed on this roof, where they are presented and explained to prospective clients.

The functions are clearly divided: a broad, projecting roof marks the approach and the attractive client entrance. The covered loading areas and the adjacent staff rooms are located to the rear. Inside, the generous reception area has been opened across two floors. It links the retail area on the ground floor with the administration zone on the upper floor. The two-story glazing is also utilized as generous showcase windows. Vertical expansion in the future has been incorporated into the structural design and construction of the building.

The office wing is the first passive house office building in Austria and was certified as such by the German Institute for Passive House Standard. The building demonstrates that compromises with regard to spatial qualities are not necessary in order to create a highly energy-efficient commercial building. Transparency, function, vertical linkages and varied vistas are not in contrast to a convincing energy balance. Some of the details in this building, unusual for passive houses, are conceived with a view to clarity of design, appropriate material selection and cost efficiency.

The technical options, which are presented to interested clients as demonstration objects, form the basis for the energy concept. All components (and sub-components, e.g. geothermal collectors) are accessible and showcased in an explanatory manner for prospective passive house clients. These include an exposed, controllable ventilation system with a high efficiency heat exchanger, an exposed geothermal collector, a biomass supplementary heating system fired with wood pellets, a solar warm water generation system, a photovoltaic power generating system, a rainwater collecting system, and many other features.

The ventilation concept includes a geothermal collector of PE pipes with heat exchanger, which pre-cools or pre-warms outside air as needed. In addition to heat recovery, the automatic reheating damper register covers the remaining heating requirements. The heating requirements, which are already drastically reduced as

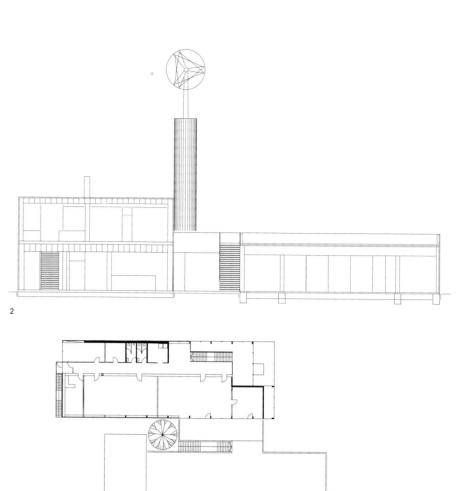

2

3

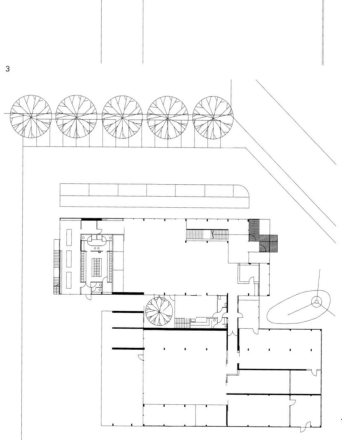

4

1 Elevation with windmill as company logo
2 Cross-section
3 Floor plan of upper floor with administration and exhibition area on the roof above warehouse and workshop
4 Ground floor plan with retail area, warehouse and workshop, drawings not to scale

a result of the constructional measures, are largely covered by natural energy sources with a heat pump and by solar collectors. The pellet-fired heating furnishes the remaining heat requirement.

Nearly one third of the power consumption is supplied from the windmill and the photovoltaic installation on the roof and the tower. In future, this installation is to be expanded to cover the entire consumption. A bio-diesel gas station has been installed in the parking lot.

The zoning map does not permit vertical building components and prominent company logos. The light- and advertising tower constructed from polycarbonate panels with photovoltaic cells and equipped with a 5-kW windmill is located at the center of these two buildings and is visible above the noise protection embankment. After considerable resistance, permission was granted for a diminished version of the slender, vertically differentiated and structurally optimized tower as an energy-gaining measure. As a nocturnal light signal, the tower represents the energy-conscious philosophy of the company. It is a confident focal point that is visible from afar.

Both building sections were assembled in a short time as a prefabricated wood construction. The building has only a partial basement. The wood construction rests on a 30-cm-thick insulated concrete slab. The structural grid measures 400 cm. The facades are constructed on a continuous 2 m grid with butt joints formed from a connecting section composed of fibrated cement strips over drainage rubber. The joints behind this layer are glued airtight and sealed. This solution is more cost efficient than aluminum connecting sections, requires less gray energy and drastically reduces the formation of thermal bridges. The results of the pressure test in a blower-door study were below 0.5 h-1 at the first attempt.

The transparent zones of the facades are covered in large triple-glazing sections of 200 x 400 cm. These large panes provide the building with stunning vistas and views into the interior.

5

6

5 Administration on upper floor and ground floor retail zone are spatially linked

6 Blower-door test: the first attempt yielded results in the optimized range

7

8

7 View of entrance with roof overhang and vestibule

8 Upper floor with spacious and attractive exhibition area on the roof above the warehouse and the workshop.

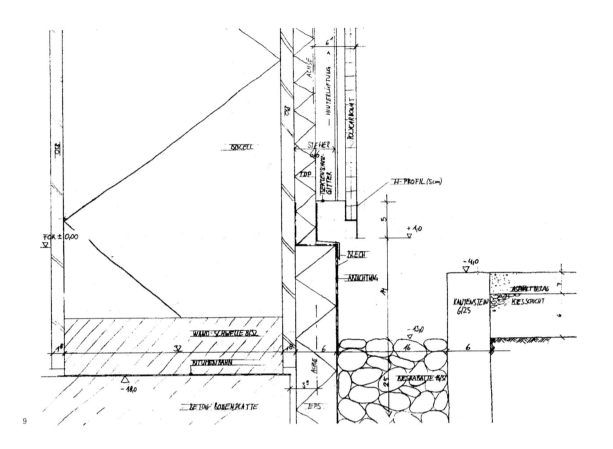

9

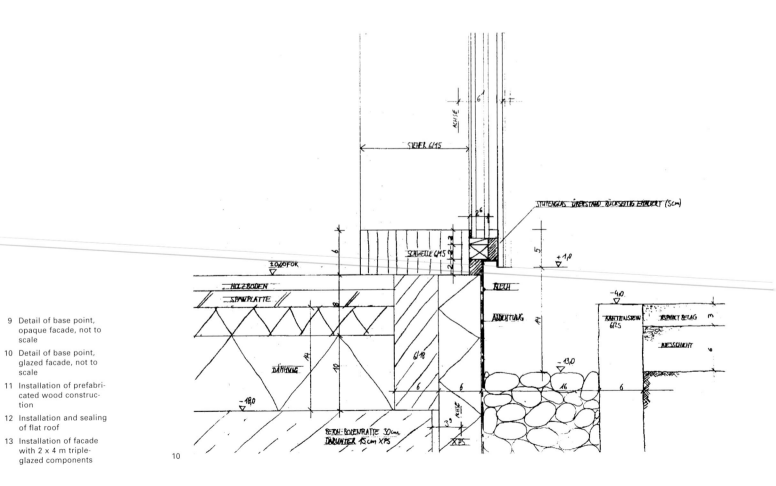

9 Detail of base point, opaque facade, not to scale

10 Detail of base point, glazed facade, not to scale

11 Installation of prefabricated wood construction

12 Installation and sealing of flat roof

13 Installation of facade with 2 x 4 m triple-glazed components

10

11

At the same time, they radically reduce the length of the joints and thermal bridges in relation to the glass area. Frames are the weak link in passive house windows, as is well known. By reducing the overall frame ratio, frames that have a lower insulating value at lower costs can be employed to achieve the same U-value for the entire window as is possible with smaller, "classic" passive house windows that have greater joint and frame lengths.

The opaque areas are post-and-rail construction in wood, with an insulated core of 32 cm and OSB cladding on both sides. On the inside, the vapor barrier is followed by an installation layer. On the outside, the walls are completed with story-high polycarbonate hollow-core panels. As a building skin, polycarbonate panels are durable, low-maintenance, cost-effective and characterized by a better eco balance than glass. They are available up to a dimension of 200 x 600 cm. The hollow-core panels employed here allow a view onto the thermal insulation of pressed hard fiberboards, which have been spray-painted in the company's signature yellow.

Economic, weather-independent prefabrication in a hall and the logistics employed throughout the construction process kept the costs within the range of conventional commercial buildings, which are far less attractive in terms of energy efficiency, achieving at the same time operation costs that are incomparably lower and a greater precision in execution.

12

13

Low-energy School Ensemble:
School Complex in Pichling

Architects:
Loudon + Habeler, Vienna

1

Selected data:

Completion: 2003
NFA: 5,015 m²
GFA: 5,901 m²
GRV: 27,351 m³

Heating energy require-
ment:
34.8 kWh/m²a

U-value roof:
0.15 W/m²K
U-value exterior wall gym:
0.17 W/m²K
U-value exterior wall classroom wing, face wall, and
along parapets:
0.19 W/m²K
U-value ground floor to
ground:
0.6 W/m²K
U-value window and frame:
1.1 W/m²K

The history of the SolarCity in Linz goes back to the early 1990s. A shortage of building ground for residential development led to the ambitious decision of carrying out an urban expansion project. Roland Rainer developed the initial urban concept, the core of which was further developed by the partners of the READ group (Foster, Rogers, Herzog) and expanded by Martin Treberspurg, who emerged as the winner of a competition. The project encompasses 1 317 residential units, which are functionally complemented by community buildings, a kindergarten and a school.

The school complex, with excellent linkages to public transportation, is situated in generous grounds that provide sufficient space for expansion, sports and leisure activities. It consists of a two-story wing with classrooms and common rooms for daycare. The gym at the front has been lowered into the ground and has an underground link to the main building. A planned second construction phase will add a comprehensive school for twelve grades with a triple gym.

An access atrium with daylight from above links the daycare rooms on the ground floor and the primary school classrooms on the second floor in a natural and pleasant manner. The longitudinal facades are fronted by suspended, adjustable shading louvers. They ensure optimized use of the solar energy. The roof area is in part accessible and offers an opportunity for classes to be held outside, weather permitting. The rest of the roof is densely planted. The daylit atrium and clerestory windows provide light from two sides to the classrooms, which therefore benefit from optimized and evenly distributed lighting.

In keeping with the building physics of the windows and the facade, the components of the low-energy system comprise a ventilation system with heat recovery and a geothermal heat exchanger employed to pre-warm or pre-cool the supply air. Fresh air enters into the classrooms from the corridor through volume flow controls and displacement ventilation flaps in the classrooms. At the same time air is removed through the open ceiling void and taken to a central ventilation collector. The excess heat contained in the ventilated air is extracted by a rotary heat exchanger. The airflow is ventilated

2

3

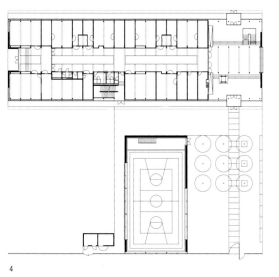

4

5

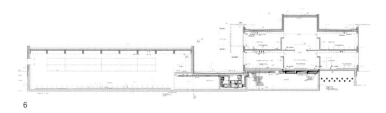

6

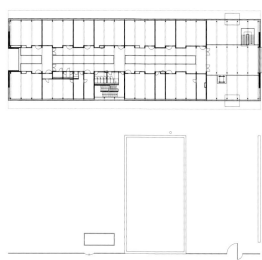

7

1 School entrance

2 View into two-story
   access atrium

3 Site plan, not to scale

4 Ground floor of school
   and gym, not to scale

5 Upper floor

6 Section of gym with
   connection to class-
   room wing, not to scale

7 Cross-section of classroom wing with build-
   ing services, not to
   scale

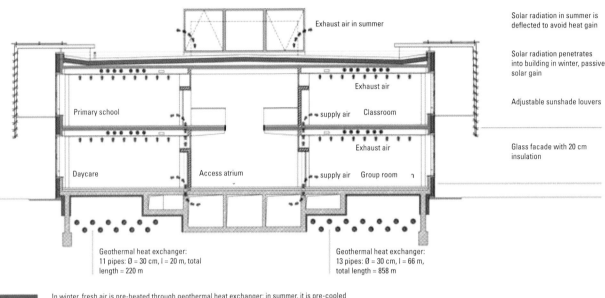

Exhaust air in summer

Solar radiation in summer is deflected to avoid heat gain

Solar radiation penetrates into building in winter, passive solar gain

Primary school

Exhaust air

Classroom

supply air

Adjustable sunshade louvers

Daycare

Exhaust air

Access atrium

supply air

Group room

Glass facade with 20 cm insulation

Geothermal heat exchanger:
11 pipes: Ø = 30 cm, l = 20 m, total length = 220 m

Geothermal heat exchanger:
13 pipes: Ø = 30 cm, l = 66 m, total length = 858 m

In winter, fresh air is pre-heated through geothermal heat exchanger; in summer, it is pre-cooled

Exhaust air is collected for heat recovery through rotary heat exchanger

Roof area above gym: 5.7 m² photovoltaics, total output of 714 watt,
16.5 m² solar collectors for water heating

8

in a draft-free manner. Window ventilation occurs via 0.35-cm-wide tall opening flaps with a series of adjustable settings for opening widths. They provide basic ventilation depending on use and an especially economic, continuous night-time ventilation in summer.

The cross-section above illustrates these components and the function of the ventilation system. The pipes for the geothermal heat exchanger are installed in the construction pit underneath the building and have a total length of 220 m. PVC pipes were employed because these can be welded to be watertight under pressure and are easy to clean. The gym is ventilated according to the same principle.

Although the heating energy requirements were largely reduced, there is a remaining requirement that is met from two supplementary temperature sources. Warm-water floor heating is envisioned for the main building and for the gym. Zone valves regulated heat transfer into the individual spaces and are centrally controlled. The gym is equipped with a heating system that is suitable for sprung floors. Solar collectors covering a total area of 20 m² are

installed on the roof of the gym to process warm water for the sanitation. The remaining requirement is drawn from the district supply grid. A bus system has been installed to record the energy consumption parameters and to optimize the operation.

The color and material concept continues the principle of conscious reduction and the use of clear, robust surfaces: terrazzo in the hallways, parquet flooring in the classrooms, wood for doors and windows.

The large open area on the east side, which merges with the natural landscape along the creek that runs nearby, is especially attractive and ideal for a school setting.

9

Roof construction:
10–22 cm substrate
22 cm storage panels
Fleece
15 cm insulation
1 cm, triple-layer moisture barrier
10 cm insulation
Vapor barrier
3–15 cm concrete layer to falls
33 cm reinforced concrete slab
Cavity
2 cm suspended ceiling

Floor construction, ground floor:
1.5 cm tiles in thin bed
30.5 cm double floor
5 cm screed/PAE membrane
3 cm impact-sound insulation
5 cm insulation
PE membrane
25 cm reinforced concrete slab

Facade construction:
1 cm glass element
2.5 ventilated cavity
2.5 cm wood-wool building slab
20 cm mineral wool
14/17 cm reinforced concrete
parapet
4 cm premixed render

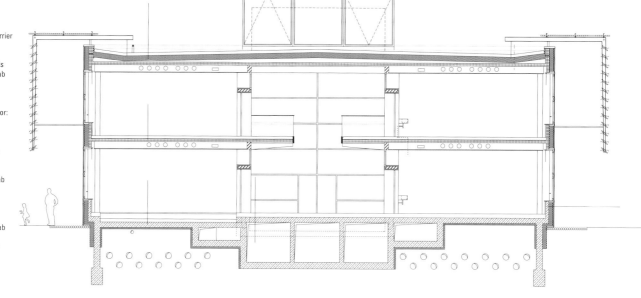

11

12

13

Passive House Standard for Children:
Montessori School in Aufkirchen

Architects:
Walbrunn Grotz Vallentin Loibl, Bockhorn

1

Selected data:

Completion: 2004
NFA: 3,614 m²
GFA: 4,080 m²
GRV: 18,976m³

Calculated heating requirement:
13.5 kWh/m²a
U-value roof:
0.10 W/m²K
U-value exterior wall:
0.18 W/m²K
U-value floor ground floor/
ground:
0.14 W/m²K
U-value glazing:
0.70 W/m²K

When planning the new Montessori elementary and comprehensive school in Aufkirchen, the architects made it their goal to create a living environment for children. The design features a two-story building that seems to grow naturally out of the ground with a curving planted roof and an organically formed plan. The friendly building which is flooded with light invites children to feel comfortable in their day-to-day school schedule and their leisure hours because of the many different uses it offers. Despite its ambitious and appealing architectural design, the building must satisfy the laws of economic viability and remain within the financing provided from public funds. The energy-conserving measures, here passive house standard, must also be realized within these parameters. The distinctive roof harmonizes with the grounds, the differing room heights merge seamlessly with one another. By virtue of the compact form, exterior surfaces are minimized in relationship to the built volume and this has a positive effect on cost-efficiency and conserves energy. The south-east side opens toward the entrance area and the school yard, while the north-west side overlooks an open landscape. The school entrance is emphasized by a rotunda penetrating through the facade and a wall running parallel to the approach. Behind the entrance lies the auditorium that reaches all the way to the roof. The adjacent dining room doubles as a student café. Mobile room dividers in the gym and the round multi-purpose room can be shifted to expand the auditorium. For large events, the gym, which is stepped down by half a story, is reconfigured by means of a mobile spectator stand between the auditorium and the gym level. The classroom wing adjoins the auditorium. On the ground floor, this section accommodates classrooms and specialist teaching rooms for six comprehensive school grades, while the upper floor houses classrooms and specialist teaching rooms for four elementary school grades and the school administration. Numerous skylights in the roof and suspended intermediate ceilings create a transparent sense of space with multiple sightlines.

Like many other details in this project, the integration of interior and exterior corresponds to

176

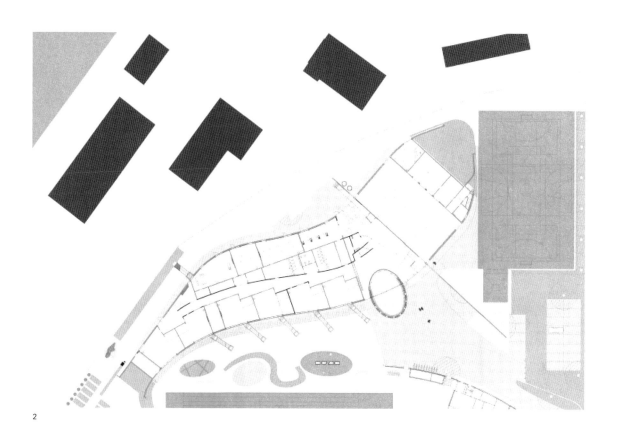

2

3

1 South elevation

2 Ground floor plan with
  site outline, not to scale

3 Detail of south facade
  with external stairs to
  classrooms on upper
  floor

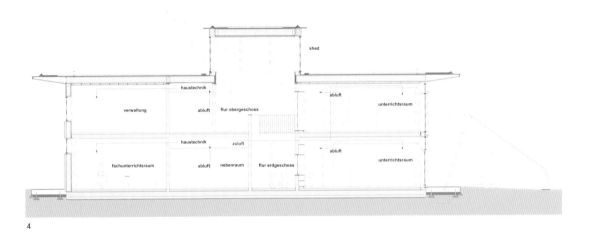

shed

haustechnik

verwaltung   abluft   flur obergeschoss   abluft   unterrichtsraum

haustechnik   zuluft

fachunterrichtsraum   abluft   nebenraum   flur erdgeschoss   abluft   unterrichtsraum

4

5

4 Cross-section, daylight
  conditions: the entire
  access core receives
  natural light through
  the central skylights.
  Ventilation diagram,
  supply and exhaust air,
  not to scale

5 View of construction
  site with shell structure

6 Grass-covered roof with
  skylight structure

7 Close up of skylights

8 Assembly of the roof
  components

9 Unfinished classroom:
  the roof incline is also
  perceptible in the
  interior

6

7

8

9

the principles of the Montessori pedagogy. For a brief albeit intense study of the school's philosophy, the architects sat in on classes at both the elementary and comprehensive level.

The Montessori school in Aufkirchen has been certified as meeting passive house criteria. The compact building skin is highly insulated: this includes the relevant glazing and passive house windows. The controlled ventilation with heat recovery supplies the required fresh air to the school building and the gym. Zoning and compactness are important aspects of the aforementioned standard. Large structures can only be realized in an energy- and cost-efficient manner by creating a highly compact fabric. In this case, the height was limited to two stories because the property is located on the edge of a small community. From the very beginning, the design was based on creating a complex with rooms on both sides of each access corridor resulting in an elongated structure. Large glazed areas on the roof compensate the disadvantages in terms of daylight penetration that are common in this type. The skylights and the open space beneath them create a spacious

interior that is flooded with light. A rigorous approach to internal zoning is equally important. The fabric has a north-south orientation to ensure that the principal rooms receive the lion's share of the solar gains and to create a plan where the auxiliary rooms are positioned on the north side. The zoning across a depth of approximately 20 to 28 m was laid out as follows: the south side is occupied by the classrooms, the multi-purpose room and the auditorium, while the core houses the internal circulation as well as auxiliary and storage rooms. Special teaching rooms and administration are located on the north side. All classrooms are linked to the schoolyard, since the classrooms on the upper floor also have direct access to the yard via escape stairs. The external stairs are part of the fire protection concept, thus fulfilling several functions. The same is true for the art and music rooms and the lunchroom.

To increase the compactness, the longitudinal side of the gym is joined directly with the auditorium. The option of connecting auditorium and gym (large opening by means of a mobile dividing wall) allows for a wide variety of uses

179

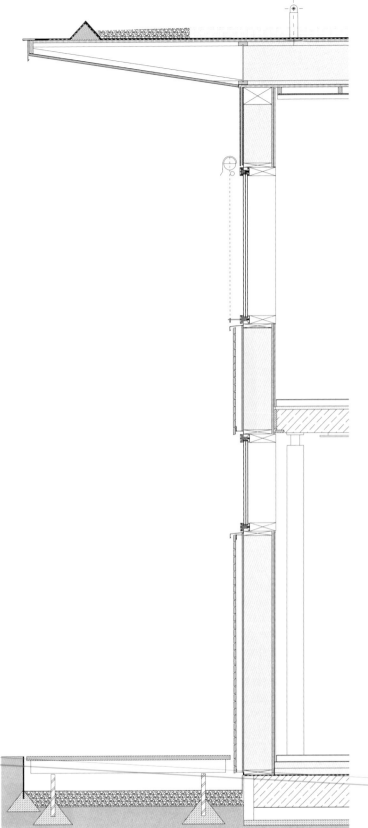

Roof construction,
from top to bottom:
100 mm grass layer,
protective membrane,
diaphragm,
separating fleece with
leak detection,
25 mm OSB panel –
airtight layer,
406 mm wood stem with
cellulose insulation
moisture-balancing
vapor barrier,
OSB panel,
cavity battening,
wood battening on
bearing plate

Facade construction,
from outside to inside:
24 mm Douglas fir planking,
cavity battening with 40 mm
facade fleece,
16 mm lining
panel DWD,
building veneer plywood
panel with 280 mm
cellulose insulation,
22 mm OSB panel,
airtight layer,
15 mm gypsum fiberboard

Floor construction on upper
story, from top to bottom:
13 mm adhesive parquet
flooring,
60 mm concrete screed
with levelling,
separation layer,
30 mm insulation,
200 mm reinforced
concrete,
Acoustic ceiling:
25 + 12.5 mm gypsum
plasterboard

Floor construction
on ground floor,
from top to bottom:
13 mm adhesive parquet
flooring,
60 mm concrete screed
with levelling,
separation layer,
120 mm insulation,
vapor barrier,
300 mm reinforced
concrete,
membrane,
120 mm perimeter
insulation,
50 mm sub-base on top
of frost blanket gravel

10

10 Detail section of facade,
    not to scale

11 Access zone on upper
    floor, flooded with light,
    promotes communica-
    tion

such as large events, school festivities and per-
formances. These are all key elements that support the Montessori philosophy.

A decision was made early on to execute the
internal load-bearing structure as a solid type of
construction. This type allows for more elegant
solutions for fire and sound protection. The
advantage of a large storage mass is also important for the energy-conserving concept and the
indoor climate. Aside from the basement story
constructed with waterproof concrete, all interi-
or walls and floors are executed in exposed
concrete. The external skin was conceived from
the outset as a wood construction, which allows
for a better and more cost-efficient approach to
thermal insulation. Prefabrication is also time-
saving. Wherever possible, wood is used not
only on the facade but in the interior as well.
The combination of reinforced concrete and
wood creates a warm atmosphere. An airtight
skin is a prerequisite for the passive house
standard. In wood construction it also serves as
a quality control strategy to prevent condensation damage caused by escaped air transport-
ing moisture by convection. The following value
was achieved during the airtightness test
(undertaken when finishing work had not been
completed; windows and glazing were already
installed): n50 = 0.09 1/h (based on the true
interior volume). The ventilation system is a
"supplementary" rather than a full air-conditioning system. It does not regulate either
humidity or temperature. When loads are high,
window ventilation can be used. A rotary heat
exchanger is a key element of the ventilation
system. The return flow heat quotient for
5,840 m^3 per hour is 86 percent for incoming
(supply) air and 74 percent for outgoing
(exhaust) air. Heat is generated in a CHP with a
gas-fired condensing boiler. In passive houses,
heating is continuous without fluctuations.

Built Participation:
Comprehensive School in Gelsenkirchen

Architects:
plus+ bauplanung, Neckartenzlingen

1

Selected data:

Completion: 2004
NFA: 16,650 m²
GFA: 19,110 m²
GRV: 77,600 m³

U-value roof:
0.23 W/m²K
U-value exterior wall:
0.33 W/m²K
U-value floor ground floor/
crawl space:
0.35 W/m²K
U-value window and
glazing:
0.23 W/m²K

"Children build their school" is the title of the project monograph on the comprehensive school in Gelsenkirchen. It is representative of the work of architect Peter Hübner. His commitment to user participation in all design stages, execution planning and implementation is exemplary and contributes greatly to the sustainability of his architecture. The children's identification with their school is the best protection against vandalism. The Protestant comprehensive school in Gelsenkirchen-Bismarck is located in an urban district that has been heavily hit by the crisis in the mining industry. The area is home to 30 percent foreign residents and an equally high percentage of unemployment. The new, multi-cultural and ecological school was conceived as a new focal point for the district. The design concept is therefore based on the idea of a miniature city complete with main street, market square with library, city hall (administration), theater (auditorium), pub (cafeteria), pharmacy (chemistry lab), studio (art) and six rows of classroom buildings on parallel side streets. From the very beginning, the participation of the students in the planning, design and even the construction was understood as an integral part of the process. As is often the case with Hübner, an imaginative narrative (explanatory report) provides the basis for the subsequent course. The jury was con-vinced by the sensible and sensuous program, which corresponded to the school's educational philosophy of creating an integrative and socially inclusive learning environment.

The school administration formulated clear ideas on an environmentally conscious school. These included: a high thermal insulation standard as a basis for utilizing passive solar energy gains and integrating them into a comprehensive energy concept, as well as a commitment to excellent daylight quality in all areas of the school. "Seasonal fluctuations, the conscious use of plants for shading or improving the indoor climate are to be the foundation for a unique aesthetic and signature of solar building." Rational rainwater management did not go unmentioned in the brief. The landscape design was to be conceived to integrate the school with a new residential development in a natural manner." As a schoolyard, the entire outdoor space is to be a place of relaxation, tranquility, balance and contemplation as well as a space to experience nature or an outdoor classroom." The result translates the brief with astonishing authenticity. Extending the use of the school to that of a cultural center for the neighborhood is only logical.

The covered "market square," into which the main street leads and to which the central facilities of the school complex such as audito-

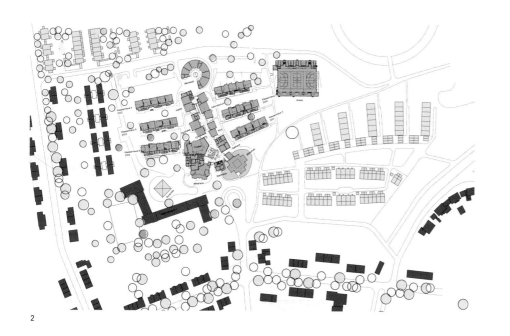

2

4

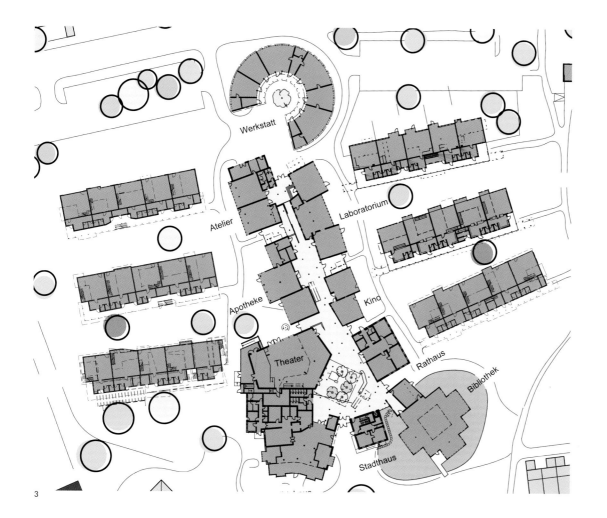

3

Werkstatt

Atelier

Laboratorium

Apotheke

Kino

Theater

Rathaus

Bibliothek

Stadthaus

1 Aerial view

2 Site plan with urban environment, not to scale

3 Plan of entire complex: the school as a small city with all necessary functional areas, not to scale

4 View of the covered market square, the focal point of the complex

183

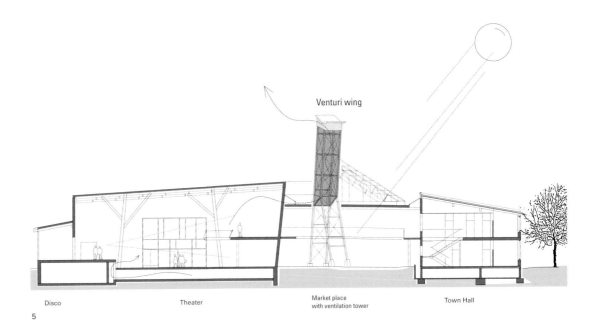

Venturi wing

Disco   Theater   Market place   Town Hall
                                              with ventilation tower

5

6

5 Section through market
   square with ventilation
   tower and adjacent
   auditorium (theater)
   and administration
   (town hall), not to scale

6 East elevation with
   town hall, chapel and
   library

rium, cafeteria, library and administration are linked, provides not only the necessary access to the school, it is also the focal point for communication. This area and the adjacent zones are naturally ventilated through a distinctly shaped exhaust shaft with Venturi wing at the center of the polygonal atrium. In the auditorium, a geothermal tunnel and the exhaust shaft are the key elements of the natural ventilation scheme. When the difference between internal and external temperature is sufficiently high, no additional measures are required to achieve adequate air change rates for a maximum occupancy of eighty persons. The required air volume flow is controlled by a system of flaps. The ventilation is based on the principle of cross-ventilation and provides comfortable ventilation with low air velocities.

The air enters at the parapet level and flows in the direction of the auditorium stage. When outdoor temperatures are low, the air is prewarmed as it passes through the geothermal tunnel, thereby reducing the heating energy requirement. Conversely, when outdoor temperatures are high, the supply air is cooled in the tunnel. When occupancy rates exceed the norm (eighty persons) or if the natural air change is too low, supplementary ventilation can be activated and adjusted by a unit equipped with two settings for this purpose. The supply air is distributed in the auditorium through wide-angle nozzles.

The gym, which is shared by external groups from the neighborhood, is not only notable for the ventilation concept, but also for its clever daylighting scheme.

7

7 View of library overlooking the pool, part of a rainwater management concept that has been integrated into the landscaping. Classroom wing with "studio" (art classes) and "pharmacy" (chemistry) and part of a classroom wing are visible to the right in the foreground.

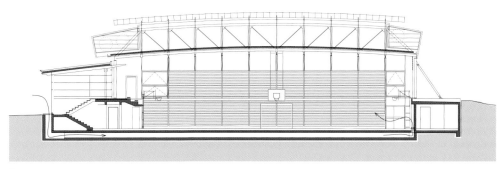

8

9

The hall is heated via radiant ceiling panels with a rapid response time to the fluctuating loads (occupancy) in the gym. The supply air is pre-warmed in the earth ducts and conventionally heated to the required temperature by supplementary damper registers prior to being distributed into the hall. In summer, the supply air is cooled by as much as 5 K in the same earth ducts. Operable windows and skylights prevent overheating in summer.

A series of daylight simulations was executed to establish the ideal balance between investment in glazing and visual comfort, that is, between daylight quotient and uniform light distribution, resulting in a daylight quotient of 5.9 percent and an excellent uniformity g of 0.96, calculated for one meter above floor level. The energy concept is based on a premise that includes the following strategies: minimizing the use of fossil fuels; minimizing the invest-

ment costs for technical equipment for building systems; minimizing potential cooling loads; minimizing transmission and ventilation losses; optimizing thermal and visual comfort; and minimizing the energy and material consumption. This was achieved through an intelligent concept of integrating natural heat sources (sun), natural cooling sources (soil and night air) and activating accessible storage masses as thermal buffers.

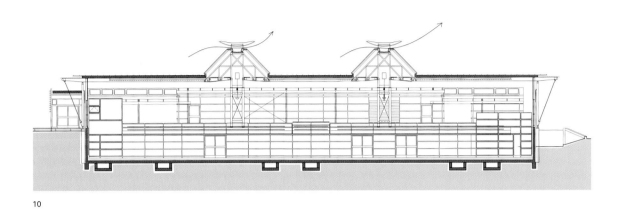

10

Response to Extreme Conditions:
School Complex in Ladakh

Architects:
Arup Associates, London

1

Selected data:

Completion:
1st construction phase:
2001

School without WC
and bathrooms:
NFA: 607 m²
GFA: 725 m²
GRV: 2,306 m³

Boarding school without
WC and bathrooms:
NFA: 340 m²
GFA: 453 m²
GRV: 1,540 m³

Since the data provided for
other projects would be
misleading in this case –
the data in this instance
cannot be compared to
European passive house
standards – the graph on
page 192 has been included
instead. It clearly illustrates
how perfectly the imple-
mented technology is
performing.

Ladakh is situated high up in the Indian Himalayas on the western edge of Tibet. In valleys with altitudes as high as 3,500 m above sea level, temperatures drop to -30° C in winter in some areas. During the brief summer, however, these fertile valleys come alive in the sun. The Drukpa Trust, a non-profit organization in Great Britain, is the initiator and administrator of a school for 750 girls and boys. In 1997, a team of architects and engineers from Arup Associates began with the development of a master plan. The goal was to consciously explore new paths with the help of technology and building methods that are adapted to the local situation in every detail. Every available program for building systems simulation was utilized; at the same time, the team also focused on traditional building methods in the interest of helping people to help themselves. Thus the possible use of a Trombe wall was carefully studied at the outset, as was the use of wool as an insulating material or the installation of insulating glazing, which is still unusual in the region. Daylight studies were also undertaken. The project also benefited from extensive experience gained in the design and construction of earthquake-resistant structures. Local resources were

explored in the context of material selection. It was understood that local craftsmen would participate in the construction and that local teachers would be trained to operate the school after completion.

Since the site is located in a highly sensitive ecological environment, the plan envisioned self-regulating systems whenever possible for water and energy supply and waste management. A solar-powered pump provides water for extensively planted areas. The orientation of all buildings is designed for maximum exploitation of the solar energy at 3,700 m above sea level. The school complex is divided into a 3 x 3 grid pattern. In elevation, the plan – whose design is a symbolic interpretation of a mandala – is based on the image of villages or monasteries in the region. Student residences are located on the north side of the complex. The classrooms are rotated by 30° from south to east in order to fully exploit the morning sun. On the whole, the buildings are designed to capture the energy gained by solar radiation during the day in order to utilize the stored heat in the evening and overnight. The external bathrooms and WCs are ventilated with the help of a solar-

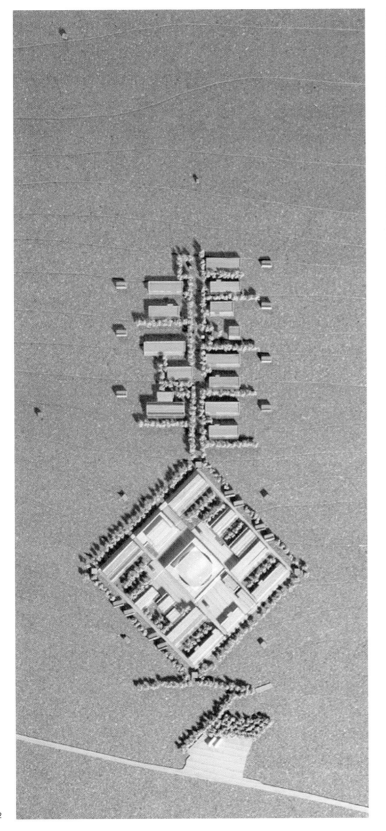

2

3

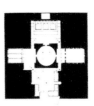

4

1 View of first completed
  section with preschool
  and elementary school

2 Site plan of entire
  complex, not to scale

3 Photovoltaic installation
  for water supply

4 Ground plan based
  on the diagram of a
  mandala

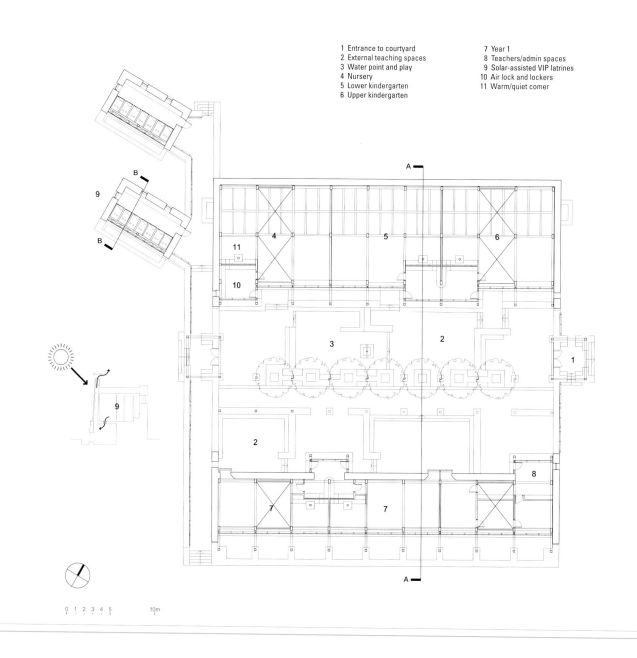

1 Entrance to courtyard
2 External teaching spaces
3 Water point and play
4 Nursery
5 Lower kindergarten
6 Upper kindergarten
7 Year 1
8 Teachers/admin spaces
9 Solar-assisted VIP latrines
10 Air lock and lockers
11 Warm/quiet comer

0 1 2 3 4 5   10m

5 Plan and section with
daycare, kindergarten
and preschool (top)
with common courtyard
for outdoor classes as
well as elementary
school with classrooms
(bottom). The WCs and
bathrooms are separate
from the main struc-
ture, located along the
side. Plan not to scale.

5

6

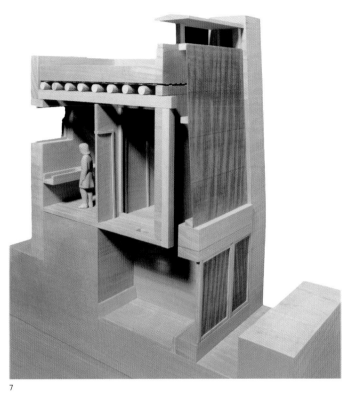

7

powered system. The student residences are heated by means of Trombe walls. This type of wall, named after its French inventor Felix Trombe, is constructed of solid masonry with a black, heat-absorbing surface and a glass facade in front of a 100-150 mm cavity. The absorbed heat is stored in the masonry and penetrates gradually into the interior. Narrow openings at the top and bottom in the cavity between glass and wall are linked to the heat-requiring space. They promote convection and increase the efficiency of the system. The living areas are enclosed by a kind of double facade. The building materials are sourced from the immediate surroundings: stone, clay rendering, clay bricks, wood and grass. The granite stones were gathered from the building site or the immediate vicinity. They are dressed and sorted and then walled up, keeping the consumption of valuable clay to a minimum. For the roof sealing, however, clay is indispensable. The exterior walls of the buildings are composed of stone, rendered

with clay on the inside. The internal partition walls are built of clay bricks. A separate structure of heavy timber beams provides safety in case of an earthquake. Massive wooden joist ceilings support the traditional clay ceiling insulated with mineral wool. On the south side, daylight penetrates into the classrooms through large windows. Priority was given to natural cross-ventilation, passive shading and glare-free light distribution. Sustainable successes in development aid projects can only be achieved by immersing oneself in the local traditions of building and living.

6   WC and bathroom building with solar-assisted exhaust air: solar radiation is absorbed via a dark-painted galvanized steel sheet, the resulting ascending convection current assists the ventilation of the septic pit.

7   Model illustrating and explaining the details

8

9

Nr. 5: Temperatures in class room and in hostel room 1

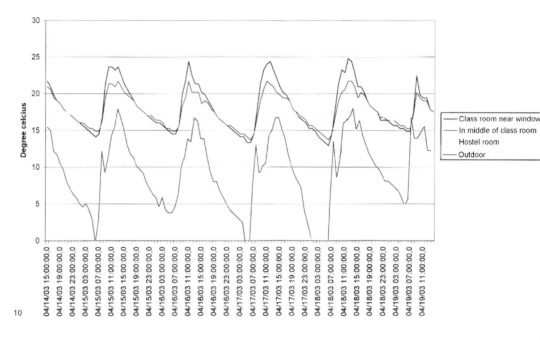

Degree celcius

Class room near window
In middle of class room
Hostel room
Outdoor

10

11

8 Children in traditional dress

9 Detail showing a window constructed according to local building traditions

10 Temperature curve in classroom and student residence, measured between March 14 and March 19, 2004, proves the effectiveness of the chosen building structure.

11 Children resting during a break – the room-defining load-bearing timber structure ensures safety in case of an earthquake.

12 View into one of the brightly lit group rooms

Adjustable Daylight Technology:
Art Museum in Riehen

Architects:
Renzo Piano Building Workshop, Paris/Genoa

1

Selected data:

Completion
1st construction phase:
1997, 2nd construction
phase: 2000
GFA: 6,225 m²
GRV: 46,450 m³

Since the energy consumption depends on a wide range of parameters in this case, these data are not included. The system is ideally adaptable to the relevant requirements for changing exhibitions and the number of visitors.

U-value glass roof:
0.60 W/m²K
U-value exterior wall ground floor:
0.24 W/m²K
U-value exterior wall basement:
0.60 W/m²K
U-value basement floor:
0.40 W/m²K

Without a doubt the art museum in Riehen can be mentioned in the same breath as the Kimbell Art Museum in Forth Worth by Louis I. Kahn and the Menil Collection in Houston. All three museums are impressive for the rigor of the structure on the outside and the equally convincing lighting strategy in the interior. Each of these buildings perfectly fulfils its intended task in complete harmony with its environment and is nevertheless an unmistakable formal prototype.

One of the unique features of the Beyeler Museum in Riehen is its status as a so-called "green building," despite the fact that the brief was focused first and foremost on creating an ideal environment for exhibiting art. Energy efficiency was therefore not nearly as prevalent among the design priorities than one might assume. It emerged during the development of the technical detail, indeed in some aspects only during the technical adjustments once the building was operational. The extraordinarily sensitive treatment of daylight was at the core of these deliberations. As so often in Renzo Piano's work, a preliminary sketch already contained the fundamental idea behind the design: "filtering" direct sunlight through a series of *brises-soleil* comprised of inclined glass panes. A climate buffer, the transparency of which can be adjusted,

separates the outside world and the exhibition space. All that remained was to devise the technical solutions that would translate this idea into reality.

The elongated structure is placed in an efficient manner parallel to the road long the edge of the lot, automatically screening the park from traffic noise. The exhibition spaces are divided across three parallel axes. While the longitudinal sides are fully enclosed, the spaces at the end walls can be extended with a view into the park and the landscape beyond when the need arises. The sculptures in the park complement the permanent exhibition. Transitions from inside to outside are fluid. In the evenings, visitors are afforded a glimpse of the interior to whet their appetite. Access is centralized and this makes it possible to separate or connect the permanent exhibition with temporary exhibitions or events. A long, glass-fronted gallery facing east offers a tranquil space for contemplation after one has experienced the exhibition. The unobstructed view of the landscape beyond sustains this quality. At no point does the reduced "neutral" material canon enter into competition with the exponents. The enormous stream of visitors has confirmed the success of the building in form and function.

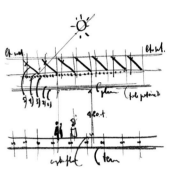

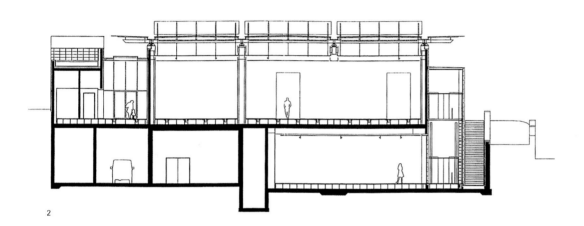

2

4

The functions are clearly legible in the section reproduced here. Following a narrow auxiliary zone, the main lobby, which is open at both ends, leads into the series of exhibition rooms. A 12-m extension realized in the second construction phase was added in such a natural manner that it blends perfectly with the original structure. The longitudinal walls are of solid concrete construction only on the outside and at the ends; they are faced in natural stone. In the interior, they consist of braced reinforced concrete supports and multi-layered plasterboard shells amenable to the integration of technical installations. The system chosen here offers the greatest degree of flexibility in terms

of transparency and floor plans for large spaces along two internal axes. The floor plan is equally suited to pre-determined tours through traveling exhibitions or linkages between individual rooms and the spaces housing the permanent collection. The orientation, which had been specified in the brief, is achieved in all areas through the clear building structure and the constant contact with the outside.

In addition to the service and maintenance rooms, the basement houses a large multifunctional room for traveling exhibitions, lectures and similar events.

Direct daylight only has an influence on the atmosphere in the exhibition space in those

3

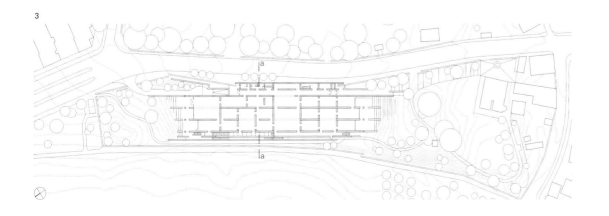

1 South elevation
2 Cross-section, not to scale
3 Site plan, not to scale
4 Renzo Piano: sketch for daylight system, 1993

5

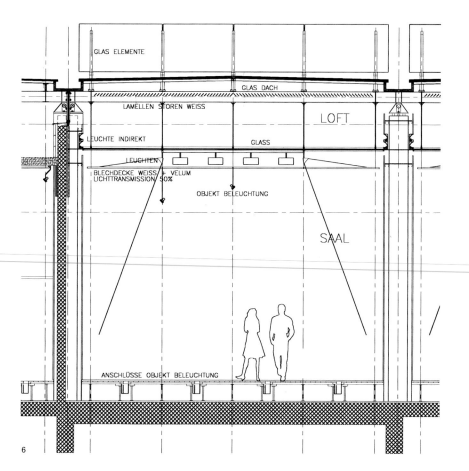

GLAS ELEMENTE

GLAS DACH

LAMELLEN STOREN WEISS

LOFT

LEUCHTE INDIREKT — GLASS

LEUCHTEN

BLECHDECKE WEISS + VELUM
LICHTTRANSMISSION 50%

OBJEKT BELEUCHTUNG

SAAL

ANSCHLÜSSE OBJEKT BELEUCHTUNG

6

5 External sun protection
  with white-enamelled
  glass panes on an
  incline

6 Section through one of
  the exhibition rooms
  with sun protection,
  installation space and
  suspended ceiling

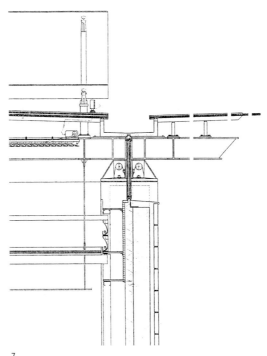

7

8

rooms that are open to the outside. In the core of the building, the light is maintained virtually without fluctuations with the help of a cleverly designed control system.

An array of *brises-soleil* comprised of inclined, parallel glass panes that seems to float above the building filters out the direct sun. To this end, the undersides of the glass panes are coated in white enamel. This highly effective sun protection was optimized during the planning stage by means of computer simulation. The diffuse northern light can penetrate freely to the next filter level above the exhibition spaces. Underneath the *brises-soleil* lies the actual upper completion: a glass area composed of three shallow saddle roofs. Rainwater is collected by gutters made of steel sheeting. These gutters are aligned with the wall axes and run the entire length of the building. Immediately below the glass roof, at the height of the girder grid, light is filtered by means of adjustable louvers linked to Lux sensors that are mounted on the glass roofs at regular intervals for this purpose. The installation space beneath the louvers terminates in an accessible laminated safety-glass floor. The exposed underside of the suspended ceiling is composed of

7 Detail of roof and roof edge, not to scale
Components, from top to bottom:
Sun protection, toughened safety glass, white enamelled on the underside, 12 mm insulating glazing with toughened safety glass, 16 mm cavity, 18 mm laminated safety glass, ceramic printed and alarm-proof in thermally separated aluminum sections, load-bearing girder grid, filtered light through automatically driven louvers, installation cavity, laminated safety glass, accessible for maintenance, "velum" fabric-covered metal grid

8 Longitudinal facade with roof overhang

197

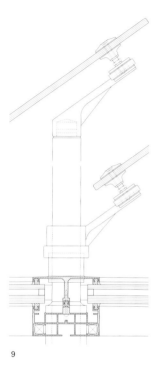

9

10

the so-called "velum": a fabric-covered metal grid ceiling. In combination with the control mechanisms, daylight can be regulated – and combined with artificial light when needed – to such a degree that the natural changes in light over the course of a day are no longer perceptible. These are excellent conditions for exhibiting art, although they may induce a sense of fatigue in visitors. However, visitors need only step into the winter garden or into one of the spaces overlooking the park to experience a beneficial variation in light.

The interior climate can also be ideally regulated by the layered roof components described above. The space between the glass roof and the accessible suspended ceiling accommodates all the components relevant to the security and lighting installations; it also acts as a highly effective climate buffer. The climate and ventilation concept was also optimized with the help of simulation models. The tremendous popularity of the museum put the climate technology to a hard test. Within one-and-a-half to two years, however, the required air volumes and hence the energy requirements of the building were drastically reduced by 30 to 40 percent in the context of optimizing the energy systems

without diminishing the quality of the exhibition parameters. The technology is virtually invisible in the interior. The sensors for the climate controls are hidden in the walls behind discrete openings covered with perforated sheet-metal plates.

On the narrow sides of the building, the glass-covered load-bearing grid projects beyond the building edges, creating shaded outdoor zones. The projecting glass roofs on the longitudinal sides protect the natural stone walls from the elements. The entire roof seems to float as a result of the slightly upward curving form. In this manner, a technical building component serves to create a unique aesthetic. Indeed, it becomes the signature of the museum.

9   Sun protection fastening with aluminum elements and point fasteners, not to scale

10 View of *brises-soleil*, gutter and roof edge

11 View from exhibition space into park

12 Elevation (page 200)

11

ENERGY-EFFICIENT DETAIL DESIGN AND TECHNICAL COMPLETION

ENERGY-EFFICIENT DETAIL DESIGN
AND TECHNICAL COMPLETION

Measures and Materials

Point of Departure

The building skin acts as a kind of clothing for human beings. It protects them from extreme temperatures and climate fluctuations. The more efficiently this function is fulfilled the lower is the energy consumption for heating or air conditioning. Technical components and construction should therefore be harmonized in every detail with the requirements determined by use and climate.

The heating requirement of a building is largely determined by the heat losses through the building skin. The transmission heat losses of a building component are proportional to its area and its thermal transmittance. The first factor can be reduced by means of compact design, the second through qualitative and homogeneous thermal insulation. The quality of thermal insulation is especially important for elements that cover a large area.

The building skin is usually composed of transparent and non-transparent building components. As a result of their high U-values, glass areas have much higher heat transmission losses than non-transparent building components. Windows must fulfil a variety of different functions, such as natural ventilation and lighting, visual contact with the outside and architectural articulation or accents. At the same time, these components – if they are correctly planned and designed – also provide the basis for the passive use of solar energy.

Glazed Areas

The quality of the frame and the glass are important for the construction of glazed areas. The glass industry has made tremendous progress in recent years. Triple glazing with gas filling and special surface coatings achieve excellent U-values. These types of glass are barely 25 percent more expensive than conventional thermal panes and the prices are falling even further as the components are coming increasingly into use. Even with conventional thermal panes, the frame was the weaker link by comparison to the glass. For this reason, the good U-values achieved with triple glazing demanded that frames, too, be improved accordingly.

The response came with the development of frame structures with integrated layers of thermal insulation (usually PUR although other materials, such as cork, have also been employed). These are far more expensive than the frames of earlier windows. Moreover, the thickness of triple glazing and hence the increased weight of windows where such panes are employed call for deeper cross sections in the frame, a factor that is seen as a disadvantage in terms of design and aesthetics. In such cases, large uniform window areas can reduce the overall requirement for frame components. Differentiating between fixed glazing and carefully planned opening lights also makes it possible to restrict the use of wider frames to a lesser number of elements. Post and rail facades with few adjustable elements can be combined much more successfully in a cost-efficient manner with triple glazing in harmony with slender load-bearing sections.

Integration with the remaining facade sections in order to prevent thermal bridges and to ensure airtightness is especially important in the context of improved window standards. As most blower-door tests demonstrate, most permeable spots in the building skin are usually located in this area.

Walls

Non-transparent building components must often fulfil a variety of requirements at the same time. Some forms of construction and materials can respond to different requirements: translucent thermal insulation is one such solution, which has insulating properties while allowing the ingress of light. Problems arise when the same constructional principle or the same material must meet requirements that spring from fundamentally oppositional physical principles. Employing one and the same material, for example, for both thermal insulation and thermal storage tends to lead to compromises that are less than ideal for either function. In this case, the right approach is to employ materials or designs that are characterized by differing properties in a complementary manner. High U-values can be achieved by combining a light form of construction for exterior walls with light thermal insulation materials across the entire wall cross section. This design relies on

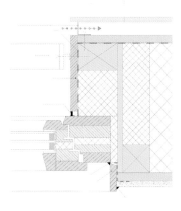

1

2

1 Wind-proof joint window to facade: special attention is required for energy-efficient detail design in this area.

2 Student residence in Wuppertal, Architektur Contor Müller Schlüter, 2000/2003, (see p. 116). Insulation is carried across the window frame, thus reducing the thermal bridge.

3

the thermal storage capacity of internal building components to compensate for the temperature fluctuations. The multi-layered design of the external skin also allows for the solid wall components with thermal storage function to be placed on the inside, while the insulating layer itself can be installed on the outside. An external, homogeneous thermal insulation across the entire building skin also helps to avoid weakness in the skin in terms of thermal properties. In an energy-efficient structure, the joints between building components deserve particular attention, especially with regard to preventing the formation of thermal bridges.

Insulating Materials
The trend in developing insulating materials is to focus on specific applications rather than covering a wide range of applications with a single product or system. Many of the newly developed product and systems are based on biotechnology. This science takes nature as a model in order to respond to specific requirements by technical means that emulate nature. There are countless similarities between technical and natural forms of development. Thus, translucent thermal insulation is comparable to the fur of a polar bear. Despite the analogies in form and function, there is usually a lack of correspondence in terms of internal structure. Here, nature is far more efficient: it functions using the minimum of energy (usually a temperature of no more than 40°), operates at a higher performance ratio and is fully recyclable.

Translucent insulating materials, or TIM, combine the excellent insulating properties of the material with transparency for solar radiation. Installed in front of a solid wall, it allows the wall to collect solar radiation and release it into the interior after some time has elapsed. This decreases energy consumption and shifts the effective balance of the walls toward the positive side of the scale.
This system evolved out of the Trombe wall in which glazing installed in front of a solid wall serves as a passive solar collector and prevents heat losses. In cold climates, the insulation provided by the glazing is insufficient to achieve a positive energy balance for the wall as a whole.

The greatest obstacle to a broader application of TIM is the high costs of these materials arising from the transparent protective layer and the regulating components such as sun protection in summer. Placing the TIM elements in a post-and-rail facade simplifies the frame construction. Polycarbonate panels can be used as cladding. With composite thermal insulation systems with a translucent coating there is no need for protective glazing or, depending on the total area covered, sun protection.

Honeycomb insulating boards are similar to TIM in appearance and to some degree in function. Once again a glazed external surface provides protection from the elements; in contrast to TIM, however, the honeycomb insulating boards do not allow light to penetrate into the interior. They absorb the heat and act as a buffer for the underlying structure. Depending on the solar altitude (winter/summer), solar radiation can penetrate to a greater or lesser depth into the honeycomb structure and warm it accordingly. The horizontal elements in the honeycomb structure also prevent convective heat losses, thus increasing insulating properties of the material. And finally, all material components of this system are recyclable.

Due to a thermal conductivity reduced by a factor of 10 (Lambda-value approx. 0.004 W/mK), vacuum insulation achieves extremely low U-values in a space and material-efficient manner. The core of this newly developed material, usually microporous silicic acid, is wrapped in an envelope composed of glass, metal or metal-coated synthetic membranes and evacuated, which prevents heat transfer through the material. Certification for these materials is still outstanding. Permission must be requested on a case-by-case basis.
The products used in construction thus far are designed as panels with a thickness of a few centimeters. Some of the problems in the practical application are related to solving the issue of thermal bridges at the panel joints and the care with which the material has to be handled. Any damage to the delicate protective membranes destroys the vacuum and thus the high insulating properties of the material. Mechanical fixing is only possible along the edge of

3 House Estevez in Mendoza, Argentina, C. de Rosa, 1985. The Trombe wall as solar facade represents the original principle of translucent thermal insulation.

4 Components of a solar facade with translucent thermal insulation.

5 Translucent thermal insulation

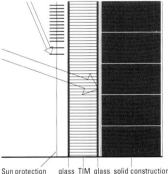

Sun protection   glass TIM glass solid construction wall

4   5

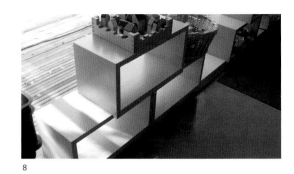

8

the panels. To protect the panels against damage during the assembly and installation, they are often covered in a harder protective layer. Manufacturing tolerances in the dimensions of the panels or the protective coating as well as the adhesive fixing of the membranes along the edges result in weaknesses along the panel joints. These areas are frequently bridged with conventional insulating materials, which are insufficient because they are not thick enough. For this reason the panels are usually covered in an additional insulating layer, which also protects the panel surface. Thus far these panels are primarily used in areas where the necessary thickness of the insulating layer cannot be achieved with conventional materials or is uneconomical. These applications include the floors of existing buildings with limited height, patios above heated spaces with a barrier-free transition between interior and exterior, heritage buildings that have been placed under conservation orders, as well as building components such as entrance doors or parapet panels in glazed facades. In the facade application, the reduced construction depth makes it possible to increase the potential usable area, which can be a financial advantage especially in multi-story buildings in downtown cores.

Thermal Storage
Energy requirements are minimized by building skins with good thermal insulation and compact building form. Solar energy can cover much of the requirements that remain. On bright days and above all during the transitional seasons, the passively collected solar energy cannot be utilized in full. Overheating does occur and the excess heat must be ventilated or solar incidence prevented in the first place. The better the thermal storage capacity of the internal storage mass, the less heat is lost. The thermal storage mass also allows for the regulation of temperature fluctuations in the rooms in summer as well as in winter. This is where the risk of overheating, especially as a result of internal heat loads, is at its greatest. In combination with overnight ventilation, the thermal storage mass can also serve as a "cold storage." The thermal storage mass alone is insufficient, however; other design parameters, such as sun protection, must not be neglected.

6

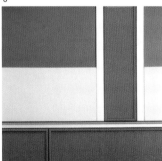

7

9

To increase the thermal storage capacity in the interior of the building, phase change materials, or PCM, have recently been introduced as latent heat storage components. A latent heat storage component absorbs a great amount of thermal energy to effect a change in the aggregate state (liquifaction) of the material while maintaining the temperature of the material. When the temperature drops, this (stored) energy is released during the reverse process of crystallization. Water is perhaps the most familiar latent storage element, used in the form of ice for cooling and refrigeration.

Building applications, however, require materials whose phase change occurs within the range of room temperatures. These properties are currently achieved with salt and paraffin as PCM. Phase change materials are available in a wide range of formats. They are used for solar walls with high storage capacity in the form of pouches, containers or double-webbed panels. They can be integrated into floors or ceilings in the form of napped sheeting. And micro-encapsulation makes it possible to add the material to plaster.

These materials are capable of storing a large amount of heat even when temperature fluctuations are minor. The heat storage is entirely passive in nature, without any additional energy supply. The most important advantage is the reduced weight and the diminished space requirements. Just 2 cm of gypsum plaster with a 30 percent admixture of PCM equals the average diurnal thermal storage capacity 18 cm of

6 Office complex in Duisburg, SchusterArchitekten, 2002, detail of facade with honeycomb insulation board (see p. 134).

7 same as 6: Facade detail

8 Energy-efficient renovation and conversion of a 1970s kindergarten in Lochham, Pollok + Gonzalo, 2003. Vacuum insulation panels as insulation of the floor without basement.

9 same as 8

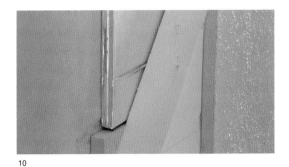

10

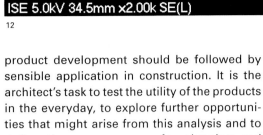

ISE 5.0kV 34.5mm ×2.00k SE(L)   20.0um

12

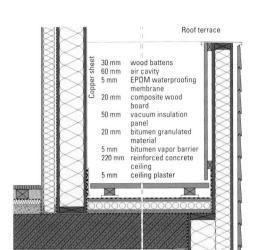

30 mm	wood battens
60 mm	air cavity
5 mm	EPDM waterproofing membrane
20 mm	composite wood board
50 mm	vacuum insulation panel
20 mm	bitumen granulated material
5 mm	bitumen vapor barrier
220 mm	reinforced concrete ceiling
5 mm	ceiling plaster

Copper sheet

Roof terrace

11

concrete. The material can also make a considerable contribution to compensating temperature fluctuations. However, most residential buildings already have the necessary building mass. PCM do not make a considerable difference in this area, provided the building has good thermal insulation and is subject to low temperature fluctuations. The opposite is true for office buildings: in summer, the use of PCM can go a long way toward preventing overheating from solar incidence or internal heat loads, especially in buildings realized with a lightweight form of construction. Targeted night ventilation completes the regenerative cycle and evacuates the heat stored during the day.

Future Goals
Researchers and the industrial sector are working feverishly to develop new components and building systems. The phase of innovation and product development should be followed by sensible application in construction. It is the architect's task to test the utility of the products in the everyday, to explore further opportunities that might arise from this analysis and to define the consequences for planning and design.

It would be even better to take on the role of forerunner and to formulate requirements for further development from a technical, structural and aesthetic perspective. We should take a critical look at the passion for innovation. It is important to define the real needs before developing new approaches:

"The opinion that everything that is technologically doable should actually be done is a childish dream of omnipotence, touching in a child but criminal in an adult. This opinion is above all an expression of a fundamentally non-technical mentality. Technology is the science of providing means for a purpose. Where there is no purpose, the means is unnecessary. Anyone who fails to take the purpose into consideration acts counter to the spirit of sensible technology."(1)

An overly technocratic approach to specific issues tends to lead to a one-sided understanding of architectural interactions. This type of development may be justified in the case of optimizing a system or developing a specific solution. It is dangerous, however, if it leads to the indiscriminate optimization of individual aspects in the overall concept and design. Creating a design is a complex process. It requires recognition of interactions and setting priorities. The integrative role of the architect is vitally important in this context.

10 Apartment and office building in Munich, Martin Pool, 2004. Vacuum panels as composite thermal insulation system (see p. 62).

11 Housing complex in Wolfurth: insulating the patio above a heated space with vacuum components allows for a seamless transition between interior and exterior (in: Krapmeier, Drössler: CEPHEUS, Springer, 2001).

12 Plaster rendering with micro capsules: electron scan microscope image.

(1) Carl Friedrich von Weizsäcker: Bewusstseinswandel, Munich 1991

15

Ventilation Concepts and Energy Systems
Andreas Lackenbauer

Ventilation Concepts

Mechanical ventilation systems combine hygienic and basic physical requirements with energy efficiency and should be used wherever conventional window ventilation is insufficient because of user requirements (e.g., school buildings), structural configurations (e.g., rooms located in the core) or high energy requirements (e.g., passive house standard).

Although window ventilation as a simple and proven approach can be part of a sustainable building solution, it is important to remember that it is largely "accidental" because of thermal lift and wind pressure, and also requires a very high degree of attention and consistency on the part of the users.

In housing, the flow direction within the unit changes as wind directions shift. Warm humid air from kitchen and bathroom can collect as condensation in cooler rooms or in permeable building components.

In office buildings the requirements for ventilation are chiefly determined by the internal floor plan. Individual offices can be comfortably ventilated by opening a window. Open-plan offices with a large percentage of work areas located at a greater distance from the facade require at least some mechanical ventilation. Large open-plan offices require both mechanical ventilation and supply air systems because of the high density of occupation and the different room zones. In all cases, savings can only be achieved when mechanical ventilation systems are combined with heat recovery.

Ventilation Zones

When mechanical ventilation systems are chosen, the building must be divided into zones. This is a planning principle aimed at ensuring that all rooms and room areas receive identical amounts of air change. Every room in a residential or office unit is allocated to one of the following ventilation zones:

Outgoing air zone: drawing off spent air from rooms that are characterized by high odor, humidity or contaminant loads (e.g., kitchen, bathroom). The extraction of the spent air results in a slight negative pressure of 4 to 10 Pascal in these rooms.

Supply air zone: supplying fresh air to living room, studies and bedrooms. In pure extraction systems this is achieved as a result of the slight negative pressure created by slipstream elements in the facade. In ventilation systems, supply air must be blown in with a slight positive pressure.

Overflow zone: areas and rooms that are located between the supply and outgoing air zones in such a manner that they are sufficiently ventilated without individual outside-, supply- or extraction vents (e.g., corridors, dining nook in the kitchen).

Ventilation Systems with Heat-Recovery

Ventilation systems in energy-efficient buildings are usually designed as supplementary systems rather than complete air-conditioning systems. Such systems can neither humidify nor cool and require additional window ventilation. In the interest of quality assurance, all ventilation systems should meet the so-called passive house standard. The criteria established for this standard not only improve the energy efficiency of the system but also its economic efficiency over the course of the lifecycle. The principal criteria are:

Supply air comfort: the minimum supply air temperature must be higher than 16.5°C.

Heat-recovery: the effective readiness for supply heat must be greater than 75 percent.

Power efficiency: the power absorption of the ventilation system must be less than 0.45 W/m³/h of distributed air.

Room air hygiene: external air filters and extraction air filters are required to meet this criterion.

Sound: the sound pressure level in living areas must not exceed 25dB(A).

Additional requirements for the ventilation equipment are related to aspects such as airtightness, frost protection, thermal insulation and adjustability.

Depending on use, building type and air volume, a variety of different heat exchange models are used. In housing, supply and extracted air must be strictly separated: cross-reverse-flow plate heat exchangers are predominantly

13

14

16

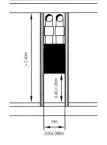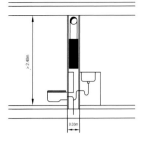

17 IN STORAGE ROOM   WALL-INTEGRATED

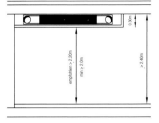

CEILING-INTEGRATED

used for this application. Rotating heat exchangers are often more economical in large public buildings or office buildings (roughly 3 000 m³/h and more). Composite by-pass systems can be employed when there is very little installation space; the disadvantage of these systems is that they have a lower degree of readiness for supply heat and should only be used in combination with other pre-warming systems (earth pipes, geothermal systems).

Ventilation Systems:
Centralized or Decentralized
Centralized ventilation systems supply several units and allow for user-specific settings for air volume and temperature by decentralized volume flow regulators and heating registers if needed.

When advantageously arranged, centralized ventilation systems can be more efficient than decentralized or individual ventilation units for single rooms or apartments even in cases where only a few user units are supplied. The key lies in the placement of the central ventilation system. Since rooms within the heated volume are usually too valuable to be used as utility spaces, the central ventilation system is commonly installed on the roof or in the basement. From those locations, air is transported to vertical shafts and distributed from these into the individual units. Centralized ventilation systems must be incorporated into the building concept from the outset.

Some of the key parameters in support of decentralized installations are the frequently expressed wishes for fresh air intake directly through the adjacent facade, for simplifying the integration of technical systems in the building, for reducing the fire protection requirements and for improving flexibility in terms of furnishing individual rooms and user zones. However, maintenance costs are considerably higher for decentralized systems, which can moreover result in increased energy consumption if malfunctions go unnoticed.

In housing, compact ventilation units must be installed in an area that is separated from the living areas for sound protection and for aesthetic reasons. Room-specific devices are not recommended in the interest of energy efficiency (ventilation requirements kitchen, bath-

room). In individual offices, decentralized units are integrated in the balustrade or double floors, whereby the return heat value of the heat exchanger must be sufficiently high.

Heating and Cooling Concepts: Energy Carriers
Fossil fuels and conventional heat generators are still the most common heating systems on the market. Fossil fuels can be employed if the heating requirements of a building are extremely low (e.g., passive house) or if the parameters do not allow for the use of an alternative system. The following applies to all systems: the relevant fuel should be utilized as efficiently as possible and pollutant emissions should be kept to a minimum; condensing boilers are recommended for liquid and gaseous fuels.

Electrical energy is the highest grade of available energy carriers. In conventional generation, three times the amount of primary energy is required for thermodynamic reasons to generate one kilowatt hour of current. Electricity should therefore be substituted whenever possible by other energy carriers for heat generation and should be employed for heating purposes only in a few exceptions where heating requirements are very low (e.g., frost protection, heat pump in a passive house).

Power-Heat Coupling (PHC)
According to forecasts published by the Fraunhofer Society, power generation will be decentralized in the future. "Large power plants are gradually being replaced by a complex network of combined heat and power plants (CHP), wind power generators, photovoltaic installations and fuel cells."

By comparison to conventional supply, the CHP offers tangible advantages in terms of energy efficiency. Thus the simultaneous generation of power and heat can make a considerable contribution toward CO_2-reduction. The savings in primary energy are up to 40 percent.

CHPs are most efficiently operated with natural gas. Heating oil, rapeseed oil or rape methyl esther (RME) can also be used for fuel. Higher investment costs and more frequent maintenance requirements translate into considerably higher operating costs.

13 Apartment building Am Ackermannbogen, A2-Architekten, NEST GmbH, 2004. Placement of supply and exhaust air openings on the facade.

14 same as 13

15 Office and apartment building in Schwarzach, Vorarlberg, Lenz-Kaufmann, 1999. Adjustable supply air vents (see p. 122).

16 Apartment and office building in Munich, Martin Pool, 2004. Supply- and exhaust-air grille (see p. 62).

17 Options for installing decentralized ventilation systems

18 Blower-door test: the airtightness of the building must be tested when controlled ventilation is used.

18

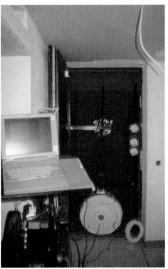

20

19 Housing complex in
    Munich, H2R, 2001.
    Solar collectors as roof
    above suspended balco-
    nies also function as sun
    protection (see p. 56).

20 Office and apartment
    building in Schwarzach,
    Vorarlberg, Lenz-
    Kaufmann, 1999. Solar
    collectors integrated into
    the patio balustrade
    (see p. 122)

Roughly one third of the transformed energy is available as power. When such plants are correctly designed, scaled and integrated, much of the generated power can be used first hand. The high power supply costs, which can be avoided in this manner and the tax advantages for power-heat coupling plants make it possible to amortize the investment for the installation within a few years.

In conventional office and residential buildings, CHPs are run in parallel operation; emergency power supply is not possible with this type of system for technical reasons (asynchronous generator).

Regenerative Fuels (Biomass)

Regenerative fuels are solid (wood, straw), liquid (vegetable oil) or gaseous (biogas) and the amount of CO_2 they release during combustion does not exceed the amount they absorbed from the atmosphere during their growth. With sustainable management, this results in a closed emission cycle.

Solid fuels in the form of cut wood, wood chips or pellets manufactured from untreated timber remnants are the primary choice for heat generation. Pellet-fired systems are a sensible choice for single-family houses and for smaller plants up to roughly 100 kW.

Like heating oil, the fuel is delivered in trailer trucks; unique characteristics are the flexibility with regard to loading, feeding and problem-free combustion. Wood chips are available directly from the forestry and timber-processing sector. Due to the somewhat more elaborate loading and clearing-out processes, they are more commonly employed in agricultural operations and district heat plants.

19

Given its many uses as food, fuel or lubricant, vegetable oil is too valuable to be used for heating. It can be used for power generation in CHPs.

Solar Power and Photovoltaics

Thermal solar plants can heat water for heating and hot water supply by means of solar collectors and store this resource in thermal buffers over longer periods of time. Such installations should provide at least 1m² of collector area and 100 l of buffer storage volume per 30 m² of gross story area. The systems should be scaled to minimal requirements and simply designed in order to minimize idle periods, downtimes and the costs of upkeep. Large systems for potable water heating or pre-heating in heating grids can supply solar heat at a cost of 0.10 to 0.13 €/kWh far more cost-effectively than small installations.

Photovoltaic systems are employed to generate power. They are operated as stand-alone systems or tied into an existing grid. Batteries are required for stand-alone systems, for example for mountain chalets or decentralized supply for technical units. Systems that are tied into an existing grid utilize the public grid for storage. Whenever the power generated exceeds the power used, the excess energy is fed into the grid via current inverters. In the case of systems that are coupled with the grid, the photovoltaic installation does not feed the building itself or other building systems; the purpose in this case is essentially to utilize roof areas.

Heat Pump and Refrigerating Machines

Heat pumps utilize the temperature contained in a local heat source (air, groundwater, soil) and raise it to the temperature required for space heating usually by means of power-operated compressors. The higher and the more constant the temperature of the heat source is, the less power is needed to achieve the required target. Heat pumps can be used in energy-efficient buildings if the heating water temperature is low as a result of area heating (<28°C) while the groundwater, or the soil, act as a heat source with a constant high temperature (>10°C). Favorable operating conditions will deliver an average of 4.5 kWh heat from one kilowatt hour of power. However, the greatly increased effort for heat generation and heat transfer is neither economical nor energy-efficient in pure heating applications. Heat pumps become an interesting proposition only when area heating and groundwater/soil can also be utilized to cool the building.

For cooling in summer, the excess heat of the building can be diverted directly or indirectly via a refrigeration machine to the ground. The most comfortable form of cooling via radiant exchange with low temperature differences is also the most efficient in terms of energy use. In the case of direct cooling, power is only required to dis-

tribute or circulate the primary cycle. Although the cooling requirements by means of refrigerating machines are higher, coefficients of more than 5.0 kW cooling energy per kW power can still be attained.

Cooling

In the Central European climate, cooling is most common in office and administration buildings or in public gathering places.

Cooling is required in the case of high internal heat loads linked to the use of a building or high external loads as a result of too many transparent components and too few shaded external surfaces.

The principle of adiabatic cooling has surpassed mechanical air-conditioning systems in the field of climate control in buildings. Adiabatic cooling systems such as chilled ceiling, building component cooling (concrete core activation) and downdraft cooling offer far greater user comfort and acceptance and make it possible to reduce the air change to the hygienic minimum – another important factor for comfort. Chilled ceilings are large cooling surfaces attached to the underside of the ceiling. The heat sources in the room transfer excess heat to the cooler enclosure surfaces, either directly as radiation or indirectly by convection. The ceilings absorb sound and can be integrated into acoustic concepts. They must be harmonized with the interior design and the lighting scheme. Chilled ceilings are simple to regulate. Energy consumption can be tracked for individual users. Chilled ceilings can also be retrofitted or integrated step-by-step into existing buildings. Depending on the water temperature, these surfaces can be utilized for cooling or heating. Utilizing this dual function obviates the need for a separate system with radiators.

PVC pipes filled with running water are concreted into the concrete ceiling for concrete core activation. The ceiling structure, which is cooled in its entirety, functions in the same manner as the chilled ceiling described above; however, due to the large thermal storage mass, this system also allows for thermal phase delays from peak daytime temperatures to cooler hours at night. This makes it possible to reduce peak loads and utilize overnight re-cooling systems where applicable.

In energy-efficient buildings, thermo-active ceilings can cover a large portion of the required space heating and some cases even provide all the necessary heating. The required water temperatures range from 18°C in summer to 26°C in winter and can be provided via geothermal systems. Concrete core activation systems are far more efficient than chilled ceiling systems in simple structures.

Due to thermal inertia and the upward and downward flow of heat, temperatures cannot be regulated for individual rooms. In winter, the heat is transferred in a self-regulating manner. When the ceiling temperature is kept at a constant of 23°C, the transition between heating and cooling is seamless. Once the room temperature falls below 23°C, the room is heated via the ceiling; as soon as the room temperature rises above 23°C, the room is cooled.

With some restrictions, floor and wall heating systems can also be employed as thermo-active systems.

Heating Systems

Given the decreased need for heating, the requirements on the heating system are lower than in conventional buildings. The basic thermal comfort in a house with good insulation and ventilation is high, and the remaining heating requirement is low. While conventional heat generators are always possible options under these conditions, they are by no means necessary. In this case, the key questions with regard to building systems are: which areas can be simplified and which systems can be utilized in multiple ways and thus reduce the overall effort?

Forced-air heating: forced-air heating as a monovalent spatial heating system is a viable option for rooms that are in constant use and have very low heating requirements. Excessive air change, especially in winter with very low outside air humidity, leads to dry internal air conditions. Forced-air heating should be employed in residential and administration buildings only if these meet passive house standards. It is only in this building type that the low remaining heat requirement can be covered with the hygienically required amount of air.

21 Housing development in Affoltern am Albis, Metron Architektur, 1998. Biomass (wood) as supplementary heating source (see p. 50).
22 Office and workshops in Weidling, Reinberg, 2004. Integration of photovoltaic panels into the facade (see p. 158).

22

23 Apartment and office
building in Munich,
Martin Pool, 2004.
Drastically reduced
energy requirements
lead to minimized
radiator dimensions
(see p. 62).

24 Average speed of cold
air drop on window
surfaces dependent on
the U-value and win-
dow height: blue 1.2 m,
red 1.8 m, black 3.0 m
(after Feist, 1998).

25 (overleaf) Office and
apartment building in
Schwarzach, Vorarlberg,
Lenz-Kaufman, 1999.
Office interior: the
installation lines are
concentrated in the
central corridor
(see p. 206).

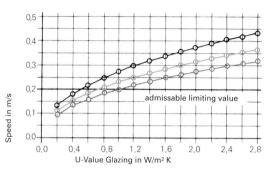

24

23

Even in passive houses, forced-air heating systems are usually complemented by additional
heating systems in individual rooms. Bathrooms
in residential buildings are usually equipped
with individual radiators because of considerably higher room air temperatures and fluctuating times of use. For large glass areas and in
the entrance areas of lobbies, one should ana-
lyze the need for installing additional radiators
or radiant heating. Forced-air heating systems
are quick response heating systems. The positioning of the outlet vents in the room is based
on ventilation principles.

Radiators: irrespective of the terminology (radiator, convector, radiovector), radiators emit
most of their heat into the room by convection.
Radiators are characterized by fairly short
response times dependent on their weight and
the amount of water they contain. They should
be positioned in such a way that the cold building component surfaces are compensated by
warm heating surfaces placed next to or in front
of them. When thermal insulation standards are
good, this generally applies only to window
areas. On cold days with external temperatures
below -10°C, temperatures on the internal surface of the pane may be lower than 15°C, even
in the case of standard double glazing with thermal insulation. In these conditions, cold air
drop takes place at the window, making a radiator necessary there. However, if the criteria
shown in Fig. 24 are maintained, the radiator
can be placed at any location in the room.

Radiant panel heating: floor, wall or ceiling
heating systems have considerably larger heat-
radiating areas in combination with low heating
water temperatures. The radiant component of

the supplied heat rises, although it no longer
plays a key role because the internal surface
temperatures in buildings with good thermal
insulation are already very high. Radiant panel
heating systems can also be employed in energy-efficient buildings; however, when used
purely for heating purposes (see also cooling),
they are considerably more expensive than
comparable systems that employ radiators or
forced-air heating systems. When considering
floor heating for energy-efficient buildings, it is
important to remember that the floor is often
perceived as being uncomfortably cold because
of the low heating requirement and the influence of passive heat gains (downtimes, low
average heating temperatures). If warmer floor
temperatures are desired, it is better to provide
them through a simple system via return flow
temperature limiters. However, only a small
percentage of the total heated area should be
equipped in this fashion to avoid overheating.

210

Glossary

Air change	Air change (ac/h) indicates how frequently the volume of air in a room is exchanged in one hour.
Available supply energy	Amount of energy purchased by the user to operate devices or amount of energy that is directly available prior to use by consumers. The sum of the available supply energy determines the total demand for energy. Statistically, energy is best measured at this stage.
Blower-door test	Method of measuring the airtightness of a building skin by creating negative or positive pressure in the rooms.
Calorific value	The calorific value or gross calorific value of an energy carrier is that carrier's maximum energy content. As with the combustion of fossil energy carriers, water vapor is also produced as a result of the energy transformation. In contrast to standard boilers burning oil or gas, condensing boilers utilize the energy contained in the water vapor as part of their heating output. Efficiencies of over 100 percent are therefore possible by comparison to applications where the lower calorific value is utilized.
Consumed energy	Energy that has been utilized in the form of light, power, heat and processes.
Convection	Heat transfer by air movement
Convection systems	Air collector systems in which heat transport is realized by convection, that is, air.
Demand ratio	Ratio of contribution by an installation or system to meeting the relevant demand (heat, heating energy, warm water or power).
Earth pipe	Heat exchanger in which horizontal pipes are laid into the uppermost earth layer. The cooler or warmer air that is injected through these pipes withdraws heat from the soil or, conversely, transfers heat to the soil.
Emissions	Solid, liquid or gaseous air-polluting materials of all kinds and origins emitted to the outside air as well as odors, noise, vibration, heat, radiation and similar manifestations.
End energy	Amount of energy purchased by the consumer to use his or her devices, or amount of energy that is available immediately prior to use by the consumer. The sum of end energies determines the total demand for energy. At this stage, energy is best measured statistically.
End energy requirement	Amount of energy required to heat a building, taking the following parameters into consideration: heating energy requirement, losses incurred through the heating system, requirement for hot water heating, losses incurred through the hot water processing system and auxiliary energy required to operate the system.
Energy balance	Balance of energy flows in a building, e.g. energy losses (transmission, ventilation) and energy gains (solar radiation, occupants, devices).
Energy carrier	Energy in its material form. Examples: heating oil, steam, electricity, gasoline, etc. Comment: energy carriers are not energy in the physical sense; they contain potential energy. Their potential energy must be transformed and released as thermal, chemical or mechanical energy to meet the consumer demand for heat, power, light, etc
Energy consumption	Amount of energy in the relevant form consumed in order to meet the energy requirement.
Energy losses	Portion of supply energy that is emitted from a system but not utilized in the sense of the process. Energy losses occur during generation, transmission, distribution and application. Some of these losses are physically unavoidable, while a certain amount of energy loss is partially avoidable by technical means and/or personal behavior.
Energy quotient (E)	Annual energy consumption for heat generation (space heating, warm water) and for lighting, power and processes in relation to the ERA (energy reference area, indicated in $kWh/(m^2a)$). The energy quotient can be broken down into the following subcategories: energy quotient for heat (E_h), energy quotient for space heating (E_{sh}), energy quotient for warm water (E_{ww}) and energy quotient for lighting/power/process (E_{lpp}).
Energy reference area	The energy reference area is the sum of all floor areas above and below ground for the use of which heating or cooling is required. The energy reference area is calculated as a gross area, i.e. based on the outer measurements including boundary walls and parapets.
Energy-saving house 40/60	Building with a primary energy requirement of 40 kWh/m^2a or 60 kWh/m^2a according to the EnEV (Energy Conservation Act), a defined subsidy category in Germany.
Enthalpy (h)	Enthalpy (h) is a thermodynamic variable for the total heat content of a system. It is composed of the internal energy plus the product of the system's volume and pressure on expansion. $H = U + Pv$
Fuels	Fossil and recent fuels: materials from which chemically bonded energy can be released. Fossil fuels: coal, peat, wood and combustible solid waste. Liquid fuels: mineral oil and products, combustible liquid waste. Gaseous fuels: natural gases and manufactured gases including biogas. Nuclear fuels: materials from which physically bonded energy can be released.
3, 4 or 7-liter house	Building with a heating requirement of 30 kWh/m^2a, 40 kWh/m^2a or 70 kWh/m^2a (1 liter of heating oil equals 9.95 kWh)
Heat exchanger	A device in which heat is transferred from a warmer to a cooler heat carrier (e.g., air or water).
Heat for heating purposes	Heat that is supplied to a heated room to compensate for heat losses. It does not include losses incurred by the heating system and during distribution.
Heat recovery	The recovery of heat losses from ventilation by a mechanical ventilation system and a heat exchanger.
Heating energy	Amount of end energy that has to be supplied to the heating system in order to provide warmth for heating.
Heating energy consumption in kWh/m^2a	Recorded annual end energy consumption for space heating and warm water (excluding operating power but including the losses of the heating system), referenced to the heated building area.
Heating energy requirement	Amount of energy that is required to heat a building in consideration of the heating requirement and the losses of the heating system.
Heating requirement in kWh/m^2a	Calculated annual heating requirement in reference to the heated area of the building. The variable is calculated by balancing heat losses (transmission Q_t and ventilation Q_v) against heat gains (solar Q_s and internal Q_i) and characterizes the heat insulation quality of the building skin.
Hybrid systems	A combination of different energy systems that complement one another.
Infrared thermal imaging	Photographic depiction of surface temperatures employed, for example, to analyze thermal bridges.

Low-energy house	A building with a heating quotient < 70kWh/m²a for single-family low-energy houses and < 55 kWh/m²a for multi-family low-energy houses.
Low-temperature heating	A heating system with low flow temperatures (< 40° C).
MINERGIE	Defined standard for low-energy houses in Switzerland taking warm water and electricity into consideration. (Heating + warm water for new buildings: 45 kWh/m²a, for buildings constructed prior to 1990: 90 kWh/m²a; electricity for both: 17 kWh/m²a). MINERGIE P: see passive house
Night cooling	Free (or adiabatic) cooling overnight refers to a ventilation concept that utilizes the cool outside air at night during the summer months to cool building components with large thermal storage capacity in order to utilize the same components as "thermal buffer zones" during the day.
Passive house	Building with a heating requirement of 15 kWh/m²a, corresponds to the MINERGIE-P standard in Switzerland.
PCM	PCM stands for Phase Change Material. Among other materials, salt hydrates and paraffin can absorb or discharge relatively high amounts of heat during the transition from a solid to a liquid aggregate state without undergoing noticeable temperature changes. PCMs can be integrated as latent thermal storage components in conventional building materials and open up new possibilities for temperature regulation in buildings.
Perceived temperature	Perceived temperature is composed to equal parts of the radiant temperature and the air temperature in a room. It is perceived on the level of human comfort; there are no technical means of directly measuring this temperature. Globe thermometers measure both a radiant portion and the air temperature on its own and can thus be employed as measuring instruments for perceived temperature. However, humidity, air velocity (drafts), clothing and activity of occupants also play a considerable role in perceived comfort.
Photovoltaics	A photovoltaic system consists of several PV modules (solar modules), which convert sunlight into direct current. This direct current is usually transformed into conventional 230 V alternate current. PV modules are composed of individual solar cells (usually 36 or 72 cells for crystalline silicon). The cells in turn are composed of doped semiconductor materials.
PHPP	Passive House Planning Package. Calculation package developed by the Passiv Haus Institut in Darmstadt, Germany, Dr. Wolfgang Feist
Power-heat-coupling	Power-heat-coupling is understood as the simultaneous conversion of fuel energy (e.g. heating oil or gas) into electrical energy and available heat. By comparison to separate power generation (e.g. in a power plant) and heat (e.g. in a boiler), power-heat-coupling consumes considerably less raw material (e.g. oil, natural gas) and decreases emissions that are harmful to the environment or the climate.
Primary energy	Energy stored in a natural source: for example, sun, water, crude oil, natural gas, coal, etc.
Primary energy requirement in kWh/m²a	Calculated annual primary energy requirement (for space heating, warm water processing and operating power for heating systems) with reference to the heated building area.
Renewable resources	Forms of energy that are permanently available (solar energy, wind energy, hydrodynamic power, etc.) or that are provided from regenerative raw materials.
Solar supply ratio	Annual ratio of heating energy demand or of the utilization energy demand for warm water that is covered by systems designed for the active utilization of solar energy.
Solar thermal power generation	The conversion of direct and diffuse solar radiation into heat.
S/V ratio	Ratio of exterior surface of a building to heated volume.
Supply energy	Energy content of all energy carriers that supply energy to the consumer.
Thermal bridges	Thermal bridges occur when there is a notable drop in temperature on the internal surface of external building components during the heating period. Causes for thermal bridges may lie in the geometry of a building, the building materials or poor workmanship. The most frequent occurrence of thermal bridges is at or near roller shutter housings, embrasures, radiator recesses, ceiling end faces, joints between reinforced concrete ceilings or balcony slabs of reinforced concrete, roof joints and along the edges of external walls. Thermal bridges not only have a negative effect on the heating requirements of a building, they also diminish comfort and hygiene in the interior. Thermal bridges are frequently the cause for moisture damage with subsequent mould formation.
U-value (W/m²K)	Thermal transmittance indicates the amount of heat (in W) that passes through a building component per square meter toward the colder side when there is a temperature difference of 1 Kelvin.
Utilization ratio	The utilization ratio is the ratio of consumed energy to end energy consumption for generating, distributing and storing heat.
Vapor barriers	The water vapor diffusion equivalent thickness of air (s_d) of a construction material is calculated from its layer thickness (s) and the water vapor diffusion resistance coefficient (μ) of the material. DIN 4108, Part 4, contains the values for common building materials. The greater the resistance (s_d), the less vapor penetrates through the building material layer. Vapor barriers are characterized by high resistance to the passage of vapor (i.e. high s_d). When placed correctly, they prevent warm, humid room air from penetrating external building components, which would result in condensation. The resistance values of vapor checks are considerably lower and they should only be employed in combination with precise calculations of the building physics.
Waste heat	Portion of energy flow that cannot be utilized.
Thermal conductivity λ	Amount of heat that flows through an area of 1 m² and a thickness of 1m per unit of time and per Kelvin temperature difference.
Zero-heating-energy house	Building that does not consume additional energy for heating.

Bibliography

Ajuntament de Barcelona, Area d'Urbanisme
Estudide L 'Eixample, Barcelona 1988

Banham, Reyner
The Architecture of the Well-Tempered Environment, Chicago 1969

Bobran-Wittfoht, Ingrid; Schlauch, Dirk
Dämmstoffe für den baulichen Wärmeschutz - (k)einer für alle Fälle
Detail, Munich 7/2001, pp. 1290ff

Carter, Brian; Warburton, Peter
Die Entwicklung einer Solararchitektur
Detail, Munich 6/1993, pp. 671ff

Compagno, Andrea
Intelligent Glass Facades, Material, Practice, Design
5th, revised and updated edition, Basel 2002

Cornoldi, Adriano; Los, Sergio
Hábitat y Energia, Barcelona 1982

Daniels, Klaus
Low Tech, Light Tech, High Tech, Basel 1998

Daniels, Klaus
The Technology of Ecological Building, Basel 1999

Danner, Dassler, Krause (eds.)
Die klima-aktive Fassade, Leinfelden-Echterdingen 1999

Deutsches Architekturmuseum und Volz, Michael (Hrsg.)
Die ökologische Herausforderung in der Architektur, Tübingen 1999

Duikergroep TH Delft
J. Duiker Bowkundig Ingenieur, Rotterdam 1982

Dunster, Bill; Pringle, John
Michael Hopkins & Partners Research into Sustainable Architecture
Architectural Design, Vol 67, No 1/2, Jan-Feb 1997, pp. 26ff

Ebel, Eicke-Hennig, Feist, Groscurth
Energieeinsparung bei Alt- und Neubauten, Heidelberg 2000

Fathy, Hassan
Natural Energy and Vernacular Architecture, Chicago 1986

Feist, Wolfgang
Das Niedrigenergiehaus, Neuer Standard für energiebewusstes Bauen
4th edition, Heidelberg 1997

Feist, Wolfgang
Gestaltungsgrundlagen Passivhäuser, Darmstadt 2001

Feist, Dr. Wolfgang– Passivhaus Institut
Stadtplanerische Instrumente zur Umsetzung von Passivhäusern,
Proceedings, Vol 10, June 2000
Arbeitskreis Kostengünstige Passivhäuser Phase II

Feist, Dr. Wolfgang– Passivhaus Institut
Architekturbeispiele: Wohngebäude, Proceedings, Vol 21,
December 2002
Arbeitskreis Kostengünstige Passivhäuser Phase III

Feist, Wolfgang
Passivhäuser Kronsberg und der Einfluss des Nutzerverhaltens
Bauzentrum/Baukultur 12/2002, pp. 36ff

FHBB Fachhochschule beider Basel
Proceedings on the 6th European Conference on Passive Houses,
Basel 2002

Fisch, Norbert; Möws, Bruno; Zieger, Jürgen
Solarstadt. Konzepte - Technologien - Projekte, Stuttgart 2001

Flagge, Herzog-Loibl, Meseure (eds.)
Thomas Herzog, Architektur + Technologie, Munich 2001

Forster, Norman
Towards the Modern Vernacular
Detail, Munich 6/1993, pp. 664ff

Gauzin-Müller, Dominique
Nachhaltigkeit in Architektur und Städtebau: Konzepte, Technologien,
Beispiele, Basel 2002

Gesellschaft für rationelle Energieverwendung e.V.
Hauser, Gerd; Stiegel, Horst; Otto, Frank
Energieeinsparung im Gebäudebestand - Bauliche und anlagentechni-
sche Lösungen, Böhl-Iggelheim 1997

Givoni, Baruch
Man, Climate and Architecture, Second Edition, London 1976

Gonzalo, R.E.; Gonzalo G.E.
The Bioclimatic Design in the Traditional Architecture of North
Argentine - Determining and Conditioning Factors, Porto 1988

Gonzalo, Roberto
Passive Nutzung der Sonnenenergie. Grundlagen für den
Gebäudeentwurf, Munich 1990

Gonzalo, Roberto
Wege zum energiesparenden Bauen und Wohnen
Detail, Munich 6/1992, pp. 554ff

Gonzalo, Roberto
Kritische Anmerkungen zur Solararchitektur
Detail, Munich 6/1993, pp. 676ff

Gonzalo, Roberto
Energiebewusst Bauen - Wege zum solaren und energiesparenden
Planen, Bauen und Wohnen, Edition Erasmus 1994

Gonzalo, Roberto and Johannes Herold
die teile + das ganze - Computergestützte Strukturanalyse der Siedlung
Halen von Atelier 5, Darmstadt 2000

Gonzalo, Susana
Höhlenwohnungen. Seminarbericht TUM, Munich 1991

Habermann, Karl J.
Low tech, high tech, intelligent Das Experiment in der Architektur
Detail, Munich 6/1992, pp. 552-553

Habermann, Karl J.
Baukonstruktion - Technischer Ausbau - Gestalt
Detail, Munich 6/1990, pp. 574ff

Habermann, Karl J.
Zur Entwicklungsgeschichte des technischen Ausbaus
Detail, Munich 2/1995, pp. 158ff

Hascher, Rainer - Jeska, Simone - Klauck, Birgit (eds.)
Entwurfsatlas Bürobau, Basel 2002

Hausladen, G.; de Saldanha, M.; Nowak, W.; Liedl, P.
Einführung in die Bauklimatik, Munich 2003

Gerhard Hausladen, Michael de Saldanha, Petra Liedl et al.
ClimaDesign, Munich 2005

Hawkes, Dean; Forster, Wayne
Energieeffizientes Bauen. Architektur, Technik, Ökologie, Stuttgart 2002

Hawkes, Dean; Yannas, Simos; Hinsley, Hugo; Dunster, Bill
Sustainability
AA files, London 32/1996, pp. 66ff

Hénard, Eugène
Les villes de l'avenir, Paris 1910

Herzog, Thomas (ed.)
Solarenergie in Architecture und Stadtplanung, Munich 1996

Herzog, Krippner, Lang
Fassaden Atlas, Munich 2004

Kaiser, Yvonne; Hastings, Robert S.
Niedrigenergie-Solarhäuser. Systeme, Projekte, Technologien, Basel
1998

Kennedy, Margrit
Öko-Stadt, Frankfurt a.M. 1986

Kolb, Bernhard
Beispiel Biohaus, Munich 1984

Krapmeier, H., Drössler, E.; Cepheus
Wohnkomfort ohne Heizung, Vienna 2001

Krehwinkel, Heinz, W.
Glasarchitektur, Basel 1998

Krusche, Althaus, Gabriel
Ökologisches Bauen, Wiesbaden 1982

Landeshauptstadt München
Leitfaden zum Geschosswohnungsbau mit Niedrigenergiestandard,
Munich 1999

Landesinitiative Zukunftsenergien NRW
50 Solarsiedlungen in NRW. Planungsleitfaden, Düsseldorf 2002

Le Corbusier
Vers une Architecture, Paris 1922

López de Asiain, Jaime
Arquitectura, Ciudad, Medioambiente, Seville 2001

Moewes, Günther
Weder Hütten noch Paläste - Architektur und Ökologie in der
Arbeitsgesellschaft. Eine Streitschrift, Basel 1995

Oberste Baubehörde im Bayerischen Staatsministerium des Innern
Wohnen in Bayern - 7. Arbeitsblätter zum Wohnungsbau
Umweltverträgliches Bauen und gesundes Wohnen im Bestand
Munich, 2nd edition September 2004

Oberste Baubehörde im Bayerisches Staatsministerium des Innern
Wohnmodelle Bayern 1984-1990. Beispiele des Sozialen Wohnungbaus
Erfahrungen aus der Vergangenheit - Wege in die Zukunft, Munich 1990

Passivhaus Institut
Proceedings on the 6th European Conference on the Passive House,
Basel 2002

Passivhaus Institut
Proceedings on the 7th European Conference on the Passive House,
Hamburg 2003

Schlaich, Sibylle; Schlaich, Jörg
Erneuerbare Energien nutzen, Düsseldorf 1992

Schreck, Hasso
Energiebewusstes Bauen
Ökologischer Wohnungsbau - Dokumentation der Vortragsreihe vom
Herbst 1992, Urbanes Wohnen e.V. Munich

Schwab, Hubert; Heinemann, Ulrich; Fricke, Jochen
Vakuumisolierpaneele - ein hocheffizientes Dämmsystem der Zukunft
Detail, Munich 7/2001, pp. 1302ff

Thornton, J.A.; Deavy, C.P.; Mitchell, D.M.
The new parliamentary building - Portcullis House
The Structural Engineer, Vol.78/ No 18, Sept 2000, pp. 17ff

UIA Berlin 2002 – XXI World Congress of Architecture
Basel, 2002

Usemann, Klaus W.
Entwicklung von Heizungs- und Lüftungstechnik zur Wissenschaft.
Hermann Rietschel - Leben und Werk, Munich 1993

Voss, Karsten; Löhnert, Günter; Herkel, Sebastian; Wagner, Andreas;
Wambsganß, Mathias
Bürogebäude mit Zukunft Konzepte, Analysen, Erfahrungen, Cologne
2005

Wuppertal Institut für Klima, Umwelt, Energie, Planungs-Büro Schmitz
Aachen: Energiegerechtes Bauen und Modernisieren, Grundlagen und
Beispiele für Architekten, Ingenieure und Bewohner
Herausgegeben von der Bundesarchitektenkammer, Basel, 1996

Zentrum für Bauen und Umwelt, Donau-Universität Krems
Proceedings on the 8th European Conference on the Passive House,
Krems, Austria 2004

Institutions

Bayerisches Zentrum für angewandte Energieforschung (ZAE), ISOTEG
E-mail: info@zae.uni-wuerzburg.de
Internet: www.zae-bayern.de; www.energieundbau.de

BINE-Informationsdienst
(Bürgerinformation Neue Energietechniken, Nachwachsende Rohstoffe,
Umwelt) Fachinformationszentrum Karlsruhe
E-Mail: bine@fiz-karlsruhe.de
Internet: www.bine.info

Bund der Energieverbraucher (BdE) e.V.
E-Mail: BDE.EV@t-online.de oder info@energieverbraucher.de

Bundesindustrieverband Heizungs-, Klima-, Sanitärtechnik e.V. (BHKS)
Weberstraße 33, 53113 Bonn
E-Mail: info@bhks.de
Internet: www.bhks.de

Bundesministerium für Umwelt, Naturschutz und Reaktorsicherheit
E-Mail: service@bmu.bund.de
Internet: www.bmu.de
Im Geschäftsbereich des BMU: Umweltbundesamt (UBA)
Internet: www.umweltbundesamt.de

Bundesministerium für Verkehr, Bau- und Wohnungswesen (BMVBW)
E-Mail: info@bmvbw.bund.de
Internet: www.bmvbw.de

Bundesministerium für Wirtschaft und Technologie (BMWi)
E-Mail: info@bmwi.bund.de
Internet: www.bmwi.de
Note: Responsible for the federal energy program. Downloadable data-
base with current subsidy- and sponsorship programs offered by the
Federal Republic, the Federal States and the European Union.
E-Mail: foerderberatung@bmwi.bund.de
Internet: www.bmwi.de

Bundesverband Solarenergie e.V. (BSE)
E-Mail:info@bse.solarindustrie.com
Internet: www. bse.solarindustrie.com

Deutsche Bundesstiftung Umwelt (DBU)
E-Mail: info@dbu.de
Internet: www.dbu.de

Deutsche Energie-Agentur GmbH (DENA)
E-Mail: info@deutsche-energie-agentur.de
Internet: www.deutsche-energie-agentur.de

Deutscher Fachverband Solarenergie e.V. (DFS)
E-Mail: dfs.freiburg@t-online.de
Internet: www.dfs-solarfirmen.de

Deutsche Gesellschaft für Sonnenenergie e.V. (DGS)
E-mail: info@dgs.de
E-Mail: info@dgs-solar.org
Note: Journal *Sonnenenergie*

Energieinstitut Vorarlberg
E-Mail: info@energieinstitut-at
Internet: www. energieinstitut-at

EUROSOLAR e.V.
E-Mail: inter_office@eurosolar.org
Internet: www.eurosolar.org

Fraunhofer-Institut für Bauphysik IBP
E-Mail: info@ibp.fraunhofer.de
Internet: www.ibp.fraunhofer.de

Fraunhofer-Institut für Solare Energiesysteme ISE
E-Mail: info@ise.fraunhofer.de
Internet: www.ise.fraunhofer.de

Fraunhofer-Institut für Systemtechnik und Innovationsforschung ISI
E-Mail: isi@fhg.de
Internet: www.isi.fraunhofer.de

Gesellschaft für Rationelle Energieverwendung e.V. (GRE)
E-Mail: gre@gre-inform.de gre@gre-online.de
Internet: www.gre-online.de

International Solar Energy Society e.V. (ISES)
E-Mail: hq@ises.org
Internet: www.ises.org und www.wire.ises.org
Note: WIRE Internet information system (World-wide
Information System for Renewable Energy).

Internationales Wirtschaftsforum Regenerative Energien (IWR)
E-Mail: info@iwr.de
Internet: www.iwr.de
Note: Extensive Internet documentation (numerous information pages,
links and national and international subsidiary contacts, subsidies, etc.).

IWU-Institut für Wohnen und Umwelt Forschungsbereich Energie
E-Mail: info@iwu.de
Internet: www.iwu.de

Passivhaus Institut Deutschland
E-Mail: passivhaus@t-online.de
Internet: www.passiv.de

United Nations Environment Programme (UNEP)
Regional Office for Europe
E-Mail: roe@unep.ch
Internet: www.unep.ch/roe

Wuppertal Institut für Klima, Umwelt, Energie GmbH
E-Mail: info@wupperinst.org
Internet: www.wupperinst.org

Zentrum für rationelle Energieanwendung und Umwelt
GmbH (ZREU) OPET-Beratungsstelle Bayern-Österreich im Auftrag der
Europäischen Kommission
E-Mail: info@zreu.de
Internet: www. zreu.de

216

Index

Project Participants

Housing Complex in Kriens
Switzerland

Client:
Luzerner Pensionskasse

Architects:
Lischer Partner Architekten Planer AG,
Lucerne

Planning technical building systems:
BW Haustechnik AG, Hünenberg

Load-bearing structure, wood construction:
Jung-Pirmin Ingenieure für Holzbau GmbH, Ran

Housing Development in Affoltern
Switzerland

Client:
Kurt Schneebli, Affoltern

Architects:
Metron Architekturbüro AG, Brugg

Planning technical building systems:
Nanotech AG, EnnetbadeW+S AG , Rohr, Bösch
AG, Aarau

Load-bearing structure:
F. Steinmann, Hausen

Multi-family House in Munich
Germany

Client:
WOGENO München eG, Munich

Architects:
H2R Architekten BDA
Hüther, Hebensperger-Hüther, Röttig, Munich

Planning technical building systems:
ITEM, Richard Kramer, Munich

Load-bearing structure:
Dr. Ing. Gernot Pittioni, Weilheim

Office- and Apartment Building in Munich
Germany

Client:
Bauherrengemeinschaft Meinhold und Laufer

Architect:
Martin Pool, Munich

Planing technical building systems:
Ingenieurbüro Lackenbauer, Traunstein

Electrical: Christian Gibis, Munich

Load-bearing structure:
Georg Weinzierl, Schwarzach

Apartment- and Office Building in Wiesbaden
Germany

Client:
A-Z Architekten

Architects:
Altmann-Zimmer Architekten BDA, Wiesbaden

Planning technical building systems:
Holger Zimmer, Joachim Altmann

Load-bearing structure:
Schmitt & Thielmann, Wiesbaden

Residential Building in Madrid
Spain

Client:
Empresa Municipal de la Vivienda (Madrid)

Architect:
Guillermo Yañez, Lydia Yañez Lopez del Amo,
Madrid

Planning technical building systems:
Transformadora de Gas S.A.; ROEMA
Instalaciones SL. Monedero Instalaciones y
Servicios

Load-bearing structure:
Jesús Chomón Ingeniero. E.T.E.S.A.

University Campus in Nottingham
United Kingdom

Client:
University Estates Office

Architects:
Hopkins Architects, London

Planning technical building systems:
Arup

Load-bearing structure:
Arup

Landscape design:
Battle McCarhty

Student Residence in Wuppertal
Germany

Client:
Hochschul-Sozialwerk Wuppertal

Architects:
1st construction phase: PPP in partnership with
Christian Schlüter and Michael Müller,
Düsseldorf, Wuppertal
2nd construction phase: Architektur Contor
Müller Schlüter, Wuppertal

Planning technical building systems:
Ingenierbüro Landwehr GmbH, Dortmund

Load-bearing structure:
Carsten Tichelmann in PTT, Darmstadt
Rüdiger Klumpp, Weikersheim (facade)

Office- and Apartment Building in Schwarzach
Austria

Client:
Miterrichtergemeinschaft Kaufmann Lenz
Gmeiner, Schwarzach + Revital GmbH, Dornbirn

Architects:
Christian Lenz, Hermann Kaufmann

Planning technical building systems:
IBN Ingenieurbüro Naßwetter, Batschuns

Load-bearing system:
M+G Ingenieure, Feldkirch
Statikbüro Galehr, Feldkirch

Office- and Apartment Building in Sursee
Switzerland

Client:
St. Georg Immobilien AG, Sursee

Architects:
Scheitlin - Syfrig + Partner, Lucerne

Planning technical building systems:
Bucher + Dillier AG, Luzcerne

Building physics:
Ragonesi, Strobel & Partner, Emmenbrücke

Load-bearing structure, wood construction:
Makiol + Wiederkehr, Beinwil

Office Complex in Duisburg
Germany

Client:
Bau- und Liegenschaftsbetrieb NRW

Architects:
Schuster Architekten, Düsseldorf

Energy concept:
Stahl, Büro für Sonnenenergie, Freiburg

Planning technical building systems:
Ingenieurgesellschaft Kruck mbH,
Mühlheim a.d. Ruhr

Load-bearing structure:
Kunkel + Partner, Düsseldorf

Office Building in Munich
Germany

Client:
Fraunhofer-Gesellschaft zur Förderung der
angewandten Forschung e.V., Munich

Architects:
Henn Architekten, Munich

Total energy concept:
Fraunhoferinstitut für solare Energiesysteme
ISE, Freiburg

Planning technical building systems:
Kuehn Bauer Partner, Halbergmoos

Facade design:
Hussak Ingenieurgesellschaft, Lauingen

Load-bearing structure:
Sailer Stepan und Partner, Munich

Office Building in Wiesbaden
Germany

Client:
Zusatzversorgungskasse des Baugewerbes
VVaG, Wiesbaden

Architects:
Thomas Herzog und Partner, Munich

Energy concept:
Kaiser Consult, Prof.Dr.Ing. Oesterle, DS-Plan,
Prof.Dr.Ing. Hausladen

Planning technical building systems:
Zibell, Willner & Partner, Ingenieurbüro
Hausladen

Lighting design:
Bartenbach Lichtlabor

Load-bearing structure:
Sailer, Stepan & Partner, Munich

Parliament Buildings in London
Untited Kingdom

Client:
The United Kingdom Parliament, House of
Commons Commission

Architects:
Hopkins Architects, London

Planing technical building systems:
Arup

Facade design:
Arup

Load-bearing structure:
Arup

Office and Workshops in Weidling
Austria

Client:
Firma B!otop, Weidling

Architect:
Georg W. Reinberg, Vienna

Planning technical building systems:
BPS Engineering, Vienna

Simulation and energy concept:
Patrick Jung, Cologne

Building physics:
Nikolaus Bruck, Vienna

Commercial Building in Steyr
Austria

Client:
Schloßgangl Immobilien GmbH, Steyr

Architect:
Walter Unterrainer Atelier für Architektur,
Feldkirch

Planning technical building systems:
E-Plus, Egg; Schloßgangl Energiesysteme, Steyr

Load-bearing structure:
Merz-Kaufmann, Dornbirn

School Complex in Pichling
Austria

Client:
Magistrat der Stadt Linz

Architects:
Architekten Loudon & Habeler, Vienna

Planning technical building systems:
Altherm Engineering, Baden

Load-bearing structure:
Anton Harrer, Krems/Vienna

School Complex in Aufkirchen
Germany

Client:
Montessoriverein Erding e.V., Erding

Architects:
Walbrunn Grotz Vallentin Loibl, Bockhorn

Planning technical building systems:
Ingenieurbüro Lackenbauer, Traunstein

Load-bearing structure:
G. Jochum H. Kutsch, Alling

School Complex in Gelsenkirchen
Germany

Client:
Evangelische Schule in Westfalen e.V.

Architects:
plus+ Bauplanung GmbH
Hübner-Forster-Hübner, Neckartenzlingen

Climate concept:
Transsolar Energietechnik, Stuttgart

Planning technical building systems:
Inco Ingenieurbüro, Aachen
Building Physics:
GN Bauphysik, Stuttgart

Load-bearing structure:
Weischede und Partner, Stuttgart

School Complex in Ladakh
Nepal

Client:
Drukpa Trust

Architects:
Arup Associates, London

Planning technical building systems:
Arup

Art Museum in Riehen
Switzerland

Client:
Beyeler-Foundation, Riehen

Architects:
Renzo Piano Building Workshop, Paris/Genoa

Planning technical building systems:
Arup
Jakob Forrer AG, Buchrain (HKL)
Bogenschütz AG (S)
Daylighting:
Arup

Load-bearing structure:
Arup

HOLZBAU WEISE

Founded by Gottfried Renggli in Schötz, Switzerland in 1923, the enterprise has grown to over 120 employees and has become a leader in the Swiss market for system building in wood. The history of the company is characterized by a passion for innovation and a pioneering spirit. Renggli has been a forerunner in the field of MINERGIE and passive house construction, expanding its reputation beyond Swiss borders.

Renggli brings the philosophy of energy-efficient and sustainable system building in wood to a wide range of applications from individual homes and housing developments to commercial and public buildings. Numerous awards and certificates bear witness to our outstanding standards, which we are committed to upholding in the future.

Our prestige projects in the field of sustainable building in wood include the new residential and office building for Renggli AG in Sursee, Lucerne district (see pp. 128 ff) and the "Senti" passive house development in Kriens, Lucerne district, comprising eighteen housing units (see pp. 44 ff). Other examples of energy-efficient comprehensive solutions in wood are featured on the Internet at www.renggli-haus.ch.

The Trade Association of Building Materials and Building Components for Suspended Ventilated Facades (Fachverband Baustoffe und Bauteile für vorgehängte hinterlüftete Fassaden e.V.) or FVHF represents the interests of manufacturers of cladding, insulating materials, anchors, fasteners and connecting devices for suspended ventilated facades (VHF). The association, which is based in Berlin, was founded in 1993 and today counts forty-five members.

In recent years, subscribing and affiliated members have played an increasingly important role for the association. Specialists in facade technology, expert facade installers and research institutions are now actively involved in the work of the FVHF. One of the goals of the association is to educate all relevant target groups about the architectural variety and the unique technical advantages that suspended ventilated facade systems offer.

The German Facade Prize for suspended ventilated facades ("Deutscher Fassadenpreis VHF"), which was awarded for the 6th time this year, acknowledges this system within the convention of the Federal Foundation for the "Culture of Building." The foundation has highlighted this renowned architecture prize as one of the "most important prizes to be awarded in the field of architecture in Germany." The FVHF is a permanent guest member of this assembly.

As a member of the Climate Alliance, also known as the Alianza del Clima, the FVHF actively supports the implementation of the German energy conservation act (EnEV) and is committed to supporting measures that minimize heating energy requirements. In this field, which is tremendously relevant to the

future, the FVHF promotes a comprehensive information policy through its facade system: VHF: Die Energieeinsparfassade®.

The FVHF is a co-founder of the EU-CLAD Working Group, founded in 2003. It is the task of this group to monitor the development of suspended ventilated facades and to ensure harmonization across Europe.

The FVHF collaborates with the bodies of the German Institute for Standardization (DIN), the German Institute for Building Technology (DIBt) and the Joint Committee on Electronics in Building (GAEB). In addition, the association cooperates with numerous universities and technical colleges, training and continuing education schools as well as with other associations and organizations.

Most recently, the association has also begun to collaborate with the German Natural Stone Academy (Deutsche Naturstein Akademie or DENAK) in Mayen. Thanks to the wide-ranging activities of the FVHF, the VHF has become established among experts in the field as a recognized facade system. Today, the suspended ventilated facade is a system whose significance continues to grow from year to year.

RENGGLI AG
St. Georgstrasse 2
CH-6210 Sursee
Tel. +41 (0)41 925 25 25
mail@renggli-haus.ch
www.renggli-haus.ch

Fachverband Baustoffe und Bauteile für vorgehängte hinterlüftete Fassaden e.V. (FVHF)
Kurfürstenstraße 129
10785 Berlin
Tel. 0049 30 21286281
Fax. 0049 30 21286241
www.fvhf.de

Xella
Neues Bauen

Fermacell gypsum fiberboards in combination with building materials in wood are an ideal response to the demand for sustainable and energy-efficient building. The projects presented in this book are a case in point: the housing developments in Kriens (see pp. 33 ff) and Affoltern (see pp. 50 ff), the student residence in Wuppertal (see pp. 41 ff) and the Montessori school in Aufkirchen (see p. 101). The boards, which can be used for floors, walls and ceilings alike, are manufactured from ecological raw materials in an environmentally friendly production process. Given their building-biological properties, which were tested by the Institut für Baubiologie Rosenheim (IBR) and verified with the IBR stamp, these boards are an excellent complement for other natural building materials. The homogenous structure and fiber reinforcement render these boards unusually stable and capable of bearing extreme loads. The boards are suitable for structural, fire-protection and damproom uses; this allows for a wide range of applications, both in the existing fabric and in new construction, and also simplifies planning and logistics. Cost-efficient processing and handling techniques complement these qualities. Fermacell constructions can be realized in a rational and rapid manner and offer the highest degree of structural stability, fire protection as well as sound protection and insulation.

Dimensional precision, harmonized board material and accessories, all of which are provided from a single source, facilitate assembly and installation. The Fermacell brand has made Xella Trockenbau-Systeme GmbH, a subsidiary of Xella International, a leader in the German market for gypsum fiberboards. The boards are distributed throughout Europe. In addition to their complete range of products for dry interior construction, the company, whose headquarters are located in Duisburg, also offers the cement-bonded Powerpanel HD for exterior wall construction: this panel offers structural stability and above all weather protection for wood construction. The Powerpanel H2O, also cement-bonded, is suitable for all types of damp and wet rooms and can withstand constant exposure to water. The panel can be installed on relevant substructures in the same manner as a standard Fermacell board.

The product range offered by Xella Trockenbau-Systeme also includes non-combustible, cement-bonded Aestuver fire protection boards, which are employed in highly specialized applications for fire prevention. They are waterproof and frost-resistant, which makes them suitable for exposed installation. The Aestuver T fire-protection boards were developed especially for fire protection in underground traffic facilities.

Multipor mineral insulation boards also form part of the impressive product range. These insulation boards, based on natural raw materials, can be utilized for residential and commercial applications, in old buildings and for new construction, for renovation and retrofitting, in all areas of a building from the basement to the roof. In the context of composite insulation systems, Multipor is also suitable as insulation for interior walls, for ventilated aerated concrete solid roof constructions and flat roofs or for ceilings in basements and underground car parks. Xella International operates within the umbrella of Franz Haniel & Cie. GmbH and handles the worldwide activities of the company in the areas of building materials, raw materials and fastening systems. Today, Xella is the largest global provider of aerated concrete and calcium silicate blocks represented by the brands such as Ytong, Hebel and Silka, and a leader in gypsum fiberboard with the Fermacell brand. The raw materials division is headed by the Fels Group, the leading European supplier of lime and limestone. Halfen-Deha, in Langenfeld, is a leading manufacturer of fasteners, anchors and assembly systems.

Xella International GmbH
Franz-Haniel-Platz 6 – 8
47119 Duisburg
www.xella.de
kommunikation@xella.com

Thomas Sohm, the owner of Sohm Holzbautechnik, has been fully committed to the renewable raw material wood since 1991 and now heads a carpentry workshop with the latest in modern equipment and some forty employees. The history of the company is characterized by innovation and the readiness to cooperate with architects, structural engineers and experts in building physics in the realization of newly developed ideas. The diagonal-dowel construction is an excellent example. This method makes it possible to realize solid ceiling and wall components without using glue or steel in the joints. This innovative system was awarded a prize at the competition "Fabrik der Zukunft." Sohm Holzbautechnik also placed third in the competition "Trio des Jahres 2003/Gewerbe."

The company handles some eighty buildings per year. Sohm is active in all areas of wood construction: housing, public and commercial building, agricultural building and special applications. Prestige projects include the office and residential building by the architects Lenz and Kaufmann in Schwarzach (see p. 122), the Tschabrun logistics center in Rankweil, the Klaus-Weiler-Fraxern public school, the highway service station in Hohenems, the Doppelmayr manufacturing hall in Wolfurt, and the Lechblick apartment building in Warth (which was awarded the State Prize for Tourism and Architecture).

Buildings with Eternit facades have been awarded the "Deutscher Fassadenpreis" (German Award for Facade Design and Construction) for the fifth consecutive year. Two projects featured in this volume are among these award-winning buildings. They are: the student residence in Wuppertal realized by the planning team Petzinka Pink and Partner in cooperation with Müller/Schlüter architects (p. 116) and the office building in Duisburg by Schuster Architekten (p. 134). Both buildings are outstanding examples of energy-efficient architecture utilizing fiber cement panels in the facade. Eternit products are distinguished by longevity, ecology, and efficiency; they also possess outstanding properties with regard to building physics. Today, the company's product range encompasses large-format panels composed of fiber cement, wood cement and calcium silicate, as well as corrugated sheet panels, roof panels and design objects. Architects and engineers have been creating remarkable buildings with Eternit products for more than a century. The company also commissioned renowned architects such as Paul Baumgarten and Ernst Neufert for its own buildings. For the current modernization of its headquarters, the company has once again awarded the contract to young architects: Astrid Bornheim and Peter von Klitzing from Berlin.

Eternit publishes an architectural magazine documenting the multi-faceted applications and uses of the material.

TRNSYS 16 is a comprehensive and expandable simulation environment for the dynamic simulations of buildings, solar energy systems and systems for rational energy exploitation. It is employed by engineers and scientists throughout the world to validate new energy concepts. In addition to the modular structure and flexibility, the success of TRNSYS lies in the ongoing development and improvement by an international R & D team.

TRNFLOW, a newly developed TRNSYS module, achieves an integral linkage between thermal simulation and the simulation of air movement. Linked or coupled simulation is indispensable for systems such as passive night-time cooling, double-facades, solar chimneys, atria, etc., in which the reciprocal influence of thermal and air-flow processes is especially pronounced. The integrated multi-zone air-flow model is based on the familiar COMIS program. In addition to entering the thermal model parameters, the user-friendly interface also allows for a quick definition of the air-flow grid composed of nodes and flow transmissibility. An equation solver, newly integrated into the building model, provides an iterative calculation of the solutions for both models. For additional information on the simulation environments of TRNSYS 16 and TRNFLOW, go to http://www.trnsys.de or direct your enquiries to:

Sohm Holzbautechnik GesmbH.
Bühel 818
A-6861 Alberschwende
Tel. +43 5579 71150,
Fax +43 5579 711511
office@sohm-holzbau.at
www.sohm-holzbau.at

Eternit AG
Ernst-Reuter-Platz 8
10587 Berlin
Service-Line Dach: 01805-659 659
Service-Line Fassade+Ausbau:
01805 - 651 651
info@eternit.de
www.eternit.de

TRANSSOLAR
Energietechnik GmbH
Curiestr. 2
70563 Stuttgart
Tel. 0711 / 679 76-0
fax. 0711 / 679 76-11
hotline@transsolar.com
http://www.trnsys.de

e·on | Energie

E.ON Energie AG is the leading private energy supplier in Europe with headquarters in Munich. Within the E.ON umbrella, E.ON Energie has over 36,000 employees and supplies power and gas to subscribers throughout Central Europe. Seventeen million customers subscribe to E.ON Energie for power, gas and multiple energy-related services. With an efficient power station park based on a balanced mix of energy resources – primarily fossil fuels, nuclear power and hydro power – the annual delivery of current is more than 240 billion kilowatt hours, while gas delivery exceeds 240 billion kilowatt hours.

E.ON Energie is a multinational enterprise, whose decentralized structure is ideal for responding to the regional differences in the European energy market. We provide services throughout Central Europe. In addition to Germany, we are especially active in the Czech Republic, Slovakia, Hungary, Bulgaria, Rumania and Poland, as well as in the Benelux countries, Switzerland and Austria.

In Germany alone, we are represented by seven regional supply companies with locations stretching from southern Bavaria to the Danish border. Performance-related energy supply means above all delivering on-site service to our customers. For this reason, we have consciously pursued a decentralized company structure. Our greatest advantage is to maintain an international presence in combination with a regional and local focus on clients.

E.ON Energie AG is actively committed to the energy-efficient use of resources, among other initiatives as a financial partner of the study group for cost-efficient passive houses.

There are excellent reasons for this committment. Germany has formulated an ambitious climate protection goal in which CO_2-emissions into the atmosphere play a central role. E.ON Energie has studied various options for reducing the amount of CO_2 that is released into the atmosphere today. One indisputable result is that the enormous CO_2-emissions resulting from generating heat for buildings, which account for 26 percent of the total CO_2-emissions in Germany, can be diminished in a relatively easy fashion by comparison to other options.

If one takes a look at energy transformation in Germany as a whole, an essential perspective in the context of CO_2-emissions, savings are possible with very little effort above all in building applications. The required measures can be implemented at especially low costs for each ton of CO_2 that is not emitted. E.ON Energie is therefore committed to this topic in order to achieve the common climate protection goal with the most effective means available.

E.ON Energie AG
Briennerstraße 40
D-80333 München
Tel +49 89 1254 01
Fax+49 89 1254 1401
info@eon-energie.com
www.eon-energie.com

Picture Credits

Imprint

Artur/Thomas Riehle
p. 4, 103 (top), 116, 118 (top left), 119 (2), 121

Arup
p. 84 (left), 111 (center), 188, 189, 191, 192, 193

Atelier 5
p. 24, 29, 90 (top right)

Baer, Steve
p. 17 (top right) (2)

Berendt, Guenter
p. 56

Bonfig, Peter
p. 110 (top) (2), 146, 148, 151

Bräuning Niggi
p. 199

Carrier
p. 14 (top left)

Carter, Brian
p. 15 (bottom)

Davies, Richard
p. 153, 154, 155, 157

Denancé, Michel
p. 114 (top right)

Dix, Thomas
p. 114 l., 196/197, 198

Drexel, Thomas
p. 176, 179 (top) (2), 181

Elsner, Gert
p. 23

Faller, Peter
p. 91 (top right)

Fink + Jocher
p. 21 (bottom)

Gonzalo, Roberto
p. 10 (3), 17 (bottom right), 18 (top and center), 19 (3), 21 (top) (2), 27 (top right), 28 (top) (3), 30 (4), 31 (3), 32 (3), 33 (3), 34 (left) (3), 36 (top right) (2), 37 (top and bottom) (2), 39 (bottom left), 40 (3), 41 (3), 42 (bottom left and top right), 88, 89 (top), 90 (left) (2), 91 (top left and bottom right), 92 (2), 93 (top left), 94 (top), 95 (top and center), 96 (4), 97 (4), 98 (4), 99 (top and bottom), 100 (left and center), 101 (3), 102 (3), 103 (bottom), 104 (3), 105 (4), 106 (2), 108 (left and center) (3), 109 (3), 113 (bottom right), 114 (bottom), 202 (top left), 203 (3), 206 (bottom left) (2), 207 (top left and bottom right), 209 (bottom right), 210 (bottom left)

H2R Hüther Hebensperger-Hüther Röttig
p. 100 (bottom left)

Habermann, Karl J.
p. 6, 9 (top), 11 (3), 13 (3), 16 (top), 20 (3), 23, 65 (top), 127 (bottom right), 131 (bottom) (2), 140, 145 (left), 179 (bottom right), 194, 197 (bottom right), 200, 206 (top right), 208 (top right)

Hamilton Knight, Martine
p. 80-81, 82, 86

Hasit
p. 205 (top left)

Heinrich, Michael
p. 63, 66-67 (top)

Hempel, Jörg
p. 28 (bottom), 68, 70, 72, 73, 112 (top right)

Hübner, Peter
p. 112 (bottom left) (2)

ISE Freiburg
p. 142 (top) (2), 145 (center left), 205 (top right)

Jarisch + Myrzik
p. 108 (top right), 111 (top), 142, 143, 145 (right)

Klomfar, Bruno
p. 110 (bottom) (2), 170, 171, 173, 174, 175

Krapmeier, Helmut
p. 205 (center left)

Krusche, Per W.
p. 16 (center and bottom), 17 (center right)

Lackenbauer, Andreas
p. 207 (top right), 210 (top right)

Lundgaard, Boje
p. 18 (bottom)

Mair, Walter
p. 107 (top left), 129, 131 (right) (3), 133

Martinez, Ignacio
p. Seite 99 (center), 111 (bottom), 123, 124 (2), 127 (top left and right), 211

MRG Vierthaler & Braun
p. 27 (top left)

Petersen, Poul
p. 21 (center)

Pollok/Gonzalo
p. 36 (top left) (2), 118 (bottom left), 204 (top right) (2)

Pool, Martin
p. 62, 66 (bottom), 118 (top left),

Reinberg, Georg W.
p. 42 (center right)

Renggli AG
p. 128

Rogers, Richard
p. 5

Roos Architekten
p. 95 (bottom)

Rudolfsky, Poul
p. 22 (top)

Springer, Frank
p. 107 (bottom) (2), 134, 136, 137, 138, 139, 204 (left) (2)

Steiner, Rupert
p. 158, 159, 160, 161 (top left), 163

tr architekten
p. 39 (center left)

VIEW London, Raf Makda
p. 22 (bottom)

Warne, Bengt
p. 17 (top left)

Wogeno
p. 58 (left) (2), 59 (right) (2), 100 (top right), 208 (bottom)

Detail, Munich:
Permission to reproduce the following drawings:
p. 149, 150, 197, 198

Illustrations without detailed credits reproduced in the chapters on project examples were made available by the architects and engineers who participated in the various projects. We would like to extend our deepest thanks to them for their practical support. Thanks are also due to the featured companies, who have generously supported this work. Their profiles can be found on pp. 220ff.

Translation from German into English: Elizabeth Schwaiger, Toronto

Layout design: Roberto Gonzalo, Karl J. Habermann, Munich

Front cover: Sentihäuser in CH-Kriens (photo: Beno Dermond, Zurich)

A CIP catalogue record for this book is available from the Library of Congress, Washington D.C., USA.

Bibliographic information published by Die Deutsche Bibliothek
Die Deutsche Bibliothek lists this publication in the Deutsche Nationalbibliografie; detailed bibliographic data is available in the internet at http://dnb.ddb.de.

This book is also available in the original German language edition (ISBN 3-7643-7255-9 / 987-3-7643-7255-2).

© 2006 Birkhäuser – Publishers for Architecture, P.O. Box 133, CH-4010 Basel, Switzerland.
www.birkhauser.ch
Part of Springer Science+Business Media Publishing Group.

Printed on acid-free paper produced from chlorine-free pulp. TCF ∞

Printed in Germany

ISBN-10: 3-7643-7253-2
ISBN-13: 978-3-7643-7253-8

9 8 7 6 5 4 3 2 1